Leisure and Entertainment in America

This publication was made possible
by a grant from the
National Endowment for the Humanities,
a Federal Agency,
Washington, D.C.

LEISURE
and Entertainment in
AMERICA

Donna R. Braden

Based on the Collections of
Henry Ford Museum & Greenfield Village

Henry Ford Museum & Greenfield Village
Dearborn, Michigan

Editor: Fannia Weingartner
Designer: Sharon Blagdon-Smart
Composition: The Print Shop,
Lincoln Park, Michigan
Printing: Wicklander Printing,
Chicago, Illinois

Library of Congress Catalog Card Number 88-080580
ISBN: 0-933728-32-8
©1988 by Henry Ford Museum & Greenfield Village
All Rights Reserved. Published in 1988.

Printed in the United States of America
Distributed nationally by
Wayne State University Press,
Detroit, Michigan

Cover and title page illustration taken from a
1928 trade catalog published by the Hill-Standard Co.,
Anderson, Indiana, manufacturers of playground,
swimming pool, and beach sports equipment.

CONTENTS

PREFACE 6

INTRODUCTION:
The Emergence of Leisure 8

1. *GETTING TOGETHER:*
Community Gatherings 14

    Bees and Frolics 16
    Camp Meetings 22
    Rural Fairs 23
    Food Gatherings 25
    Community Music and Dancing 30
    Clubs and Organizations 37
    Public Celebrations 43
    Community Gathering Places 50

2. *STAYING IN:* Home Amusements 62

    Visiting and Entertaining 65
    Home and Family Celebrations 70
    Reading 77
    Family Members' Pastimes 87
    Home Music 110
    Radio and Television 117

3. *GOING OUT:* Public Entertainment 124

    STEP RIGHT UP: BEGINNINGS 126
    The New City Audience 126
    "Strictly Moral" Entertainment 134
    Traveling Shows Emerge 136
    THE GREATEST SHOWS ON EARTH:
    CIVIL WAR TO WORLD WAR I 138
    All Manner of Variety 138
    The Proliferation of Traveling Shows 143
    Arbiters of Taste 152
    Embracing New Forms of Entertainment 157
    THE SHOW MUST GO ON:
    SINCE WORLD WAR I 168
    The Decline of Live Performance 168
    Entertainment for All 174

4. *COMPETING:* Sports to 1915 194

    PREINDUSTRIAL SPORTS 196
    SPORTS IN ANTEBELLUM AMERICA:
    1820S TO THE CIVIL WAR 199
    City Sports 199
    Early Spectator Sports 200
    Team and Field Sports 203
    The Growing Importance of Exercise 205
    Enthusiasm for New and Earlier Sports 206
    SPORTS MIRROR INDUSTRIALIZATION:
    CIVIL WAR TO WORLD WAR I 211
    Technological Changes 211
    Changing Attitudes 213
    The Urge to Organize 217
    Team and Spectator Sports 222
    Sporting Pastimes 237

5. *TAKING PART:*
The Shaping of Modern Sports 252

    New Influences 254
    Spectator Sports 260
    Sports for Everyone 271

6. *GETTING AWAY:* Travel and Tourism 286

    AMERICANS BECOME TRAVEL CONSCIOUS:
    TO THE CIVIL WAR 289
    Destinations 291
    TOURISM GETS ORGANIZED:
    1865 TO 1915 295
    Heading Farther Afield 305
    THE ERA OF MASS PLEASURE TRAVEL:
    SINCE WORLD WAR I 323
    Expanding Horizons 342

SELECTED BIBLIOGRAPHY 358

PICTURE CREDITS 366

Library purchase, 5-1-91

PREFACE

Much has been written about the history of work and the workplace in the United States, but surprisingly little attention has been paid to the history of leisure and leisure-time activities. As leisure activities have come to occupy a growing proportion of people's time, however, it has become increasingly evident that their evolution is related to profound changes in American work and family patterns and values. With few exceptions, it is only recently that the change in the ways Americans have used their leisure time has become a subject of historical rather than sociological scrutiny.

This publication traces the development of leisure activities in a changing American society, drawing on and incorporating materials from the collections of Henry Ford Museum & Greenfield Village. An introductory section examines changing conceptions of leisure as well as the historical factors that shaped these changes. The six subsequent sections describe the activities themselves in the context of the community and the home, public entertainment, sports, and travel. Since the amount, availability, and type of research materials for each subject differ substantially, the manner in which they are presented varies from section to section.

This publication does not attempt to present a comprehensive history of leisure activities; rather, it offers a perspective on the subject based on the extensive collections of a major American museum. It focuses primarily on the period between the early 19th and mid-20th centuries, when the most dramatic changes both in the amount of leisure time available and in the nature of leisure activities occurred. While all segments of society are discussed to some degree, the chief emphasis is on activities engaged in and supported by the general public at the national level. The text and illustrations reflect the fact that until recent decades some ethnic and minority groups and the less prosperous remained on the periphery of many of these activities.

The histories of various leisure-related industries (among them television and movies) and products (including toys, games, and sports equipment) are extensively covered in other books. This work focuses on the people who were responsible for, responded to, and were affected both by changes in attitudes toward leisure and by the resulting proliferation of leisure activities.

As is well known, visual evidence is extremely powerful in evoking a sense of a particular time and in capturing the nuances of social behavior. In many ways, the illustrations constitute the core of this publication. An extensive search through the Henry Ford Museum's collections for relevant illustrations and artifacts coincided with the writing of this work. As in the case of other holdings, the leisure-related materials in the collections are rich in diversity and depth. Obviously, space permits use of only a small portion of the thousands of two- and three-dimensional items in the collections. The high proportion of graphic materials in relation to the three-dimensional artifacts included in this publication results from the decision, whenever possible, to depict people actually taking part in the various activities. In some cases, illustrations were drawn from other sources to complete the story.

A project of this scope requires the collaboration of numerous colleagues and support staff. The project would not have been possible without the support and encouragement of Harold K. Skramstad, Jr., president of Henry Ford Museum & Greenfield Village. Steven K. Hamp, chairman of the Collections Division, continually supported both my own and the Museum's commitment to the project, as well as providing insight into specific subjects covered in the publication. John L. Wright, director of Public Programs, and James R. Van Bochove, Jr., manager of Education, also participated actively in the conceptual discussions. Historical consultants John F. Kasson, Bernard Mergen, and Robert C. Toll provided invaluable assistance and constructive criticism. Incorporating the wide range of materials for this project would not have been possible without the work of research assistants Jane N. Law and LuAnne Gaykowski Kozma, who searched and helped organize the collection of leisure-related materials with exceptional thoroughness and unflagging enthusiasm.

Many other members of the Museum staff deserve recognition. I am especially grateful to former curator Robert E. Eliason, Jr., for help with music history and to curator William S. Pretzer, both for reviewing the manuscript and for offering moral support. All of the curators lent valuable assistance in identifying appropriate materials for illustration, including Nancy E. Villa Bryk, John Bowditch, Peter H. Cousins, Michael J. Ettema, Larry C. McCans, and Randy Mason, as well as former curators Walter E. Simmons II, Donald W. Matteson, and Christina H. Nelson. Kenneth M. Wilson, former director of Collections and glass specialist, helped identify objects as well as providing more general support. G. Donald Adams, director of Public Affairs, helped with his expertise on bicycles.

The Library and Archives staffs deserve special thanks for their help. I would particularly like to thank curator of prints and photographs Cynthia Read-Miller for her continuous and ungrudging assistance. Judith E. Endelman, Benson and Edith Ford librarian, and Jennifer M. Heymoss, assistant librarian, former librarian Joan W. Gartland, and former coordinator Julia T. Chesley were especially helpful in tracking down materials related to the wide-ranging topics of this book. Curator David R. Crippen gave aid and encouragement. Archivist Jeanine M. Head, as well as several technical assistants and volunteers, helped locate and process the hundreds of two-dimensional artifacts illustrated in this book.

I am indebted to talented photographers Rudy T. Ruzicska, Tim Hunter, Alan R. Harvey, and former manager of Photographic Services Carl L. Malotka for producing the hundreds of photographs needed for this project and for their helpful suggestions. Virginia A. Morrow tirelessly processed photograph requests and cheerfully answered questions. I would also like to thank Ann M. French and Geraldine Ferraiuolo of the collections support staff for their assistance, and David C. DeVore, director of Development, and his assistant Lannette M. Nabb for their support.

Staff members from several other institutions were helpful during the research stages of this project, particularly at the University of Michigan libraries and the Popular Culture Library at Bowling Green State University. I would also like to acknowledge the help of those who aided me during my visits to search the holdings of their institutions: Joyce Lee at The Schomburg Center for Research in Black Culture; Rob Wright at The Harvard Theatre Collection; and the staffs of the Film Stills Archives at the Museum of Modern Art, the Prints and Photographs Division of the Library of Congress, and the Still Pictures Branch of the National Archives.

This project would not have been possible without the talents and spiritual guidance of substantive editor Fannia Weingartner, who worked closely with me during the tedious editing process and who saw the project through its various stages of production from its initial conceptual stage to its completion. My warm thanks to the editorial and production staff who worked on this project, including Carole Presser, Sarah Mollman, and Jan Kozora Less. I am especially grateful to graphic designer Sharon Blagdon-Smart for applying her artistic and technical skills to create the striking appearance of this book, as well as for helping to keep the production schedule on track and for always lending an open ear.

Special thanks go to my husband Curt for his continual encouragement, helpful suggestions, and unfailing patience throughout the painstaking process of writing and organizing the materials for this book, especially during the many times when we could have been pursuing leisure activities instead. Thanks, also, to my good friend Deborah Berk, for letting me stay with her during my trips to New York and for adding her special brand of insight to the project.

Finally, on behalf of the entire Museum, I wish to thank the National Endowment for the Humanities, whose generous support made possible *Leisure and Entertainment in America*.

Donna R. Braden, Curator
Henry Ford Museum & Greenfield Village

INTRODUCTION:
The Emergence of Leisure

What is leisure? It is not merely time away from work, which is often used to fulfill duties and obligations. Nor is it idleness, with its connotations of "wasted time." In fact, the meaning of leisure has changed dramatically over time and must be viewed within a cultural and historical context.

For centuries, leisure was primarily identified with a "leisured" class, a group free of any obligation to work. The changed meaning of leisure to relate to everyone rather than to a privileged few is integrally connected with economic, technological, and social changes; above all, it relates to changes in the nature of work and the workplace.

In America this shift was set in motion in the 19th century, as urbanization and industrialization altered the existing fabric of society. As rapid technological innovation and the spread of the factory system made workers' tasks more routine, they tried to find new forms of relief from the monotony of repetitive work. Inherent in the factory system was a strict adherence to the clock. By the mid-19th century, the intrusion of "clock time" separated "work" from "not work" more clearly than ever before.

Mechanization, the more efficient use of time, and the growing demand for better working conditions eventually led to the reduction of hours in the workday and workweek. (Between 1850 and 1950, the average workweek of 66 hours for a laborer in the manufacturing sector had been reduced to 40 hours.) Eventually, mechanization not only allowed those outside the home more time away from work, but also helped free women and children from some of their traditional domestic chores.

Although it is difficult to quantify an actual decrease in work and increase in leisure, the growing separation between the two became decidedly pronounced. As a distinct realm of leisure emerged, public attitudes toward its relationship with work changed dramatically. By the end of the 19th century, social reformers of the Progressive era, building on earlier attempts to breach the stern Calvinist work ethic, were trying to persuade Americans of the value—indeed the necessity—of leisure time. They recommended this as the way for workers to renew their physical energy, attain mental health, and solidify family relationships. They hoped it might even prevent social unrest.

Facing page: *Bicycling enjoyed tremendous popularity during the last few decades of the 19th century. This 1887 trade card advertisement for Columbia bicycles depicts a hardy group of cyclists on a nighttime ride.*

The Fourth of July in the Country, *an engraving from* Harper's Weekly, *July 6, 1867, conveys the variety of entertainment offered during such celebrations, including eating and drinking, music and dancing, and parades and patriotic oratory. A strong community spirit characterized such gatherings.*

Since World War I, leisure has become an end in itself, signifying the freedom to choose activities that are voluntary, satisfying, and restorative. Embodying a set of attitudes that value self-fulfillment, it has become a crucial element in a widely shared vision of "the good life."

Closely related to, and often considered synonymous with leisure, is the term recreation. Since recreation is generally an organized and goal-oriented activity that people pursue during their leisure time for pleasure and satisfaction, recreation is, in a sense, a subcategory of leisure. Also related to leisure is the concept of play, a less easily defined form of behavior, most often associated with spontaneity and some separation from the demands of the everyday world. Generally applied to children's activities, the term implies a happy, unfettered spirit.

Leisure time, attitudes, and activities changed most dramatically as America moved from being a rural-agrarian to being an urban-industrial society. These changes will be described in more detail within the framework of three broadly chronological phases: before the Civil War; between the Civil War and World War I; and since World War I.

The Intermingling of Work and Amusement

In preindustrial America, amusements were largely informal and frequently associated with work activities. Generally dictated by custom, they tended to differ according to region, ethnic and religious grouping, and social class.

The strict attitudes of the New England Puritans "in detestation of idleness" are well documented, although it is difficult to discover how closely these settlers actually obeyed the laws established by their moral leaders. Puritan theology did, however, leave a deep impression on American life well into the

By the end of the 19th century, Progressive-era reformers were urging people who lived in cities to participate in organized social programs and recreational activities. This Children's Day pageant was held in Detroit's Belle Isle Park during the first decade of the 20th century.

19th century. Other settlers of Colonial America had more positive attitudes toward amusements. In particular, wealthy settlers in the South and in towns along the East Coast (especially New York, Philadelphia, and even the New England town of Boston) helped formalize many activities later taken over by a broader public.

In the early 19th century, urbanization and the beginnings of industrialization profoundly influenced the growth of amusements. In spite of a rigid adherence to the work ethic, a renewed religious fervor, and the disapproval of many social leaders, this period was marked by the beginning and gradual expansion of popular amusements that have since played an increasingly important part in the leisure life of Americans. Faced with long, highly regimented workweeks, the remoteness of the countryside, and the loss of the traditional sense of community, city dwellers especially sought diversion through new, commercialized amusements.

An Antidote to ''All-Consuming Busyness''

In the period between the Civil War and World War I, the choice of activities Americans could engage in during their nonworking hours expanded tremendously. Although there was increasingly widespread involvement in leisure activities by Americans, an individual's choices were often restricted by gender, background, geographical location, income, and social rank.

In the decades after the Civil War, the status and wealth sought by members of the middle class led them to emulate the upper class in as many ways as possible. Since the wealthy organized and participated in many leisure activities, they provided models for the middle class to imitate, and eventually helped mitigate some of the latter's prejudices and highly moralistic attitudes. By this time a distinct working-class culture, characterized by preferences for particular leisure activities, also had emerged.

By the end of the 19th century, leisure activities were formalized, standardized, and bureaucratized. Ironically they tended to mirror developments in the business world from which they were supposed to offer an escape.

While a growing array of amusements was available to city dwellers, the options of people living in rural areas and small towns continued to be limited for several reasons. In such places the emphasis on "edifying" activities remained dominant, reflecting the Protestant ethic with its injunctions against the misuse of time. The conservative attitudes fostered by the influential role of the church in these areas lingered well into the 20th century. At the same time the isolation of such places and people's limited time and income also restricted the proliferation of amusements.

In an address at the Chautauqua Institution in New York State in 1880, James A. Garfield, soon to be president of the United States, commented that:

> *We may divide the whole struggle of the human race into two chapters: first, the fight to get leisure; and then the second fight of civilization—what shall we do with our leisure when we get it.*

Indeed, during the last few decades of the 19th century, popular opinion placed an increasing emphasis on the importance of leisure. The loss of job satisfaction experienced by employees of corporations and bureaucracies began to erode the old work ethic as the nation's economy shifted from one that was organized around scarcity and production to one that was based on surplus and consumption.

By the turn of the century, Progressive–era social reformers were tempering their rhetoric with a new realization of the need for play. At the same time, government, church, and school programs also were being reoriented toward an acceptance of leisure as an antidote to the "violent, all-consuming busyness" of Americans. Even conservative members of the middle class were supporting the notion that pure relaxation and enjoyment were important and increasingly looked for personal expression and fulfillment in leisure activities instead of in work.

Fun for Everyone

Leisure activities since World War I have been characterized by a high degree of democratization, uniformity, and commercialization, as leisure became widely available to the general public rather than being confined to the more privileged members of society. While some exceptions have persisted, leisure pursuits have increasingly tended to depend more on special interests than on gender, geographical location, or social class.

The widespread use of automobiles and the development of the mass media have reduced many regional and ethnic differences. These have led to a certain degree of standardization in leisure activities, although regional variations persist and ethnic celebrations remain important in some communities. Religious and moral objections to leisure have also diminished and many

The Woodstock Music & Art Fair, held in upstate New York in August 1969, was especially emblematic of the period. Featuring live performances by rock-and-roll, folk, and pop musicians, this outdoor event attracted a markedly youthful audience of some 500,000.

church and governmental authorities have given wholehearted support to recreational programs and facilities.

Leisure has become a commercialized, highly lucrative industry in America's modern consumer culture. The emerging consumer ethic not only has come to include the actual purchase of leisure goods and services, but also has affected the entire culture surrounding them, turning celebrities and tourist sites into commodities and molding popular taste.

Today, leisure is often regarded as more important than work as a way of giving meaning to life. It is precisely because this profound degree of significance is attached to it that leisure continues to be referred to as a "problem" or a "challenge," and endless studies seek ways in which Americans can use it wisely. Many Americans would agree with the claim of sociologist Charles Brightbill in *Education for Leisure* (1966): "Tell me what you do when you are free to do as you wish and I will tell you what kind of person you are."

A few overall patterns can be perceived in this brief survey of the emergence of leisure in America. First is the growing dominance of a middle-class culture and its influence on the democratization of leisure. Second is the commercialization of leisure—its development into an industry and its connection with America's emerging consumer society. Third is the theme of cultural assimilation—the "Americanization" of the diverse groups of people who settled in this country as certain leisure activities became popular on a national level.

These patterns, and the phases of change described above, are explored in the following text and illustrations relating to five major aspects of people's lives: community, home and family, public entertainment, sports, and travel.

THE QUILTING PARTY.

GETTING TOGETHER:
Community Gatherings

*W*hether in an isolated settlement on the edge of the frontier, a large metropolitan area, or a suburban neighborhood, festive gatherings have encouraged the kinds of close relationships that are fostered by active participation and shared experiences. Over time, community-based leisure activities have been transformed from casual gatherings of whole communities, or of people living within geographical proximity, into formally organized groups and group activities, often based on specialized interests.

In preindustrial America, closely-knit rural communities frequently combined amusements with seasonal work activities to serve a constructive end. Get-togethers were largely informal, involving active participation by all who attended. One of the earliest and most persistent organizing influences on community gatherings was the church. During the early 19th century, the scope of community activities expanded, while a renewed religious fervor and an emphasis on moral purpose led to the popularity of such gatherings as camp meetings and singing schools.

After the Civil War, the influence of urban amusements brought more organization and commercialization to many of the earlier gatherings as well as to newly created types of get-togethers. The commitment to moral purpose persisted during this time, as was evident from the popularity of church-sponsored functions. During the first two decades of the 20th century, various neighborhood and civic programs tried to revive the earlier participatory nature of community gatherings.

Since World War I, many more activities have become organized around the goals of relaxation and recreation. Urban influences have predominated in community gatherings, increasing their scale and degree of bureaucratization. While some neighborly informality lingers in small towns, urban ethnic districts, and suburban neighborhoods, the new, highly organized "communities" of special-interest clubs and organizations have largely supplanted the earlier communities based primarily on geographical proximity.

Facing page: *The quilting bee was but one of many informal gatherings that took place in preindustrial America, combining arduous labor with a spirit of festivity. When the women were finished with their tasks, an invited group of gentlemen might arrive for a pleasurable evening of games and dancing, as suggested in this September 1849 engraving from* Godey's Lady's Book, *entitled* The Quilting Party.

Bees and Frolics

Foreign travelers in the early and mid-19th century often noted the quality of neighborliness among Americans, especially in rural settlements. English traveler Charles Latrobe wrote in *The Rambler in North America* (1836):

A life in the woods teaches many lessons, and this among the rest, that you must both give assistance to your neighbor, and receive it in return, without either grudging or pouting . . . . [E]ach has learnt . . . that . . . lending a free helping-hand in the spirit of kindness is both a laudable and a natural [practice].

Among the earliest types of community gatherings were those that combined recreation with work activities. Informal in nature, these so-called bees and frolics put to good use the tradition of cooperative labor within the closely-knit, rural communities. Marked by full group participation and a spirit of friendly neighborliness, bees were amusedly referred to by foreign travelers as "assemblings" where Americans would "imitate those industrious insects."

The organizers of the bee or frolic were expected to furnish a generous supply of hospitality in return for their neighbors' labors. Feasting and drinking, dancing, music, game-playing, and storytelling were provided in abundance. "If everything has been satisfactory," English traveler Isabella Lucy Bird reported in *The Englishwoman in America* (1856), "the convivial proceedings" were prolonged past midnight. Both hospitality and labor were usually reciprocated; the givers of a bee were bound to attend those of all their neighbors.

The types of rural gatherings that people ar-

Nathaniel Currier's lithograph, American Forest Scene, Maple Sugaring, *from 1856, depicts a "sugaring-off," during which sap was boiled down until it hardened into candy or crystallized into sugar. Neighbors often were invited to help boil the sap and then join a "sumptuous feast" followed by dancing.*

ranged so as to take advantage of cooperative labor were as diverse as the large-scale, difficult, and monotonous tasks that had to be performed by farm families. Many of the bees and frolics were organized to divide or share the intensive labor involved in certain seasonal farm tasks. For example, when the maple sugar season began in New England and other Northern states in early spring, a "sugaring-off" gathering was commonplace. Englishman Thomas Nichols described this activity in 1864 in his *Forty Years of American Life:*

> *Young men and maidens gather round the fire at night, when the sap has been boiled down to the sugaring-off point, when it will harden into candy on the snow, or crystallize into sugar. These are among the pleasantest of rural gatherings.*

Corn-husking bees were perhaps the most popular types of bees, especially among young people of courting age. The husking of the annual crop of corn during the fall harvest was well suited to the bee format, with its pairing of concentrated group labor with boisterous fun. Rival teams of huskers, which sometimes included both sexes, competed in tearing the husks loose from two evenly divided piles of corn ears. Singing and conversation usually accompanied the husking, and drinking and flirtation were commonplace. Thomas Nichols described the "pleasant excitement arising from the rule that the fellow who husks a red ear of corn has the privilege of kissing the girl next to him." Yet another English traveler, S. A. Ferrall, made an interesting observation in *A Ramble of 6000 Miles Through the United States of America,* published in 1832. Witnessing a corn-husking frolic near Cincinnati, he observed two or three young Irish "rogues" exacting kisses from their female partners half-a-dozen times from the same red ear:

> *Each of them laid a red-ear close by him, and after every two or three he'd husk, up he'd hold the redoubtable red-ear to the astonished eyes of the giggling lass who sate (sic) beside him, and most unrelentingly inflict the penalty. The "gude wives" marvelled much at the unprecedented number of red-ears which that lot of corn con-*

> *tained: by-and-by, they thought it "a kind of curious" that the Irishmen should find so many of them—at length, the cheat was discovered amidst roars of laughter.*

However, William Dean Howells, in his *Recollections of Life in Ohio, from 1813-1840,* published in 1895, recalled that he "never knew it to be necessary to produce a red ear to secure a kiss where there was a disposition to give or take one."

After the husking was completed and prizes awarded, the group usually adjourned to a bountiful harvest dinner, followed by singing, storytelling, and a dance that might last several hours. Sometimes a corn-husking bee ended at the local tavern. Too often, apparently, the "fun and frolic, merriment and glee" overshadowed the work to be done, much to the outrage of hard-working farmers. According to Nicholas Hardeman in *Shucks, Shocks, and Hominy Blocks: Corn as a Way of Life in Pioneer America* (1981), one New England farmer lamented:

> *If you love fun and frolic, and waste and slovenliness more than economy and profit, then give a husking. Sing dirty songs for the entertainment of the boys, and expect your corn to be mixed, crumbled, and dirty; some husked, some half husked, and some not at all.*

In states where apple trees were abundant, apple-paring bees were popular to help prepare the apple crop for storage and preservation over the winter months. Pennsylvania Germans were particularly fond of these festive gatherings, as P. E. Gibbons recalled in his book, *Pennsylvania Dutch,* published in 1874:

> *Evening "snitzen parties" to pare apples and make apple butter, were festive occasions. Commonly a boy and a girl both take hold of the long-handle of the stirrer and stir together.*

Threshing usually required mutual help among neighbors. Fred Lape recalled his boyhood experience of a threshing near Esperance, New York, in the late 19th century in his memoir *Farm and Village Boyhood* (1980):

The corn-husking bee typically combined group labor with fun, food, drink, and a chance to mingle with the opposite sex. In this engraving from Ballou's Pictorial, *November 28, 1857, entitled* Husking Party Finding the Red Ears, *several "fortunate gentlemen" have been successful in their quest and are "insisting on their rights" to exact a kiss from "the nearest damsel." The author of the accompanying article expressed the hope that "the new-fangled husking-machines will prove an utter failure" since they would "banish" this "important resource from our calendar of winter sports."*

One of the proudest days of my early years was the day I was sent off alone with the team and an oak rack to help a neighbor in threshing. Often the women went along with the men, to help the neighbor's wife get dinner for the crew. Then the days of exchanging work became also the days of social gossip.

The threshing-day dinner and supper were generally bountiful meals and occasions for merriment. Butchering, which took place in November or December, was another task that often required neighborly assistance.

Other forms of frolics involving cooperative work were less seasonal. In new areas of settlement, neighbors assisted in constructing or "raising" log houses and barns. They helped drag and roll the logs, cutting notches and lifting and fitting them together to construct the framework of the building. Occasionally neighbors also helped to fell and dress logs.

According to Thomas Nichols, 12 to 20 men would gather, "bringing their own provisions, and make a sort of pic-nic in the forest." In addition to the frame, the wooden floor and roof were often constructed at this time, and the logs chinked and daubed with clay. With the hard work of several neighbors, a log house could be erected in one day. The sense of exhilaration felt at its completion emerges from Caroline Kirkland's description of a raising near Pinckney, Michigan, in *A New Home or Life in the Clearings* (1839):

This was the moment of triumph. The men, who had been scattered in every direction throughout the frame, giving it the appearance of an enormous bird-cage, rather aviary, now ranged themselves along the beams, and gave three thrilling cheers, presenting the most perfect image of the beautiful manoeuvre of "manning the yards" on board a vessel of war, that can possibly be conceived.

Right: *During the mid- and late 19th century, dozens of mechanical apple parers were devised to facilitate the task of peeling apples. Apple parers can occasionally be spotted in scenes of apple bees, like the one that follows.* Below: *During an apple-paring bee like the one pictured in this engraving,* Fall Games—The Apple-Bee, *from Harper's Weekly, November 26, 1859, neighbors helped pare, quarter, core, string, and hang apples to dry for the winter. The scene also illustrates the superstition, "still firmly believed in many country places" at the time, that an apple paring thrown over a young girl's shoulder would form the initial of her future husband's name when it hit the ground.*

Neighbors often got together to help raise a house or barn, especially for a newly married couple. The barn-raising at Jacob Roher's farm near Massillon, Ohio, depicted in this 1888 photograph, was probably followed by a dinner and an evening of drinking, games, dancing, and lively talk.

Other structures in addition to farm residences also were often erected by raisings. "A Boy's Story of Pioneer Life in Michigan," by Theodore Potter, published in the *Michigan Pioneer & Historical Collections* (1907), recalled the communal raising of the capitol in Lansing, Michigan, in 1847:

> *All the settlers around Lansing had been invited to the "raising" that day, jugs of whiskey provided free for all, and also dinner and supper, and the whole proceeding was after the fashion of an old style raising of the heavy hewed frame of an old-fashioned barn or house . . . .*

Residents of rural areas often held logging bees to have neighbors help roll and collect felled logs into piles for burning. According to Stevenson Whitcomb Fletcher's account of pre-1840 rural practices in

Pennsylvania Agriculture and Country Life (1950):

> *A score or more of neighbors participated. They came armed with log hooks with which to roll the logs into piles for burning. They worked in teams, each team under a captain. Captains were selected by acclamation and they then chose their teams. The team that piled the most logs was the winner. It was hard, dirty work but, as one participant put it, "the greatest of hilarity prevailed," partly because of frequent visits to a shaded nook where a jug or two of corn liquor was kept to cool parched throats. A "stump-pulling frolic" might follow a log-rolling.*

Neighbors also might organize communal bees for such tasks as grubbing out underbrush, splitting rails, or chopping wood.

Women held their own bees and frolics, especially to make and sew textiles. The best known and perhaps most common were quilting bees. Nichols wrote:

The quilting is mostly a feminine arrangement. Its ostensible object is the manufacture of a bedquilt. This involves a social gathering—talk, tea, probably a little gossip and scandal, and in the evening the accession of masculinity, with more or less of fun and frolic . . . .

As he noted, the men usually joined the women in the evening to play games or dance. Nineteenth-century accounts also frequently mentioned sewing bees as well as rag bees, organized to transform rags into usable materials for making rugs.

Although some of these rural gatherings continued into the 20th century, many declined and eventually disappeared, except in the most remote communities. Increasing population and denser settlement throughout the country reduced isolation, while machinery, hired labor, and readily available consumer goods contributed to the decreased necessity for bees and frolics. Sports, contests, entertainment, and other more urban amusements also lured rural people away from the earlier forms of work-centered recreation.

One type of quilt produced at a communal bee was the album quilt, like the mid-19th-century example shown here. These quilts, composed of a series of separately designed squares, often were fashioned to commemorate an event like a wedding or family reunion.

Camp Meetings

While the religious camp meeting did not involve the arduous labor of the bee or frolic, it did combine social activity with a serious purpose. The primary aim of the camp meeting was to bring about the spiritual regeneration of those in attendance. Beginning around 1800, the meetings were mainly organized by traveling Methodist preachers or circuit-riders, although Presbyterian and Baptist preachers also were known to take part. Especially popular in the South and on the western edges of settlement during the first half of the 19th century, camp meetings presented an attractive alternative to formal church services; in more isolated areas, they offered the only religious services available. A camp meeting created its own fellowship, unifying its participants through shared experiences and the kind of emotional release possible only among strangers.

Often having traveled long distances, participants at the meetings stayed for days or weeks, forming a closely knit camp of tents and buggies. Within this community social activity and gossip abounded. Meetings consisted of several days of services, marked by revivalist oratory, "sonorous hymns often set to popular song-tunes," and prayer. The religious fervor of these meetings tended to evoke numerous emotional outbursts. In Nichols's words:

> *They clap their hands, and shout with excitement. Nervous and hysterical women are struck down senseless, and roll upon the ground. "Mourners" crowd to the anxious seats, to be prayed for. There is groaning, weeping, shouting, praying, singing. Some are converted, and make the woods ring with joyful shouts of "Glory," and these exhort others to come and get religion.*

Camp meetings, with their combination of spiritual purpose and social activity, would later serve as the models for Chautauquas and denominationally sponsored resort communities. (*See "Going Out" and "Getting Away."*)

Camp Meeting Sketches—The Tent, *an engraving from* Ballou's Pictorial, *August 21, 1858, depicts a group in prayer under the leadership of a "distinguished preacher" at a week-long camp meeting in Millennial Grove, Cape Cod, Massachusetts. Such meetings fostered community spirit while engendering considerable excitement.*

This 1880 lithograph of a Broome County [New York] Agricultural Society Fair shows the combination of educational and recreational elements that characterized such fairs at this time. Although there were many amusements to entice visitors to this fair—including baseball and a primitive sort of merry-go-round—the biggest draw was the race track.

Rural Fairs

Since the early 19th century, annual county and local fairs have fulfilled both recreational and socializing functions for rural communities, enlisting direct participation and creating a sense of belonging. Although fairs can be traced to medieval Europe and even to earlier times, it was only after around 1800 that the combined objectives of commerce, education, and recreation evolved. Members of learned agricultural societies were the first to promote fairs as a way to stimulate agricultural improvement. The first agricultural fairs directed to the average farmer were conceived by a New York banker and agriculturist named Elkanah Watson around 1810. Watson's "practical fairs" introduced such popular and enduring features as contests and competitions, parades, and special exhibitions of agricultural and domestic products.

The scope of agricultural fairs expanded during the second half of the 19th century as new machinery, crops, and livestock breeds competed on the market. The annual local or county fair became a major means for the exchange of information, as well as a meeting place where farm families could socialize with one another.

During the last few decades of the 19th century, fairs underwent drastic changes. Such commercialized amusements as horse races, carnival rides, and side shows assumed increasing prominence, clashing with the traditional combination of recreation, work, and education as the main purpose of fairs. Increasing specialization in agriculture, the development of agricultural schools, and the rise of agricultural organizations contributed to the decline of informality in the character of county and state fairs—although this varied from region to region. On the whole, visitors to the fairs tended to be spectators rather than participants. This was offset by organizations, like the 4-H clubs sponsored by the Department of Agriculture, whose activities became significant features of these 20th-century fairs.

When Progressive-era reformers began to organize recreational programs in the decade before World War I, the planners and directors of such programs made conscious efforts to adapt features of the earlier, noncommercial fairs to neighborhood recreational activities. They encouraged local residents to take an active part in sports and amateur competitions, and in creating exhibits, rather than remaining passive spectators. These programs met with varying degrees of success, however, and largely disappeared in succeeding decades.

Street fairs both promoted local business interests and encouraged community participation. The fair shown in this photograph took place in Vicksburg, Mississippi, around 1900.

Picnics were a favorite form of social gathering. This 1880s trade card advertising Crown sewing machines and Florence oil stoves suggests that a good time could be had by all, including the lady using the Florence oil stove to prepare food.

Food Gatherings

Some social gatherings were organized around a communal meal shared in an informal outdoor setting. Picnics provided ample opportunity for social interaction, as we learn from Eliza Farnham's account in *Life in Prairie Land,* published in 1846. The picnic she describes took place on a bluff overlooking the Mississippi River in Illinois:

On the very pinnacle of the bluff . . . we found a little shaded nook, just large enough to admit our number. Here, after the vines and light undergrowth had been cleared away, we spread our white napkins, table cloths, &c., and laid out our simple refreshments . . . .

Stories, songs, and hymns followed the lunch, and when these were no more called for, one or two chess boards were routed from their repose at the bottom of the baskets, and put on duty by some, while others strolled out to enjoy the prospect . . . .

In many communities, August was a popular time for the annual church or Sunday School picnic. Della Lutes, who grew up in southern Michigan in the 1880s, recalled in *The Country Kitchen* (1946) that the Sunday School picnic in her community was always held in an upland grove. And "despite the 'programme' or any other attractions that may have been offered by teachers or pastor," people's attention mainly centered around the long table.

By the mid-20th century, picnics had become an American institution in rural areas, towns, and urban neighborhoods. Reflecting the popularity of this pastime, *The Picnic Book,* published by the National Recreation Association in 1942, suggested

numerous group activities suitable for such outings, including music, drama, and sports, as well as appropriate "themes." The book included the following warning:

> *Unless the chief purpose of your outing is the study and discussion of some immediate, important problem, make your affair a "speechless" one. If speeches have to be in the program, avoid long ones. A real picnic for fun has no long-winded speakers who have political aspirations or who have an "ax to grind." If there are any speeches to be made, insist that they be short and snappy. Picnickers want action!*

Above: *This Hawkeye Basket Refrigerator, patented in 1902, was designed to serve as an efficient container for picnic foods. It had an airtight cover and insulated lining to keep food hot or cold, and was said to be roomy enough to carry lunch for five to seven people. The metal tumblers and "insulated cup" were also designed for picnics or outings.* Below: *Gatherings centered around food often featured regional delicacies. The clam steam, which frequently included other shellfish and sweet corn as well, was a particular favorite in New England. This anonymous photograph was taken around 1900.*

Barbecues were a popular focus for communal gatherings, particularly in the South and the West. In the 19th century, a barbecue often consisted of nothing more than dining outdoors, although it usually involved the roasting of whole animals over an open fire. Some of these meals were quite elaborate and often varied between regions. Wherever they were held, however, games and dancing frequently fol-

lowed the feasting. In addition to those held in local communities, barbecues also were organized by political candidates to attract voters to their cause.

Many 19th-century travelers from abroad, including the critical Frances Trollope (mother of the English novelist Anthony Trollope), commented on the American celebration of the strawberry season. In her book *Domestic Manners of the Americans*, published in 1832, she noted that "the only rural amusement in which we ever saw any of the natives engaged" was the eating of strawberries and cream "in a pretty garden" about three miles outside of Cincinnati, Ohio. Strawberry festivals often were held at the local church or school on a warm June evening. Cakes and ice cream, handcranked at the festival, generally accompanied the strawberries. An ice-cream-and-strawberry festival held in Columbiana, Ohio, in June 1881, received the following eloquent description in the *Independent Register,* the village newspaper:

> *The tables were very tastefully ornamented with beautiful boquets (sic) of flowers, which June has so lavishly furnished. The crimson berries, plates of snowy cake and beautiful flowers, mingled in pleasing contrast, formed pictures of loveliness and reflected credit upon the fair hands which prepared and arranged them. A committee of young ladies, assiduous in their endeavors to please their guests, served at each table . . . . Our excellent Silver Cornet Band was present . . . and rendered the musical part of the entertainments in an admirable manner.*

A more formal 19th-century rural gathering involving food was the donation party or church bee, organized by congregations to collect money or foodstuffs to supplement their minister's often meager income. Caroline Kirkland described one such party held near Pinckney, Michigan, in the 1830s:

> *Two great baskets in the hall were already pretty well filled with bundles of yarns, woollen stockings of all sizes, (sure to fit, in a clergyman's family), rolls of home-made flannel, mysterious parcels enveloped in paper, and bags which*

When not held outdoors, strawberry festivals often were celebrated on the premises of sponsoring churches or schools. This unfortunate scene, captioned Accident at a Strawberry Festival, *accompanied an article in the* July 4, 1874, *issue of* Days' Doings, *fervently denouncing the flimsy construction of the newer churches.*

> *looked as if they might contain a great many precious things. Flocks of company were arriving, and no one empty handed . . . . The tea hour drew on, and now the melee began to assume a business-like air . . . . The younger gentlemen officiated as footmen . . . .*

As the need for work-related rural bees declined, so-called "sociables" and "entertainments," centering more around recreation, became prevalent. Combining the basic features of urban receptions with indoor games and refreshments, these social events were popular in rural communities, villages, and small towns, especially during the last decades of the 19th century.

Sociables might commence with a hay- or sleigh-ride that delivered passengers to a festive gathering. Church socials were organized to encourage fellowship among members of different religious congregations. Other sociables revolved solely around food, taking the form of a supper, a box social, an ice-cream social, a pie social, a covered dish supper, or a bean bake. For the box social, each female participant packed a box with food for two people. After bidding for a box or picking it by lottery, a man was entitled to share it with the woman who had prepared it. As Fred Lape recalled in his reminiscence of life in Esperance, New York:

This always produced certain rivalries and discomfitures, for certain boys wanted to eat with certain girls, and there were certain women in the community whose cleanliness was suspect and whose food nobody wanted to eat. So some sly work and some trading usually accompanied the drawing of the lots.

Bean bakes often were sponsored by local chapters of the Grand Army of the Republic (G.A.R.), the Union veterans of the Civil War. One such event, held on Thanksgiving evening 1882, in Columbiana, Ohio, was advertised in the local newspaper as follows:

Rations will be served in army style and at moderate prices. Oysters and confectionery will also be served to all who desire them. The exercises of the evening will consist of vocal and

Often centered around the roasting of one or more large animals on a spit, a barbecue might include selected families or an entire neighborhood. Stockmen and their wives were the guests at this 1941 beef barbecue at Spear's Siding, Wyola, Wyoming, photographed by Marion Post Wolcott.

The box social or supper, usually sponsored by a church or school, was a highly popular type of gathering. Both young people and their parents attended this 1940 pie and box supper, given by a school in Breathitt County, Kentucky, to raise money for repairs and supplies. Each box was auctioned off to the highest bidder, who then had the privilege of sharing it with the woman or girl who had made it.

instrumental music, army songs, army anecdotes, readings, &c. A pleasant time may be expected. All are invited . . . .

The bean bakes in Fred Lape's hometown were more of a community potluck, followed by a speech presented by a member of the G.A.R. and a dance that might last until two, three, or even four o'clock in the morning. Lape recalled that by about 1910 the popularity of G.A.R. bean bakes had dwindled because "most of the old men left in the G.A.R. were too feeble to dance."

Community "entertainments" were somewhat more formal than sociables. Church entertainments, festivals, and fetes, forerunners of 20th-century church bazaars, provided ways for the church to raise money. Often based on a seasonal or other appropriate theme, they usually featured a number of stands or places of amusement at which people purchased useful articles or paid for entertainment. Some churches, for example, staged "Harvest Home" festivals during the early fall. These celebrations, like the one described in the *American Agriculturist* of September 1878, included picnics, games, amusements, and refreshments:

Tents were pitched over tables, from which sandwiches, cake, coffee, ice-cream, and confectionery were sold . . . . Games—such as an apple race, a sack race, a foot race, and a tub race—and the ascension of fire balloons made fun for the people, and brought prizes of ice-cream and lunch for the winners. A mock art gallery and a lace maker were among the novelties. One of the marked attractions was horse-back riding by a young lady of the farm, with her instructor . . . . The day was delightful, everybody had a good time, none felt bored, and when sundown came, many felt sorry that the day was done. Some enjoyed a social party in the evening (which helped swell the proceeds), and had a pleasant drive home by moonlight.

Holiday entertainments, especially for Easter, Thanksgiving, and Christmas, usually included musical programs, recitations, and pageantry.

Singing schools like this one, held in Oregon in 1860, flourished in rural communities during the 19th century. Although they ostensibly convened their members to practice sight reading, these ''schools'' became especially popular because they offered an opportunity to meet members of the opposite sex.

Community Music and Dancing

Various regional forms of music and dance were characteristic of rural and small town gatherings. A popular form of community singing was the singing school, which flourished during the first half of the 19th century and continued in some areas until around 1890. The singing school movement began in the Colonial period as part of an attempt by Puritan ministers to promote better singing in church. Participants were convened by a traveling singing master at appointed times to learn, practice, and demonstrate sight-reading skills. Usually the songs had been transcribed into a system of notation called shape notes, developed to simplify the task of learning to read music. The course typically culminated in a public performance, which was sometimes followed by a sermon from the local minister.

The great popularity of singing schools has been attributed to the social opportunities they offered to young people. According to William Dean Howells's recollections of his boyhood in early 19th-century Springfield, Ohio:

It was understood that girls, who could generally come out with their brothers or family friends,

would accept the company of some young man to go home, as an escort. In this way, they made acquaintances and sometimes matches, as well as having a pleasant time.

Sometimes the social aspect of the singing school was shrilly criticized, as was the case in the following letter sent to the editor, and printed in the July 13, 1882, issue of the *Independent Register* of Columbiana, Ohio:

Several pieces of music were sung before and after recess to the credit of the singers, but a goodly number present, to their discredit, indulged in a whispering conversation.

During a recess of some 45 minutes, some of the class, and, if I am not mistaken, the leader also, engaged in a game known as ''Pig in the Parlor,'' which is so familiar to most of us as to need no describing. . . .

I was convinced that the young folks meet for pleasure only. I think not one of them will deny it. Therefore, I suggest that the class call it a pleasure school, instead of a singing school, so as not to murder the cause of singing.

Right: *The keyed serpent, an unusual improvement of a woodwind instrument first used in Europe to accompany church choirs, was enlisted as a bass "voice" in some American military bands during the early 19th century. Its three-foot-long body was curved in an attempt to maintain a reasonable amount of portability for a bass instrument. (If straightened, it would have been eight feet long!) Serpents like this one, made by Thomas Key of London around 1840, eventually proved troublesome to make and uncomfortable to play, and were largely replaced by powerful valved brass instruments by the 1850s. Below: This 1864 sketch of the Musical Temple in New York City's Central Park was the work of Pennsylvania artist Lewis Miller. By this time most bands were using brass instruments, valued for their effectiveness in carrying sound outdoors.*

Above: *During the 1840s and 1850s, the keyed bugle became a popular solo instrument and a leading melodic "voice" in American bands. This 1850 keyed bugle in E flat, made by E. G. Wright of Boston, was inscribed and presented by the members of the Lowell Brass Band to their bandleader D. C. Hall. Below: From the 1890s through the 1920s, composer and conductor John Philip Sousa brought the band concert to new heights of popularity in America, pleasing the public with his lively compositions. This turn-of-the-century postcard shows Sousa's band at Willow Grove Park, New York.*

While community singing, both religious and secular, was common at public gatherings—including socials, public festivals, and holidays—community bands outranked all other types of musical performers in popularity. Early bands in America, primarily composed of woodwind and percussion instruments, often were loosely connected with units of local or state militia. They played for parades and drills, gave public concerts, and sometimes provided music for dances. With technological improvements in the early 19th century, brass instruments such as cornets, trumpets, and horns became so popular that they dominated American bands for the next several decades. In the late 19th century, under the leadership of prominent bandmasters like Patrick Gilmore and John Philip Sousa, bands and band music reached new standards of achievement and acclaim. As cited in Carolyn Bryant's *And The Band Played On 1776-1976,* Sousa explained the special appeal of band music to Americans when he stated his aim as a composer: "I wanted to make a music

Above: *This 1939 photograph shows a school band marching in Dearborn, Michigan.* Right: *Franz Schwarzer of Washington, Missouri, made this zither around 1900, adding structural and decorative innovations to this traditional European instrument. Zithers were among the instruments used to accompany community dances.*

for the people, a music to be grasped at once."

By the turn of the century, local bands flourished all across America, helping to foster community pride and spirit. They played for just about every form of public gathering and amusement: they marched in military, political, holiday, and other parades; performed at festivals, picnics, sociables, and free outdoor concerts; provided the music for many local dances; and played at circuses, carnivals, minstrel shows, athletic contests, and holiday gatherings. With the proliferation of alternative forms of music and entertainment, their popularity gradually declined. Through the early 20th century, many community bands were replaced by local high school bands.

While urban dances were becoming increasingly refined, rural dances retained much of their earlier informal character. Occasionally the more sophisticated city folk played at recapturing some of the simplicity and heartiness of earlier times, as in this engraving, The Shirt and Pants Party, *from the* Days' Doings, *July 11, 1874. In this scene, Boston ladies and gentlemen "of a free and easy class" have donned rural costumes to dance amid simulated rustic surroundings.*

Despite restrictions by religious sects like the Puritans in the early years of settlement, dancing was one of the most popular rural diversions. Types of dances varied across the country, and regional styles persisted. Reflecting the high spirits of these community dances, J. M. Franks described the dances of his youth in *70 Years in Texas,* published in 1924:

> *[W]e would have a fiddler and he would rosin his bow, tune up his fiddle, and was then ready for the dance. Some fellow would shout out: "All to your places and straighten up your faces," and the dance was on. This was the old square dance, and I tell you those big-footed boys would just knock the black out of those old puncheon floors when the fiddler would start off. . . .*

Before callers became common late in the 19th century, people either knew the dances by heart or followed directions shouted out by a fiddler. Occasionally, a traveling dancing master taught the more popular dances recommended by dance manuals. Musical accompaniment varied depending on local preferences. In some regions, especially the South, dances were accompanied by singing and rhymes, since instruments were looked upon as tools of the devil. In other areas, a local band or at least a fiddler might be employed. Charles Hoffman described an unusual assortment of musicians at a tavern dance he attended near Chicago, Illinois, in *A Winter in the West* (1835):

> *[A] dandy negro with his violin, a fine military-looking bass drummer from the fort, and a volunteer citizen, who alternately played an accompaniment upon the flute and triangle.*

After the turn of the century, dancing became more formal, and earlier forms of dancing were relegated to physical education courses in schools. Ballroom dancing and dance halls came into vogue, incorporating ever-changing trends in popular music.

During the early decades of the 20th century, events organized by Progressive-era reformers to rekindle community spirit in urban neighborhoods and rural areas helped to restore and revive community-oriented music and dance. Recreation programs in these places encouraged participatory musical activities that were free of charge. Many clubs also sponsored community sings during the post-World War I years. In her 1924 study, *The Woman on the Farm,* Mary Meek Atkeson addressed the topic of community music-making as a modern form of rural recreation:

Everybody likes to sing and almost everybody can play some sort of musical instrument with a little training, so vocal and instrumental music should be a large part of the community recreation. . . . Each community group should have its active committee on music to organize choruses, duets, and quartettes, and arrange for solo singing. And every country boy and girl with musical talent should be in the local band or orchestra . . . . Many farm families can muster a small orchestra of their own, and if some of the neighbor boys and girls can drop in for the evening with their instruments, one of the best forms of community recreation can be developed.

Municipal and street dances as well were organized in order to draw young people away from public dance halls, which were generally considered to be unsavory and disreputable places.

Traditional forms of music and dance persisted in many regions and among various groups of Americans. A group of men display their proficiency to an informal audience in this turn-of-the-century photograph.

The radio and phonograph, increasingly available to the public in the 1920s, had a dual effect on community music and dance. On the one hand, they played a role in revitalizing earlier forms of community music and dancing. On the other hand, they sapped the amateur spirit and pulled people away from their local traditions. "Barn dance" music broadcast over the radio in the 1930s and 1940s, particularly helped revive public interest in square dances and related music. Fred Lape recalled that in the 1930s the standard repertoire of the dance orchestra in which he played included fox trots, waltzes, and square dances. He added that:

It soon became obvious that the square dances were the most popular numbers. They were attracting not only a few of the old timers but an increasing number of couples from the cities, persons who had never square danced before in their lives but who found the rhythms and the intricacies of the dances exciting. As the popularity of the dances increased, we added a banjo player and a second saxophone. We were much in demand, for the very reason that we could play both rounds and squares.

In the next few decades a square-dance craze swept the country, as dance magazines, records, television, and the movies acquainted the public with updated versions of earlier dance forms. More traditional dance forms persisted in some rural and more isolated regions.

The great popularity of square dancing in the mid-20th century, as depicted in this advertisement from Collier's, October 29, 1954, stemmed, in part, from the view that dancing was a constructive form of community recreation. Its adherents hoped that this participatory and thoroughly American dance form would help revive the community spirit that had become so elusive in urban settings.

Volunteer fire companies often sponsored their own social events, as can be seen by this 1857 invitation to the Excelsior Fire Company's First Annual Festival.

Clubs and Organizations

Foreign travelers in 19th-century America often remarked that Americans were a gregarious people who loved to gather into groups. In addition to church-related activities, a diverse assortment of clubs and societies provided an avenue for those who were interested in joining organized social groups. These organizations usually combined business with pleasure and invariably offered an escape from the routines of daily life.

Throughout the 19th century, local organizations thrived in both sparsely and heavily settled areas. Political societies, militia companies, and volunteer firemen admitted men, while discussion, literary, and debating societies, as well as choral groups and dramatic associations, were open to members of both sexes.

Fraternal organizations and secret societies had existed in America since the first settlement, but it was during the late 19th century that they became a major component of organized social groups for men at both local and national levels. Originally most were formed around particular trades and occupations, but eventually they came to be based on similar interests or ethnic backgrounds. Secret societies such as the Masons and the Odd Fellows emphasized mutual support and accepted members regardless of wealth or social standing. Some of the fraternal organizations furnished insurance and related benefits to their members.

After 1880, fraternal organizations grew at a phenomenal rate in number and membership. By the end of the century, close to 500 fraternal orders had been founded. The nationwide enrollment of six million men accounted for approximately 40 percent of the American male population over the age of 21. The colorful and exotic rituals developed by many of these groups were rich in religious and ethical symbolism, incorporating the sense of dignity and solemnity associated with contemporary attitudes of propriety.

Clubs and organizations sponsored and participated in many community gatherings, including fairs, socials, dances, picnics, and band concerts. They also organized similar activities for their own members. In *40 Years of American Life* (1864), Thomas Nichols noted that in New York City alone, each of the 50 or 60 companies of volunteer firemen gave one or more balls every winter, as did the 20 or 30 regiments of military volunteers. In addition, Nichols reported:

> *There are hundreds of societies and lodges of Freemasons, Odd Fellows, Sons of Temperance, Druids, and various Irish, German, trade, and benevolent societies, which must have at least their annual dance in winter, and excursion or pic-nic in summer.*

Ladies' societies also were common. Although some of these were auxiliaries to fraternal organizations, women were more inclined to form their own

First Annual Masquerade
ROBERT WAINWRIGHT SCOTT POST,
G. A. R.

464

U. S.
13,
G. L.

CASINO

Monday, February 22d, 1886.

ERIE, PENN'A.

From its founding in 1868 through the end of the 19th century, the Grand Army of the Republic organized scores of meetings and festive gatherings for the Union Army veterans of the Civil War and their families and friends. This 1886 G.A.R. Masquerade was held on Washington's birthday, a popular holiday for organizational and community affairs.

church-connected groups, such as ladies' aid and missionary societies. By the end of the 19th century, women also were involved in numerous clubs reflecting a "zealous pursuit of culture." As early as December 1880, an *Atlantic Monthly* article listed a variety of women's clubs devoted to cultural pursuits, noting:

> *We have art clubs, book clubs, dramatic clubs, pottery clubs. We have sewing circles, philanthropic associations, scientific, literary, religious, athletic, musical and decorative art societies.*

The declared goals of these women's organizations tended to stress education and moral improvement rather than recreation or entertainment.

Agricultural associations had been organized in America prior to the 19th century, primarily by gentlemen farmers and members of learned societies. During the second half of the 19th century, however, many cooperative and social organizations for the promotion of agricultural improvement sprang up in rural areas. Some were private associations and some represented specialized groups like woolgrowers, dairymen, or breeders. However, it was the organization founded in 1867 under the name of Patrons of Husbandry (although it was more commonly known as the Grange) that had the most profound effect on farmers of all kinds throughout the United States. Within six years of its founding, the Grange claimed to have 15,000 local orders, many of which were located in the Midwest and the South. The total membership of the Grange was said to be about one-and-a-half million.

Above right: *The Freemasons, a fraternal and benevolent association with roots in the Old World, became an important element in the social life of the United States during the 19th century. Masonic jewelry, like this pin made for Charles Gibson of Detroit around 1889, is rich in symbolic images associated with the tenets of freemasonry.* Right: *Fraternal organizations grew at a phenomenal rate in the United States in the latter decades of the 19th century. The ritualistic character of many of the proceedings and the exotic trappings associated with them are reflected in this 1890s carte-de-visite showing a member in the full regalia of an unidentified organization.*

Above: *The "Benevolent and Protective Order of Elks," a fraternal and charitable organization formed in New York City in 1868, became highly successful because it was able to adapt to the changing needs of its members over the years. This 1910 bowl sports the organization's official emblem.* Left: *The Patrons of Husbandry (also known as the Grange), founded in 1867, soon became the most popular agricultural organization in the United States, with thousands of local groups spread throughout the countryside. In addition to furthering political and educational goals, Grange meetings became important social gathering places for farmers and their families. The manifold purposes of the Grange movement are reflected in this 1870s engraving.*

The Grange encouraged all aspects of agricultural improvement and aided farmers through various cooperative activities. Including women and older children in its membership, it promoted extensive social and recreational activities in addition to regular monthly or semimonthly meetings. In time the Grange assumed a leading role in the social, political, intellectual, and recreational life of farm communities. Local orders organized lectures, concerts, debates, picnics, socials, box suppers, and dances. Hamlin Garland, describing his youth on the Iowa frontier in *A Son of the Middle Border* (1914), recalled the Grange's significance for his family:

My father was an early and enthusiastic member of the order, and during the early seventies its meetings became very important dates on our calendar. In winter "oyster suppers," with de-

bates, songs, and essays, drew us all to the Burr Oak Grove school-house, and each spring, on the twelfth of June, the Grange Picnic was a grand "turn-out." It was almost as well attended as the circus.

Everett Dick depicted a 19th-century Grange oyster supper in more detail in *The Sod-House Frontier, 1845-1890,* published in 1937:

The women brought big kettles or wash boilers and each family brought milk. The oysters and crackers were purchased from the order's fund. Songs, debates, recitations, essays, and other forms of entertainment often accompanied the oyster stew and coffee. Discussion of political and religious questions was strictly forbidden by the constitution of the order.

Right: *The Boy Scouts of America, organized in 1910 and modeled after a similar organization in England, combined an emphasis on good citizenship and community service with an extensive program of out-of-doors activities. The scouts in this 1946 photograph, taken in Detroit, are paying their respects at a memorial to Abraham Lincoln.* Below right: *Soon after the formation of the Boy Scouts, a number of girls' organizations with similar goals made their appearance. These included the Girl Scouts, whose commitment to community service is described in this early 1920s broadside.*

Although the number and variety of societies and organizations in the 19th century were constantly increasing, the rate of growth was actually relatively modest compared to the proliferation of clubs in the early 20th century. In their work *Middletown: A Study in American Culture* (1929), Robert S. and Helen M. Lynd noted that the town of Muncie, Indiana, had had 92 clubs in 1890, but by 1924 that number had risen to 458.

These new clubs and organizations offered a revised vision of what was meant by "community."

Rather than embracing only people living within geographical proximity, the notion of community was expanded to include those with a common heritage, profession, or interests. These types of clubs or organizations helped meet the universal need for companionship and social life, especially within larger towns and cities, where anonymity and emotional isolation were commonplace.

The newer clubs frequently were devoid of the ritualistic trappings characteristic of fraternal organizations and provided a more casual social

The Kiwanis organization, founded in Detroit in 1915, resembled other 20th-century clubs in de-emphasizing ritual and focusing on fellowship and community service. Among other activities, the Kiwanis sponsored recreational events like this 1941 ski tournament at Iron Mountain, Michigan.

English Girl Guides, was founded in Savannah, Georgia, in 1912, and incorporated nationally in 1915. An organization with a similar focus, the Campfire Girls, also was established in 1912.

Social stratification was reinforced by the development of these new clubs. As reflected in the Lynds' *Middletown: A Study in American Culture*, during the 1920s working-class men in Muncie, Indiana, tended to continue socializing through fraternal organizations and occupation-related organizations like trade unions, while middle-class families were more apt to join the new civic clubs.

During the 1920s and 1930s, growing numbers of women, especially from the middle and upper classes, joined clubs. Doris E. Fleishman drew attention to this trend in her article, "Women: Types and Movements," published in *America as Americans See It* (1932). She wrote:

American women do everything in clubs. It is astonishing to see how passionately clubminded they are. Whatever they do tends to take on more importance if it is done in such a group. A single act takes on a broad social import when it is performed by a number of women who have banded together under a name. A book read alone is just another volume perused. But a book read and discussed communally is part of an educational movement. Child care is studied in groups. Housing for workers, philanthropic work and the art of beautiful living is furthered in groups. There is a tremendous significance in the desire for personal and communal improvement as expressed by the women's club activities of America.

The national trend toward joining clubs included residents of rural communities, villages, and small towns, as well as cities. Traditional forms of rural gatherings declined in favor of the more formalized and specialized organizations. During the 1920s and 1930s, rural communities vigorously promoted civic service clubs and cooperative organizations for mutual aid and recreation. Clubs continue to serve as a means for bringing together people with similar interests or backgrounds.

ambience for their members. In an attempt to draw people away from some of the rapidly growing leisure pursuits that many considered harmful—burlesque shows, pool and dance halls, saloons, and the movies—such clubs increasingly developed their own programs of supervised recreational activities, including card and other games, music, and dancing. Amateur dramatic performances and pageants were especially popular.

While many of the 20th-century clubs retained strong business associations, they also developed community-service oriented programs. Some of the most popular service clubs were founded as national organizations from the beginning. Among these were three of the principal men's clubs: the Rotary Club (founded in Chicago in 1905); the Kiwanis (founded in Detroit in 1915); and the Lion's Club (founded in Chicago in 1917). The General Federation of Women's Clubs was established under the name "Sorosis" in New York City in 1889. The American Boy Scouts movement, emulating the British model organized in 1908, was incorporated in Washington, D. C., in 1910. The Girl Scouts movement, adapted from the

The Fourth of July 1876, the centennial celebration of Independence Day, provided the occasion for spectacular festivities in Madison Square, New York City, as this engraving from Harper's Weekly, *July 22, 1876, shows. The accompanying text referred to a "grand procession" as well as "magnificent illumination."*

Public Celebrations

Probably no activity was as effective in arousing a sense of unity and pride within a community as a public festival or celebration. National holidays, political rallies, parades, military musters, and other public celebrations offered occasions for members of diverse groups to meet for a common purpose and manifest their feelings of civic pride and patriotism.

The most widely and enthusiastically celebrated holiday of all was America's Independence Day. During the 19th century, the Fourth of July became the occasion for parades, band concerts, and patriotic orations. The formal ceremonies often began with public prayer, after which the Declaration of Independence was read. These ceremonies might be followed by community picnics or public dinners at which leading citizens proposed patriotic toasts. Formal balls, informal dances, and fireworks displays often rounded out the daylong celebration.

Describing New York City's celebration of Independence Day, Thomas Nichols remarked that great

numbers of local residents left town on that day to avoid the noise; their places were more than filled, however, by "the country people," who flocked to the city. The actual festivities began the night before with "a furious din and illumination" produced by the firing of firecrackers, guns, and cannons. This was accompanied by heavy feasting and drinking at the various booths set up by vendors along Broadway. At sunrise on the Fourth of July, the celebration began in earnest with the ringing of bells and the thunder of cannon from nearby ships and volunteer batteries, followed by the raising of the flag. All through the morning, "Chinese crackers" were fired off "by the millions and by tons" so that the air was "as full of the sulphurous smoke as that of a battlefield" and the pavements were "literally covered with the debris of exploded fire-crackers." Revelers continually fired rifles and pistols, thus adding to the general noise.

The parade that followed, made up of 8,000 to 10,000 men in military formation accompanied by

Left: *From 1897 on, Flag Day was observed every June 14, the anniversary of the day in 1777 on which America's Continental Congress adopted the flag of the United States. This Flag Day "exercise," from the 1902 book* Popular Amusements for In and Out of Doors, *suggests the type of presentation that might be prepared by a school or youth organization to celebrate this patriotic holiday. Below: July Fourth celebrations outside New York City were on an appropriately more modest scale. Nevertheless, as can be seen from this engraving entitled* Fire-Works in the Country, *which appeared in* Harper's Weekly, July 22, 1876, *the day's festivities—the parade, the speeches, the music, and the picnics—often concluded with a fireworks display.*

Decoration Day, honoring veterans of the Civil War, was first proclaimed in 1868 to encourage decoration of the graves of the Union dead. It remained a significant ceremonial holiday until the thinning ranks of the G.A.R. were replaced by veterans of World War I, at which time the holiday was renamed Memorial Day. This photograph, from Anthony's Photographic Bulletin, *July 11, 1885, depicts the celebration of Decoration Day in New York City.*

several regimental bands, constituted the grand attraction of the day. Afterward, the more formal proceedings—the orations and speeches—took place. According to James Boardman in *America, and the Americans,* published in 1833, the subsequent feasting was extensive:

> [F]rom the spacious saloons of the City Hall, to the humble dwelling of the artisan, the tables groaned with substantial viands, while the memories of the great father of the republic, and his immortal companions, were drunk in generous claret or sparkling champagne, the air resounding with the patriotic strains of "Hail, Columbia, happy land!"

The evening's fireworks displays—set off in several locations simultaneously and accompanied by band music—provided a grand climax to the celebration.

Similar celebrations occurred on a smaller scale in cities, towns, and villages across the country. English traveler Elizabeth Ellet described the celebration of Independence Day in Sodus Bay, New York, in *Summer Rambles in the West* (1853), as follows:

> The 4th of July, 1852, was here celebrated by a rural fete; an oration was delivered in one of the groves, followed by a substantial repast and a rustic dance, in a spacious arbor arranged for the occasion, with a fine display of fireworks in the evening, in front of the two hotels . . . . A calf and sheep were barbecued whole, after the primitive fashion, and huge pots of vegetables were set to boil over the fires kindled in the open air. . . . The time till dinner was spent in what might be called a regular celebration of the day. The Declaration of Independence was read by one of the citizens; then the orator was called upon for a speech; and after that a rustic poet rose and rehearsed some indifferent verses in honor of his country. This done, the banquet, the portion of the celebration certainly most relished by all present, commenced.

Many of the features of July Fourth celebrations continued into the 20th century, including the firing of cannons, band music, parades, formal ceremonies, community dinners, and fireworks. Pageantry became more common, as did participation by clubs

Parades and fireworks persisted into the 20th century as popular features of holiday celebrations. This 1926 Canada Dry advertisement emphasizes the enjoyment of the spectators at a July Fourth parade.

and local commercial and business interests. Games, sports, and other forms of community recreation also took a more important place in these celebrations.

Nineteenth-century communities also celebrated Washington's birthday, though to a lesser extent. Mrs. Trollope described a Washington's "Birth-day Ball" in Cincinnati, a gala event that she assumed took place in every town and city throughout the Union. English traveler Marianne Finch described the somewhat unusual observance of that day in New York City in *An Englishwoman's Experience in America,* published in 1853:

> *In the morning there was a procession, in which a little girl, habited in blue and silver, was car-*

ried under a canopy, and rather inadequately represented the Goddess of Liberty. In the afternoon an oration was pronounced by Senator Foote in Niblo's theatre.

After the Civil War, Memorial Day became a major holiday, for a time even surpassing Independence Day. Other essentially patriotic holidays that assumed a public character by the late 19th or early 20th centuries included Columbus Day, Lincoln's Birthday, Flag Day, Armistice Day, and Arbor Day. These holidays often called for formal public celebrations. As George A. Lundberg, Mirra Komarovsky, and Mary Alice McInerny wrote in their book *Leisure: A Suburban Study* (1934):

Community holiday celebrations often involved games and athletic competitions. As seen in this photograph from 1940, residents of Inkster, Michigan, take part in and observe a long jump contest that accompanied the July Fourth festivities of that town.

When this Goodyear advertisement appeared in the November 24, 1947, issue of Newsweek, Macy's Thanksgiving Parade in New York City was in its twenty-first year. In addition to the scores of spectators who lined the sidewalks to see the parade go by, thousands watched it on their television screens.

Parades, music, speeches, and ceremonies are on such occasions the order of the day, and they constitute major recreational events.

Although many 19th-century features of the celebration of public holidays continued into the 20th century, a general trend developed toward large public spectacles in which the majority of people were spectators rather than active participants. An extreme example of this is the gathering of New Yorkers at Times Square to ring in the New Year. Describing the scene in *The Great American Parade* (1953), H. J. Duteil wrote:

New Year's Eve is celebrated with a frenzy which is like the prefiguring of carnival week. In New York close to a million people gather in Times Square, between the Times Building and the Hotel Astor. Precisely at midnight this crowd is seized with delirium. No number of police can restrain it. All the cars in town sound their horns and klaxons, the gravest gentlemen have paper hats on and blow whistles. A panic delight, a myste-

rious need for making a noise, a grimacing super-excitement takes possession of this crowd, which moves shouting in every direction.

In addition to celebrating national holidays, many communities organized local celebrations. Until the mid-19th century, for example, legally mandated muster or battalion days served as occasions for community festivities. Volunteer militia from local communities met once or twice a year to drill and elect officers. Usually there was a three-day encampment, two days for a muster and drill and one day for a public review. Thomas Nichols recalled the "company-trainings" that took place in New England during the first half of the 19th century as follows:

The company-trainings on the green before the meeting-house were great days. The spectators gathered in crowds, drank sweet cider and New England rum, and ate molasses-gingerbread. Emulous pedlars (sic) sold tin-ware and Yankee notions at auction with stentorian lungs, and jokes that made the crowd snicker . . . . Our

Military musters and parades inspired lively community gatherings. This 1830s painting, The Gettysburg Guards, *depicts such a parade in a Pennsylvania town whose name would come to carry new meaning during the Civil War.*

citizen soldiers were dressed in every kind of homespun fashion, and as variously armed. . . . When they were tired of maneuvering, firing by platoons, and burning powder in a sham-fight, full of roars of command, rattle, and smoke, the captain, if oratorically gifted, made a speech, and the company was dismissed, satisfied that there was glory enough for one day, and that they had served their country.

At the muster of a regiment there was, of course, a larger gathering. People came ten or fifteen miles, in waggons (sic) and on horseback . . . . After the morning evolutions came the grand review . . . .

In 1848, the law mandating musters was repealed, largely because of the violence and drinking associated with these events.

Political processions, rallies, and election days also were occasions for public celebration. At these times, crowds of spectators or marchers in torch-lit parades would fill the streets. In cities parades were often followed by a mass meeting or public banquet; in rural areas picnics and barbecues were more usual. Horse races, band concerts, athletic contests, dancing to patriotic tunes, and fireworks displays often added to the enjoyment of these days.

Intense nationalism and local pride also encouraged public celebration of such events as the completion of the Erie Canal, the opening of the Atlantic telegraph, the completion of a railroad track or municipal waterworks, or the arrival of a notable foreign visitor. The increasingly passive participation of most of the people who attended these public celebrations, however, and the growing standardization of these events across the country, led to the organization of special local days devoted to encouraging active community participation. Old Settlers' celebrations, in which the early residents of an area were honored, were particularly popular in the last few decades of the 19th century. Lewis Atherton described them in his book *Main Street on the Middle Border* (1954):

People sometimes talked of erecting and equipping pioneer cabins, and old settlers occasionally baked corn pone, displayed old newspapers, and exhibited "relics" of early days, but nothing of a permanent nature resulted. In general, such gatherings took place at a county seat or village, with a morning oration, followed by a basket dinner, and then music, games, reminiscences of the past, and a reading of the names of those who had died during the preceding year.

In the early 20th century, Old Settlers' celebrations were largely replaced by special days or weeks promoting various types of community service. Among those observed in Muncie, Indiana, in the mid-1920s, for example, were "Thrift Week," "Savings Day," "Insure Yourself Day," "Share with Others Day," "Home Beautiful Week," "Clean Up and Paint Up Week," and "Fire Prevention Week."

Right: *Political rallies, which included flamboyant oratory, parades, and fireworks, were well staged and attracted thousands of spectators during the late 19th century. All manner of political accoutrements espousing the various candidates were produced for these events, including this hat made for the 1888 presidential campaign of Republicans Benjamin Harrison and Levi Morton. Below: Election day provided an excuse and opportunity for much conviviality during the 19th century, especially among the men of the community, who were the only ones to vote. One such high-spirited gathering can be seen in the 1854 engraving,* The County Election, *after a painting by George Caleb Bingham.*

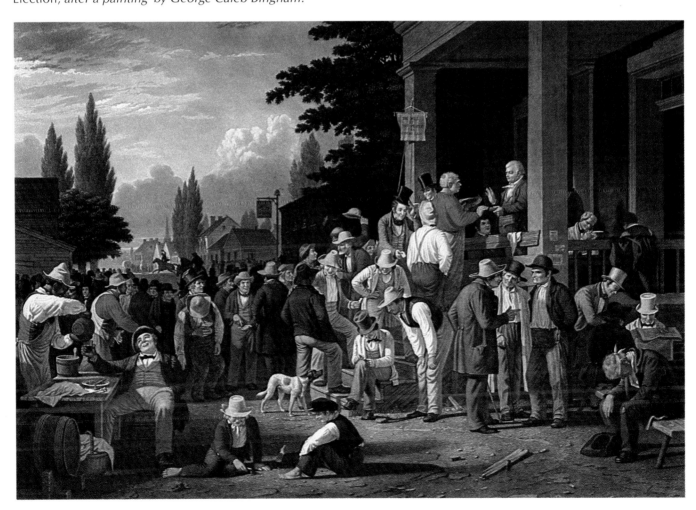

The entire nation joined in a mass celebration when the Atlantic telegraph cable was completed in 1858 (although it broke soon thereafter). On the appointed night, cannons were fired, bonfires were lit, and cities across the country were illuminated. In New York City, as this Harper's Weekly *illustration from August 28, 1858, shows, the fireworks were "of such unprecedented magnificence that they set the City Hall on fire."*

Community Gathering Places

People did not gather together only at specifically scheduled times and places to celebrate specially designated events. In many communities there were certain places where people tended to congregate for informal meetings and conversations. Churches and schools were important social centers, often providing auditoriums for a variety of recreational activities, from musical and dramatic performances to box suppers. Some churches provided their own entertainments, in some cases to make up for the recreational restraints they imposed upon their congregations.

Schools staged community spelling bees, geographical knowledge and mental arithmetic matches, dramatic programs, debates, and socials, as well as club meetings. In the 20th century, they not only continued to serve as centers for community recreation, but increasingly provided opportunities for adult education. While lodge and Grange halls also were used for diverse community activities during the latter part of the 19th century, in the 20th century these locations were largely replaced by growing numbers of newly built civic and community centers as settings for community gatherings.

Traditionally, there was a great deal of informal socializing at such locations as general stores, artisans' shops, and other service places. From the mid-19th century on, drugstores, especially ones with soda-water counters, became popular gathering places in both cities and towns. Fred Lape recalled that in Esperance, New York, the barber shop was a popular place for men to hobnob around the turn of the century:

Local Old Settlers' days were a popular diversion during the late 19th century, giving the older generation a chance to reminisce about earlier times. Such reunions attracted large crowds, as at this 1879 gathering in Bismarck Grove, Kansas.

Toward the back of the room was the usual pot-bellied stove and wooden benches and spittoon, and here even more than at the stores was the gossiping center for the men of the community.

In the 20th century, "going to town" continued to serve an important social purpose for community members, as is clear from the following excerpt from Horace Miner's study of Eldora, Iowa, *Culture and Agriculture: An Anthropological Study of a Corn Belt County,* published in 1949:

In the afternoon, or most commonly, after supper the rural families come to town in their cars. Upon arrival the families separate . . . . The women go to their favorite stores to shop and chat. Aside from the trading which is done, everyone has a chance to talk to friends. As the sidewalks around the court house square are packed with milling people from seven to eleven o'clock, the stores remain open for the trade . . . . As the people move about, groups of acquaintances form on the sidewalks. Girls parade by, arm in

Churches and schools served as important social centers in rural areas and small towns throughout the 19th century, as can be seen in this 1890s photograph of a flagpole raising in Grafton Center, New York.

During the 19th century general stores and artisans' shops served as informal gathering places for residents who had come to town to shop, as shown in this 1869 illustration.

arm, and are shouted at by the loitering groups of boys. This results in isolating acceptable double or triple couples of "dates" who later go off in cars. Conversation groups are continually forming, dissolving, and reforming. Friends from over a very wide radius are thus thrown together, and the expanded community does not have to be utterly dependent upon the "personal" columns of the newspaper for grist for its gossip.

In the developing suburban areas of the post-World War II era, outdoor shopping centers and indoor malls perpetuated traditional patterns by offering opportunities for community interaction and organized recreational activities.

Eating and drinking have always been associated with socializing, and establishments that serve food and drink have long been important gathering places. This was true of 19th-century inns or taverns which, in addition to providing food, drink, and shelter for travelers, also offered formal entertainment such as lectures, dances, and political speeches. At such places, informal conversation, card-playing, gambling, and storytelling continued throughout the day and well into the night. Taverns were particularly lively places during court days and elections, when barrooms often were filled to overflowing.

Drinking, usually heavy drinking, often went hand in hand with socializing in taverns. Frederick Marryat, an English traveler, remarked on this American characteristic in *A Diary in America: Remarks on Its Institutions* (1839):

Right: *Almost any type of establishment could serve as a community gathering place, especially if it offered a sidewalk bench. The San Diego, California, amusement store in this early 1940s photograph by Russell Lee, was probably stocked with pinball machines and other games, and possibly even gambling devices.* Below: *With increased emphasis on organized recreational activities in the 20th century, new uses were found for community buildings whose initial functions had declined. In this 1941 advertisement for Ford automobiles, a Grange hall is being used for a local square dance and supper.*

Above: *The barrooms of inns or taverns traditionally served as social clubs for the local men. However, the writer of the article accompanying this engraving from* Harper's, *November 13, 1858, disapproved of the use of barrooms as voting places.* Left: *Many foreign travelers commented on the heavy drinking that accompanied socializing in American taverns. This stoneware jug, made between 1835 and 1860, reflects this custom and undoubtedly helped incite the growing number of temperance advocates to try to combat the consumption of alcohol.* Below: *During the second half of the 19th century drinking saloons, like the one depicted in this turn-of-the-century photograph, frequently offered such amusements as card playing in addition to supplying alcoholic beverages.*

The Volk's Garten, depicted in this engraving from the October 15, 1859, issue of Harper's, was just one of several enclosed beer gardens to be found in New York's Bowery district at the time. Men and women gathered at these places on Sunday evenings to drink beer, talk, watch the entertainment, and listen to the band.

The consequence of the bar being the place of general resort is that there is an unceasing pouring out and amalgamation of alcohol and other compounds, from morning to late at night. To drink with a friend when you meet him is good fellowship, to drink with a stranger is politeness, and a proof of wishing to be better acquainted....

So much has it become the habit to cement all friendship, and commence acquaintance by drinking, that it is a cause of serious offence to refuse . . . .

The first bars in New York City are said to have sprung up as part of the business of corner grocery stores, but they soon developed into separate places devoted to drinking called saloons. Until Prohibition closed them down in 1920, saloons served an additional purpose as vital centers of neighborhood business and social life. Thomas Nichols related that the "great bar-rooms" of New Orleans:

[S]erve the purposes of commercial exchanges. They have news bulletins, and the latest telegrams, as well as the daily newspapers. Men meet here to do business, and cargoes of sugar and tobacco, corn and cotton, change owners over glasses of "Old Bourbon," or "Monongahela." Here, too, are held auctions . . . .

Reflecting the segmented nature of urban life, corner bars and saloons in cities became gathering places for local neighborhood residents, ethnic groups, and people of the same occupation or political persuasion. On the frontier and in more isolated areas, they served much the same functions as the earlier taverns, providing a central place for all sorts of people to meet for conversation, amusement, and relaxation.

An offshoot of the saloon was the German beer garden, which traced its origin to the Continental custom of enjoying Sunday afternoons outdoors with the family. In America, as in Europe, the beer garden often was attached to an inn or an outdoor recreation area on the outskirts of a major city. Characteristically, beer gardens were furnished with tables and chairs, and offered an assortment of food and some form of continuous music.

By the end of the 19th century, beer gardens had become social centers for native Americans as well as for newly arriving immigrants in search of a familiar diversion. Another type of drinking establishment introduced by immigrants was the coffeehouse, where customers could sit at small tables and converse or play cards over coffee or other nonalcoholic beverages, ice cream, and a variety of confections.

Nichols reported that ice cream, which he con-

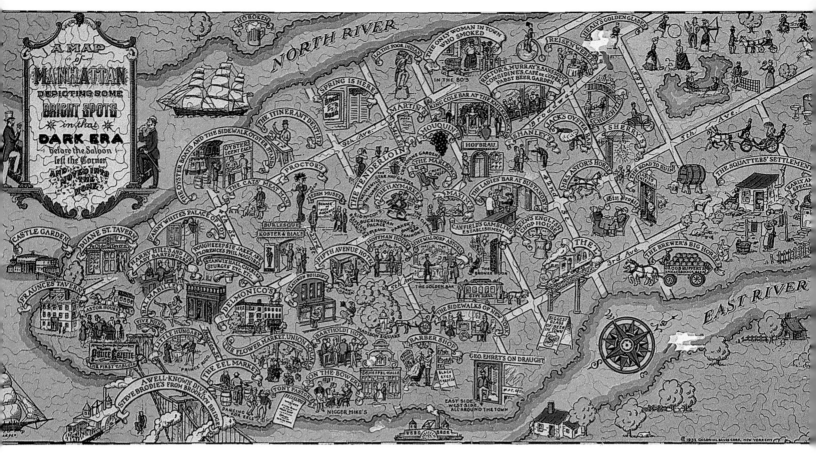

Despite the agitation of temperance advocates, the number of bars and saloons in the United States mushroomed during the late 19th and early 20th centuries. This humorous 1932 puzzle depicts the diversity of drinking establishments in Manhattan before the passage of the Volstead Act, which ushered in Prohibition in 1919.

sidered the most universal luxury in America, was served in public gardens, in saloons that held as many as a thousand people, and at large confectionery establishments in New York City. A report in the June 30, 1888, issue of the *St. Joseph County Republican,* published in Centreville, Michigan, noted that the ice cream sold at "Jack Hampson's place" made it the most crowded spot in town: "The continuous rattle of the popular milkshake could be heard at Jack's all day long." By the end of the 19th century, the specialized features of soda-water establishments, ice-cream saloons, and confectioneries often were combined to form what would become, in the 20th century, the ubiquitous and popular soda fountain.

Oysters were as popular as ice cream during much of the 19th century. Often, people got together to consume enormous quantities of oysters while enjoying each other's company at the numerous oyster saloons and cellars that sprang up in sizable towns and cities. English traveler Isabella Bird described the oyster saloons that she observed in New York City in 1854:

In the business street of New York the eyes are greeted continually with the words "Oyster Saloon," painted in large letters on the basement story. If the stranger's curiosity is sufficient to induce him to dive down a flight of steps into a subterranean abode, at the first glance rather suggestive of robbery, one favourite amusement of the people may be seen in perfection. There is a counter at one side, where two or three persons, frequently blacks, are busily engaged in opening oysters for their customers, who swallow them with astonishing relish and rapidity. In a room beyond, brightly lighted by gas, family groups are to be seen, seated at round tables, and larger parties of friends, enjoying basins of stewed oysters; while from some mysterious recess the process of cookery makes itself distinctly audible. Some of these saloons are highly respectable, while many are just the reverse.

Although barrooms and saloons held sway during the late 19th and early 20th centuries, a growing number of temperance advocates crusaded against alcoholic beverages and the places that served them. They promoted such establishments as coffeehouses, lunchrooms, and soda-water parlors, which generally offered food and an increasing number of recreational activities, as well as nonalcoholic beverages. When Prohibition forced the closing of thousands of bars across the country during the 1920s, these "substitutes for the saloon" entered their heyday. Numerous new soda fountains were built, while many existing bars converted to dispensing nonalcoholic beverages. Soda fountains began to serve hot drinks as well as light breakfast and luncheon foods. Tearooms, specializing in afternoon tea and dainty sandwiches, became highly popular with women.

After Prohibition was repealed in 1933, newer forms of eating and drinking establishments became popular. Roadhouses, located along highways and accessible by automobile, offered drinking, dining, entertainment, and socializing to young crowds from nearby towns. Cocktail lounges and taverns, located in urban areas, in towns, or adjacent to public facilities like train stations or hotels, served much the same function. Their characteristic dim lighting, high-backed booths, and small tables promoted intimacy among small groups. If live bands were not available, mechanical jukeboxes often provided music as background or as accompaniment for dancing. Socializing within small groups continued in restaurants and at the newer informal eating places like diners, hamburger stands, and drive-ins.

Outdoor areas have always provided opportunities for relaxation and socialization as well as for more formal, organized recreation and entertainment. Into the 19th century, these purposes were served by commons and greens in the centers of towns and villages, and by public squares in cities. When increasing population and new settlements began to encroach upon open spaces in 19th-century American towns and cities, public-spirited citizens and reformers urged the creation of public gardens and parks, especially for urban residents. According

Below: *Soda fountains experienced their heyday from the 1920s to the 1940s, initially due to the closing of bars during Prohibition. The social role played by drugstore soda fountains is clear from this 1943 photograph, taken by John Vachon on a Saturday afternoon in San Augustine, Texas.* Below right: *Early on, enterprising soda-fountain managers tried to entice customers with varied menu choices, including Vigoral, a mixture of concentrated beef and hot water guaranteed to make "weak people strong." The urn and mugs are from around 1910.*

Left: *After Prohibition was repealed, cocktail lounges and restaurants tried to create a sophisticated atmosphere to give drinking a positive image. The label on this bottle for "Hacker's Choice Pale Ale" was meant to convey this idea of respectability.* Below: *To provide wholesome substitutes for seemingly harmful commercialized amusements, community centers offering recreational activities began to be established around World War I. By 1943, when this photograph of a recreational facility in the workers' quarters at the Ford bomber plant in Willow Run, Michigan, was taken, such centers had become widespread.* Bottom: *As automobile ownership increased during the 1930s, young people gathered at highway roadhouses to socialize, drink, and dance. This photograph was taken by Russell Lee in a Raceland, Louisiana, roadhouse in 1938.*

During the 1930s and 1940s, dimly lit bars and cocktail lounges were characteristically furnished with small tables and high-backed booths that offered privacy to patrons. This isolation would break down for special events, like this television relay of a 1949 World Series game.

to Clarence C. Cook, in *A Description of the New York Central Park*, published in 1869, formal gardens, such as Vauxhall and Niblo's in New York City, were designed to provide:

> *Open-air inclosures where people went to eat cakes and ices, the boys and girls to meet one another, and the elders to talk gossip and politics, and to discuss the scandal of the hour.*

Landscaped cemeteries located on the outskirts of urban centers also served as park-like spaces for outings, as well as for devotions honoring the departed.

City parks like New York's Central Park, created in 1858, were designed to encourage the urban public to socialize, and at the same time to refresh and calm their "hurrying, workaday lives" with beautiful and "reposeful" sights and sounds. Discreetly positioned "Keep Off the Grass" signs preserved the unspoiled appearance of the landscape by shepherding the public from one vantage point to another. In designated places, people could walk, drive, ride, row, skate, and engage in various other sports and recreational activities. Most important, the park was available free of charge to people from all walks of life.

Above: *Beginning in the 1830s, park-like rural cemeteries were being designed to provide relaxing places for urban families and friends to visit. The Greenwood Cemetery on Long Island, pictured in this 1855 lithograph, was one of the earliest of these, incorporating the ''picturesque'' mode of landscape design then in vogue in England.* Below: *Central Park was the first and most influential of America's landscaped parks, intended to provide recreational opportunities not only for the privileged classes but for the population as a whole. This 1869 lithograph suggests the variety of activities to be enjoyed in Central Park.*

San Francisco's Golden Gate Park, shown in this turn-of-the-century stereograph, was considered exemplary among the new public parks that were designed to offer recreational opportunities as well as picturesque scenery. Not only were people encouraged to walk on the grass, but an array of cultural and natural attractions was added to draw city residents to the park.

Inspired by this and other examples of great urban parks, the public demand for more formal outdoor recreation areas gained momentum during the second half of the 19th century. By the 1890s, this movement had become a nationwide cause. Into the 20th century many local parks were equipped with a growing array of recreational facilities, including bandstands, clubhouses, pavilions, picnic tables, shelters, grills, and refreshment stands. Organized park programs included dancing, concerts, and civic pageants. In his book *Substitutes for the Saloon*, published in 1919, Raymond Calkins gave the following glowing report of the facilities of one of the most widely acclaimed parks of this type, Golden Gate Park in San Francisco:

There are many attractions besides the groves, flowers, and scenery. Music, a museum, a conservatory, an aviary, zoological garden, recreation grounds, speed tracks, drives, and walks help to draw the people. On Sunday afternoon . . . a band of fifty pieces gives a free concert to an audience of ten thousand scattered over the grounds or seated in the large auditorium. In the museum,

there are sometimes as many as three thousand people. There is the greatest freedom allowed in the park, and there are no "Keep off the Grass" signs . . . . This great gathering of people in open air is in striking contrast with the city . . . .

Parks of varying sizes and facilities across the country continue to provide open spaces for Americans to relax and to pursue recreational activities.

The changing fabric of life from America's pre-industrial years to the mid-20th century is reflected in the altered nature of community gatherings during this time. Informal gatherings of people living within geographic proximity declined in favor of formally organized groups and group activities related to more specialized interests. Following similar trends in other leisure pursuits, gatherings devoted solely to recreation also became more widespread. All of these types of gatherings, however, shared a common objective: to bind individuals together through shared experiences and the social ties necessary to ensure the well-being and continuity of a community.

Home Amusements

STAYING IN:
Home Amusements

*T*he American home has proven an enduring setting for a variety of leisure activities, from parties and family celebrations to the commercial entertainment provided by radio and television. The specific nature of these pursuits, however, has altered in accordance with a number of factors, especially with the changing role of the home in the lives of American families and in the relationships of family members to one another.

In the preindustrial period, the home provided a setting for both work and amusements, and these activities often were interrelated. The home frequently served as the place for extended social visits and holiday celebrations involving family and community members. A heavy emphasis was placed on activities that were morally uplifting or instructional.

As home and workplace became separated in an increasingly urban-industrial society, family members saw less of each other than they had before. The strict conventions of Victorian society dictated appropriate home leisure pursuits, focusing primarily on female domesticity and gentility. Many earlier pastimes, including visiting and party-giving, became highly structured, even ritualistic, at this time.

By the end of the 19th century, technological developments and mass production had tremendously widened the scope and expanded the number of home amusements. Commercialized industries sprang up in connection with a broad range of home leisure pursuits, providing such items as toys, games, sheet music, and magazines and books. The success of these industries ultimately led to a greater awareness and acceptance of their products, as well as to the standardization of these items on a national basis.

The emphasis in the post-World War I period was on treating the home as a private haven for the relaxation and entertainment of all members of the family. Activities that had been highly structured a decade or so earlier became less formal, and many of them were seen as potential ways of bringing the family together.

As more leisure-related goods appeared and families had more money to spend, home amusements became part of the consumerist culture. Manufac-

Facing page: *Industrialization and consequent social changes influenced every aspect of life in America, including the scope and scale of leisure activities in the home. This illustration, from* Queen of the Home, *published in 1892, shows some of the favored home amusements of the time.*

turers realized high profits by planning new lines of products linked to the seasons and to annual celebrations like Easter, Halloween, and Christmas, and by gearing products toward special-interest groups, from hobbyists to high-fidelity sound production enthusiasts.

Like other leisure activities, home amusements in the present century have been more focused on offering entertainment than on instruction. The mass media, which brought entertainment to American homes on a broader and larger scale than ever before, have come to dominate the nation's domestic leisure time.

Reading for information and entertainment has been one of America's chief forms of relaxation since the early 19th century. This photograph is from around 1900.

A NEW ENGLAND FIRESIDE.

This engraving from Ballou's Pictorial, March 10, 1855, *depicts one of the principal pastimes in 19th-century rural America—visiting family and friends. Referring to the "good old-fashioned New England homestead" shown here, the author of the accompanying article noted that many such "yet exist, remote from cities and large towns."*

Visiting and Entertaining

Through much of the 19th century, social visits in rural areas often required overnight, or even more extended stays because of the distances involved, the slowness of transportation, and the fact that the demands of farm life made such visits rare occurrences. During these visits, the children usually played games while the adults reinforced their ties with conversation and gossip. Such visits helped to bridge the sense of isolation imposed by rural life.

The custom of calling and receiving visitors, at first mainly observed by upper-class families in large towns and cities in America, had its origins in the social world of the European aristocracy. During the second half of the 19th century, these highly formal activities were enthusiastically imitated by the American middle class; paying calls on friends and acquaintances became a popular leisure activity for the women of the household. Such visits often had an important purpose, namely, to advance one's own or the family's social position. The material evidences of the calling ritual were printed calling cards, which expressed a range of social meanings by their design, content, and the manner in which they were presented. As John S. Locke wrote in *The Art of Correspondence,* published in 1884:

Cards, though only pieces of pasteboard, bearing simply a name, play an important part in the drama of social life.... They exhibit whatever of character or influence is attached to the name they bear, and, in many cases, become the representative of the individual.

Both the customs of extended visiting (derived from rural traditions), and calling (derived from aristocratic and urban conventions), declined after

Above: *A more formal procedure than the mere exchange of visits, calling was especially prevalent among middle-class women eager to move up the social ladder. The "calling" ritual stimulated the demand for calling cards like this one, dating from around 1880.*
Right: *This page from an 1885 sample book shows the variety of stock cards available for embossing with one's name. Below: This turn-of-the-century photograph shows a typical "call" in progress.*

World War I. With urbanization and increasing mobility, people were more likely to socialize with fellow members of special-interest clubs and associations than with those who lived nearby.

While social interaction with neighbors revived somewhat in the suburban communities that sprang up after World War I, visits with neighbors tended to be less elaborate and less time-consuming than had been customary during the previous century. This new informality was reflected in Della Lutes's *Gracious Hostess* (1923):

Formality in the use of the visiting card, as in making calls and sending invitations, has lessened with the growing intimacy and democracy of our lives. Much of this is due to the outdoor life we are now living....Formal visits and ''duty calls'' savor of dullness, and we refuse to be dull.

Although visiting has continued to be a popular activity among friends, such inventions as the telephone and the automobile have hastened the decline of lengthy social visits.

Parties, a more formal type of home entertaining, required greater organization than visiting. As in the case of the calling ritual, the formal parties of the wealthy—teas, dinner parties, and balls—were avidly imitated by the middle class in the late 19th century. However, after World War I, informal parties became popular. *How to Entertain at Home,* issued by the Priscilla Publishing Company in 1927, proclaimed, ''Informality is the note of the day, and happily so. Formal occasions are generally stiff and cumbersome, if not stupid.'' Teas were replaced by bridge parties and ladies' luncheons, while informal supper parties were favored over dinner parties. The cocktail party combined the earlier custom of receiving visi-

"I HAVE THE NICEST HUSBAND"

Many a man would like to hear his wife say that. So here's a tip.

Get her one of those new kitchen telephones that hang on the wall.

Convenience is just the half of it. She'll be so proud!

It will be a conversation piece in more ways than one. Especially if it's in color.

Above: *After World War I, the calling ritual became less formal, although many women continued to favor a more relaxed version of the custom, as depicted on the cover of this 20th-century question-and-answer game.* Left: *The telephone offered an easy way to socialize without leaving home or receiving visitors, as indicated by this Bell Telephone advertisement from* Life, *December 2, 1955.*

tors with the more informal aspects of 20th-century entertaining. Growing use of the back yard as a setting for leisure activites made outdoor parties increasingly fashionable.

A trend toward serving less elaborate meals also made entertaining easier. What had once involved tedious hours of planning, preparation, and the use of servants could now be accomplished solo by an efficient hostess. According to Ida Bailey Allen in *Successful Entertaining* (1942), the new custom of serving appetizers before the meal helped the "maidless hostess bridge over that awkward interval when the guests are arriving." Buffet-style dinners, with the guests serving themselves, offered a happy alterna-

tive to sit-down dinners requiring service. And by the 1950s, a revival in the popularity of the cooperative or potluck dinner (derived from 19th-century community gatherings) relieved many a hostess of the burden of preparing the whole meal by herself, and allowed her to devote more energy to entertaining her guests.

The availability of a profusion of ready-to-eat canned delicacies during the 1920s and the invention of mixes and fast-frozen foods in the 1930s, considerably lightened the work of entertaining at home. This trend toward using semi- or fully prepared foods for home entertaining continued in the decades following World War II.

Left: *Entitled* One O'Clock A.M., Supper Time, *this illustration from* Frank Leslie's Lady's Magazine, *April 1864, shows the breakdown of the customary formality as supper is served at this rather splendid gathering.* Above: *Specialized serving equipment was devised to help the hostess who had no servants. This late-1930s electric snack server, made by the Chase Brass & Copper Company of Waterbury, Connecticut, was designed to keep food at a consistent temperature while it stood on the buffet table. A promotional brochure pointed out that this invention gave the hostess the "welcome opportunity" to be with her guests during the entire party, and not just in "fits and starts."*

The Hungry Man's OUTDOOR GRILL Cookbook

$1.50

The expansion of suburban living in the post-World War II era helped American families rediscover the pleasure of relaxing in their back yards. Some yards were fitted out like outdoor living rooms, with special furniture, grills, picnic areas, and, in some cases, swimming pools. This cover from The Hungry Man's Outdoor Grill Cookbook, published in 1953, illustrates the types of accoutrements deemed necessary for a back-yard barbecue party.

Home and Family Celebrations

The high points in an individual's life have traditionally been celebrated at home. The announcement of a birth in the local newspaper might bring neighbors to the house with food and offers of assistance. Celebrations of religious rituals associated with birth were more intimate affairs, often confined to relatives and largely shaped by the family's religious affiliation. Baby showers—gatherings of friends and family bringing gifts in anticipation of a baby's birth—became popular in the 20th century.

In the 19th century, birthdays often were celebrated by a family dinner or simply by visits from family and friends. By the close of the century, children's birthdays were being celebrated at structured parties attended by their friends. Children's birthday parties became even more elaborate after World War I; decorated cakes, special party decorations, and gifts increasingly became the rule. Adult birthdays, when celebrated at all, continued to involve only close relatives, although the elderly were sometimes given special birthday celebrations at large family get-togethers or by old friends.

Coming-of-age rituals often were celebrated at home parties attended by family and friends. These rituals might be religious, like confirmations and bar mitzvahs, or purely social, like "coming out" parties. In the 20th century, these celebrations were supplemented or sometimes even replaced by school graduation parties.

In rural areas through the 19th century, an entire community might eagerly anticipate and attend a local wedding, since the "frolics" associated with weddings were among the few social gatherings not

By the early 20th century, children's birthday parties had become customary. Left: In this scene from a 1904 book of Buster Brown comics, the children attending Buster's birthday party have piled the requisite presents on the table in the foreground. Above: Candles for the prescribed birthday cake were often inserted into holders like these, shown with their display box.

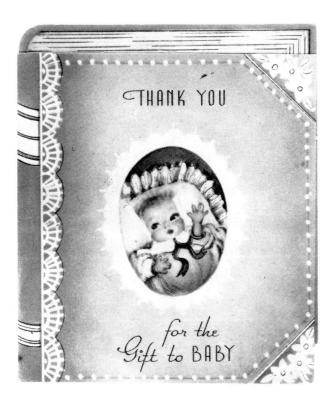

Above: *This card, dating from the 1950s, would have been sent out to acknowledge a gift received at a baby shower or after the baby's birth.* Right: *The tradition of sending out announcements of a baby's birth has been around for some time, as this humorous card shows.*

accompanied by some form of work. Some such affairs were quite boisterous, with dancing and revelry lasting far into the night. Other regional celebrations associated with weddings also took place in homes. For example, the "charivari" (a term of French origin that came to mean the creation of incessant noise outside the wedded couple's new home until the revelers were invited inside) was particularly popular in isolated settlements in the South and Midwest. The "infare" (a Scottish term, coming to mean a gathering of close friends and family members the day after the wedding at the bride's or bride's parents' house) was known to take place in some Midwestern and Western communities. After World War I, premarital gatherings like the bachelor dinner or party, bridesmaids' luncheons, and bridal showers became prevalent.

Anniversaries were sometimes celebrated at home. Such celebrations often were described in local newspapers, as in the following item from the September 7, 1882, edition of the *Independent Register,* published in Columbiana, Ohio:

Mr. and Mrs. Geo. M. Esterly celebrated the twentieth anniversary of their marriage on Tuesday evening, and a large party of their friends were there to aid in duly commemorating the interesting and joyful event. Their residence was thronged, in fact, overflowed with guests; all ages being appropriately represented.... After partaking of a variety of sumptuous refreshments, provided in lavish abundance, and passing several hours in an enjoyable way, the company dispersed with kind wishes for their courteous entertainers.

Wedding anniversary parties became even more common after World War I in step with the growing popularity of informal gatherings.

Funerals often involved socializing by relatives

Left: *Weddings and their anniversaries have long served as occasions for celebration and gifts. This tin basket was created specifically as a 10th wedding anniversary gift around 1850. Below left: The advertisement from the* Woman's Home Companion, *March 1950, depicts a bridal shower. The custom of giving bridal showers, which became prevalent after World War I, remains as popular as ever. Below right: From the early 20th century on, the betrothed couple could choose from an assortment of specialized accessories to enhance their wedding reception. This included such items as these decorative crepe-paper bride and groom figures.*

Imagine! Real Gorham silver from the kids in the office!

Lunch Hour Shower

YOU'VE BEEN HEADING all your memos with your wedding date...dreamily typing his name with a "Mrs." in front of it...not quite sure it would really happen. But now it seems real...you've been given your first two place-settings of Gorham Sterling...beautiful, permanent, so much a part of marriage.

The excitement of getting married never changes, they say. But for millions of today's brides it is more exciting, in one sense, than ever before. They know that from the first day of married life they can own Gorham Sterling. They can begin with the best. They can use it every day at every meal all their lives.

By using the modern place-setting method of buying Gorham, you can start with one place-setting—six pieces of solid silver—about $26.00 (Fed. tax incl.) depending on the pattern. Then, add to your pattern gradually. And though your tastes may change, your Gorham pattern will never be out of place or out of fashion, so honest and authentic is its design.

At your Gorham dealer's, see delicate, lace-edged Camellia* (above) and the many other Gorham* patterns. And send for our illustrated booklet "Entertaining...the Sterling Way," 10¢ (outside U.S.A., 40¢). The Gorham Company, WHC-31, Providence, R. I.

Gorham *"Camellia"*

Gorham *"Lyric"*

Gorham *"Chantilly"*

Gorham *"Buttercup"*

Gorham *"Sovereign"*

Gorham
STERLING

AMERICA'S LEADING SILVERSMITHS SINCE 1831
Also Makers of Gorham Silverplate, Gorham Silver Polish, Gorham Bronze, Gorham Ecclesiastic Wares.

*TRADE MARKS
COPYRIGHT 1950 BY
THE GORHAM COMPANY

A NEW ENGLAND THANKSGIVING DINNER.

This engraving from Gleason's Pictorial, *December 6, 1851, depicts a New England family enjoying a great feast, the hallmark of the Thanksgiving holiday. The accompanying text observed that family members "from far and near" join "in the happy festal hour . . . all feast to their very fill from groaning tables laden with the fat of the land."*

and groups of people who lived nearby or came from similar ethnic or religious backgrounds as the deceased. Relatives and friends might make condolence calls before or after funeral services, while neighbors might come by to help the mourning family prepare for visitors or might bring food for the reception usually held after the burial.

A number of formal holidays traditionally have been marked by home celebrations. Thanksgiving had been a popular day for feasting and visiting among New Englanders since early Colonial times, and after its proclamation as a holiday by the government in 1789, it came to be observed by many other communities as well. In 1864, President Abraham Lincoln designated the fourth Thursday of November as the official day for observing the holiday.

The Christmas holiday, which was at first observed only among some ethnic and religious groups, was legalized in all American states between 1836 and 1890, Alabama being the first, and Oklahoma the last of the then existing states to do so. While the closing of banks, state offices, schools, and workplaces varied from state to state (most of these closings were officially ordered several years after the holiday was legalized), the growing popularity of Christmas celebrations was a sign of increasing efforts to strengthen family ties to the home. Evidence for this can be found in the fact that 13 states legalized the Christmas holiday during the Civil War years—the period that also saw the legalization of Thanksgiving as a holiday.

Christmas customs and rituals, such as exchanging gifts, decorating the home, hanging stockings, and trimming the tree, were incorporated into family celebrations from the observances of various cultures and religious groups throughout the country. A day long associated with family reunions, feasting, and children, Christmas has retained its tradition of family togetherness to the present.

Above: *Illustrations like this scene from* Harper's Weekly, *December 25, 1858, helped popularize holiday customs, especially the display of Christmas trees. Decorations for tabletop trees (introduced by German immigrants) often included gifts for children as well as candles and ornaments.* Below right: *Although the first electrically lit Christmas tree appeared in 1882, lights were expensive and undependable well into the 20th century. This type of electric bubble light was patented just after World War II.* Below left: *By the 1950s, when this photograph was taken, Santa Claus had become more conspicuous, and commercial items had replaced home-made Christmas gifts and decorations.*

Above: *This fashion plate from* Demorest's Magazine, *January 1874, depicts a formal New Year's Day reception. Such gatherings were popular during the 19th century, especially among city dwellers with social aspirations. It was customary for the men to visit as many friends and acquaintances as possible during the day, while the women remained at home to receive visitors.* Right: *By the end of the 19th century, the exchange of Christmas gifts between adults had become more customary. This whiskey bottle from around 1900 wishes its recipient both a merry Christmas and a happy New Year.*

Calling on friends became an important aspect of celebrating the new year through much of the 19th century, particularly in cities and among people with social aspirations. British traveler Captain Thomas Hamilton described New Year's Day calling customs in New York City in *Men and Manners in America* (1833) as follows:

The ladies of a family remain at home to receive visits; the gentlemen are abroad, actively engaged in paying them. You enter, shake hands, are seated, talk for a minute or two on the topics of the day, then hurry off as fast as you can. Wine and cake are on the table, of which each visitor is invited to partake.

By 1880, the custom had spread throughout the country. Indeed, according to *Hill's Manual of Social and Business Forms,* it had become fashionable for ladies:

[T]o announce in the newspapers the fact of their intention to receive calls upon New Year's day, which practice is very excellent, as it enables gentlemen to know positively who will be prepared to receive them on that occasion; besides, changes of residence are so frequent in the large cities as to make the publication of names and places of calling a great convenience.

After World War I, New Year's Day celebrations were largely supplanted by New Year's Eve parties, and the entire week between Christmas and New Year's Day became a favored time for home entertaining. In the post-World War II era, New Year's Day has been celebrated in many American homes with parties arranged to watch college football games on television.

Like Christmas, Easter began as a strictly religious holiday, but became more secularized in the course of the 19th century. Children's activities like

Right: *Many of the Easter items produced commercially are geared to children, like this pull toy, which was meant to be filled with decorated eggs and candy.* Below: *Like Christmas, Easter has become a highly commercialized holiday since the turn of the century. The lily, egg basket, and rabbit depicted on this 1938 telegram are among the emblems that link the religious holiday of Easter to more ancient pagan festivals associated with the coming of spring.*

dyeing Easter eggs, egg hunts, and egg-rolling frolics became connected with the holiday celebration by the late 19th century. A family dinner also became part of Easter celebrations at home.

After World War I, many holidays traditionally celebrated at home, including Christmas and Easter, became increasingly commercialized. Scores of special holiday decorations were manufactured for these occasions and appropriate recipes and foods were recommended to enhance home celebrations. Greeting cards were printed by the thousands, not just for holidays like Valentine's Day traditionally associated with sending greetings, but for as many holiday occasions as the card publishers could promote. At the same time, families were encouraged to observe holidays as a way of cultivating familial closeness. Ida Bailey Allen, in *Successful Entertaining,* urged:

In households where there are children, celebrate not only Christmas and Thanksgiving but all holidays in some way. Such days become a tradition in family life and are the milestone of memory. It may not be convenient to give a party, but a special holiday cake, a little decoration on the dinner table, or a surprise now and then can surely be introduced. Valentines for everyone at the dinner table, a Washington's Birthday cherry cake, fun for St. Patrick's Day, an April-fool dinner, May baskets, a Flag-Day celebration—so we might continue throughout the year....

The celebration of Mother's Day (first observed in Philadelphia in 1910 and declared a national holiday in 1914) and of Father's Day (first observed in Spokane, Washington, in 1910 and celebrated informally across the country since then) were introduced both to encourage family unity and to promote the sale of greeting cards and gifts. Halloween, a holiday with religious origins but increasingly secularized as celebrated in America, came to assume major proportions as a children's festivity.

Top: *Halloween, designated as the eve of All Saint's Day in the 7th century, was closely linked to an ancient autumn festival with a long history of merriment and parties. In the post-World War I era it became an American custom for groups of children in costume to go out into the neighborhood to "trick or treat." In later years this netted them large quantities of candy.* Above: *Beginning in 1910, the movement to celebrate both Mother's Day and Father's Day represented efforts to reaffirm family unity. In time, the celebration of these days became highly commercialized, as demonstrated by this card, one of thousands mass produced in 1943.*

Reading

As cited in James D. Hart's *Popular Book* (1950), a London bookseller named Lackington, who had traveled across America in 1791, remarked that:

> *[T]he poorer sort of farmers, and even the poor country people in general, who before . . . spent their winter evenings in relating stories of witches, ghosts, hobgoblins, &c. now shorten the winter nights by hearing their sons and daughters read tales . . . . In short all ranks and degrees now READ.*

As Lackington observed, reading as a form of relaxation and home entertainment had been well established by the 1790s. Moreover, literacy was not limited to the upper classes, but was considered to be the right of all citizens. This high degree of literacy was primarily a consequence of the importance attached to reading the Bible from the Colonial period on.

Although they were not the only form of secular literature being produced, almanacs early on served as a major source of pleasurable reading. Aimed at the general public, they were intended for readers of all ages. They provided information pertaining to daily work, including calendars; tide tables; harvest suggestions; and recipes (then known as receipts); but also included proverbs; riddles; humorous anecdotes; poems; exotic-adventure and sentimental narratives; and humorous art work. As more almanacs were produced during the late 18th and early 19th centuries, publishers added increasing numbers of these entertaining features to the contents in order to outsell their competitors.

From the mid-19th century on, the scope of reading materials expanded immeasurably. The demand for books increased as more people became educated. Major advances in printing, paper making, and publishing made books readily available to a major segment of the population. Improvements in transportation expanded their distribution, while innovations in home lighting increased the number of hours in the day that could be devoted to reading.

Of all the types of books published for the American public, fiction soon became and remained the most popular. Responding to accusations that novels were "polluting the imagination," publishers at first promoted them for their value in teaching moral lessons. By the mid-19th century, however, popular fiction had achieved respectability and middle-class women in particular became avid readers of domestic novels directed at them. The best-selling novel before the Civil War was Harriet Beecher Stowe's two-volume anti-slavery novel, *Uncle Tom's Cabin,* published in 1852. Within three weeks of its publication, 20,000 copies of this work had been sold.

The penchant for novelty and adventure that had developed as part of the American tradition of oral storytelling furnished many of the major themes for popular novels. After the Civil War, adventure stories, especially about the opening of the West, gained a ready audience among men. Although an inspirational and moralistic viewpoint remained evident in these works, the authors introduced an abundance of drama and excitement into their books as well.

Throughout the 19th century, books became less expensive and, therefore, more accessible to the general public. By the last few decades of the century, paperback adventure-story books were being sold as parts of nickel, dime, and twenty-cent "libraries" or series. Some of the more sensational stories were popularly referred to as "dime novels" or "dime shockers." "Pulp" magazines, introduced in the 1890s and so called because they were printed on cheap and poor quality wood-pulp paper, supplanted dime novels by the first decade of the 20th century.

Toward the end of the 19th century, historical romances, meant to amuse and interest rather than to instruct their readers, found an eager following among women. These types of stories dominated American popular fiction between the 1880s and the 1920s, offering an escape from the uncertainties of a changing society by evoking an earlier, supposedly simpler time.

In the post-World War I era, the publishing industry became highly commercialized and concerned with mass marketing. Popular fiction was influenced by current events, more permissive canons of behavior, more sophisticated advertising, and the mass media. Adventure stories (especially Westerns), romances (especially historical romances), domestic

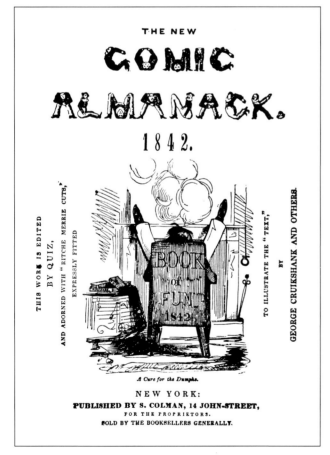

THE NEW

GOMIC

ALMANACK.

1842.

THIS WORK IS EDITED
BY QUIZ,
AND ADORNED WITH "RITCHE MERRIE CUTS,"
EXPRESSLY FITTED

TO ILLUSTRATE THE "TEXT,"
BY
GEORGE CRUIKSHANK AND OTHERS.

BOOK of FUN! 1842

A Cure for the Dumps.

NEW YORK:

PUBLISHED BY S. COLMAN, 14 JOHN-STREET,
FOR THE PROPRIETORS.
SOLD BY THE BOOKSELLERS GENERALLY.

As almanacs found themselves increasingly in competition with other forms of popular literature during the first half of the 19th century, they became more entertaining and less prosaic. The publishers of this 1842 almanac went so far as to call their offering a "comic almanack" and a "book of fun."

Above: *Compulsory public schooling and technological innovations in paper production and printing made books accessible to an increasingly wider American public as the 19th century progressed. This 1860s engraving suggests the spaciousness and substantial inventory of John P. Jewett & Company's bookstore in Boston around the time of the Civil War.*
Right: *Novels outstripped all other books in popularity, providing an escape from the routine of daily life. The gentleman in this turn-of-the-century photographic postcard is likely to have chosen an adventure-filled Western or mystery-detective story to entertain him.*

novels, exposes, and mystery and detective novels remained most in demand; science fiction acquired a growing readership from the 1930s on.

"Pulp" magazines experienced their peak of popularity during the 1920s and 1930s. Following a formula derived from the dime novels, they delivered action-packed adventure, romance, and detective stories as well as a growing number of science-fiction and fantasy tales.

Although best sellers had existed during the 19th century and the Book-of-the-Month Club had been established as early as 1926, it was the mass manufacture of paperback books in the 1930s that most significantly expanded the scope of popular

IDLE HOURS

NOVELETTE

Composed by
JOHN T. HALL
Composer of
"WEDDING OF THE WINDS" WALTZES
"MURMURING WATERS" WALTZES
Etc.

6

JOHN T. HALL MUSIC PUB CO INC
1285 BROADWAY
NEW YORK

1905

Facing page: *Novels for women tended to be quite different in character from those directed at men. Women like the one depicted on the cover of this 1905 sheet music were likely to read historical romances, moral or religious tales, or novels centering around domestic life.* Above: *Improvements in home lighting stimulated reading in a number of ways. It increased the hours during which one could read comfortably and expanded the areas that could be lit by a single lamp. This illustration from the 1919 Coleman Quick-Lite catalog was meant to demonstrate that "every member of the family can read or write at any distance from the fixture."*

reading. Using technological advances developed for the production of magazines, the publishers of paperback books increased the sale of books to the American public to an unprecedented level. According to Russel Nye in *The Unembarrassed Muse* (1970), Pocket Books sold 600 titles and 260 million books in paperback between 1939 and 1949, its first 10 years in business. The move to paperback publication and reading accelerated after World War II and continues to the present.

Alexis de Tocqueville, whose *Democracy in America* recounted observations made in the course of a ten-month tour of the United States in 1830-31, wrote that Americans were addicted to reading news-papers. Within a decade of Tocqueville's visit, technological improvements were speeding the production and distribution of local newspapers and reducing their price substantially. As competition between rival newspapers grew, editors paid ever more attention to methods of increasing circulation. Many newspapers came to include such special features as sports and society news, and introduced photographs, drawings, and editorial cartoons to attract even more subscribers.

Throughout the 20th century, newspaper publishers continued to add special sections and features, made more vivid by a liberal use of colored inks and photographs. A growing emphasis on the

By the first half of the 20th century the habit of reading newspapers was well established throughout the United States. Dorothea Lange took this photograph of a black tenant farmer in Chatham County, North Carolina, relaxing with the paper on a hot Saturday afternoon in July 1939.

ephemeral, and a trend toward the publication of succinct articles and features, satisfied the American public's desire for reading materials that could easily and quickly be understood and would simultaneously provide enjoyment.

To further entertain readers, colored comics (introduced with "The Yellow Kid" in the October 25, 1896, issue of the *New York World*) were added as a regular feature of Sunday supplements. Evolving from editorial cartoons in the late 1890s, comics served as a vehicle for social satire and helped promote circulation. Humorously illustrating the daily lives, activities, and fantasies of their readers, comic strips became increasingly popular during the early decades of the 20th century. They have gone on to reflect changing public tastes and national preoccupations. The most recent trend in newspaper comics has been toward a large variety of strips aimed at satisfying a broad spectrum of readers.

Comic strips have continually reached a vast audience, estimated at three times the number of readers who follow the daily news.

Despite the continued popularity of books and newspapers, it is magazines that have become America's major source of reading since World War I. With their heavy emphasis on feature articles and illustrations, they provide information to broad and specialized audiences in an easily manageable, highly visual, and entertaining way.

Early on, magazine publishers recognized the importance of design and illustrations as a way of attracting and holding readers. *Frank Leslie's Illustrated Newspaper* (introduced in 1855) and *Harper's Weekly* (introduced in 1857) added visual interest to their articles by using engravings, a format that competing magazines soon followed. Between 1865 and 1885, the number of periodicals published in the United States increased from 200 to 3,300. During this time the scope and variety of magazines also expanded rapidly, beginning a trend toward specialization that would become even more pronounced in the 20th century. With the exception of a few successful general-interest magazines like *Life* (which first appeared in 1936), magazines have become increasingly geared toward specialized interests. In the post-World War II period the distinction between feature writing in magazines and newspapers has become somewhat blurred.

The development of the rotary press, of cheap wood-pulp paper, and of speedy typesetting machinery by the 1890s made it possible to mass produce magazines and to offer them to the public at a reasonable price. Between 1900 and 1950, families subscribing to one or more periodicals rose from 200,000 to more than 32 million. Many magazines published quality fiction to boost their sales, while technical developments in photography and typography increased their visual appeal.

By the time that this early 1900s photograph of a periodical stand at 23rd Street in New York City was taken, a tremendous variety of general- and special-interest periodicals were supplementing the daily newspapers with in-depth articles, quality fiction, and an increasing number of illustrations.

THE USEFUL SHOULD BE PREFERED TO THE AGREEABLE.

Playthings can please but a moment, while books are always amusing.

This page from The Child's Pictorial Preceptor, *published in 1841, shows the importance attached to moralistic teachings in the children's literature of the time.*

Children's reading materials have shown somewhat similar tendencies as literature for adults. Throughout much of the 19th century, stories for children often were based on Scripture and were viewed as instructional tools to be used to instill virtue and proper values in the young. Late in the 19th century, many children's stories shifted their emphasis from promoting piety to stressing more secular virtues like thrift, neatness, and kindness. Collections of rhymes and fairy tales gained popularity, and by the turn of the century, children were turning to dime adventure novels, much to their parents' distress.

Light-hearted, entertaining stories for children became more prevalent after World War I, influenced by the general fashion in mass media entertainment. A growing awareness of child psychology also led to an increased sophistication in children's reading materials. The development of high-speed color presses made possible the production of cheaper books with an abundance of color illustrations.

Pulp magazines, like dime novels, soon attracted

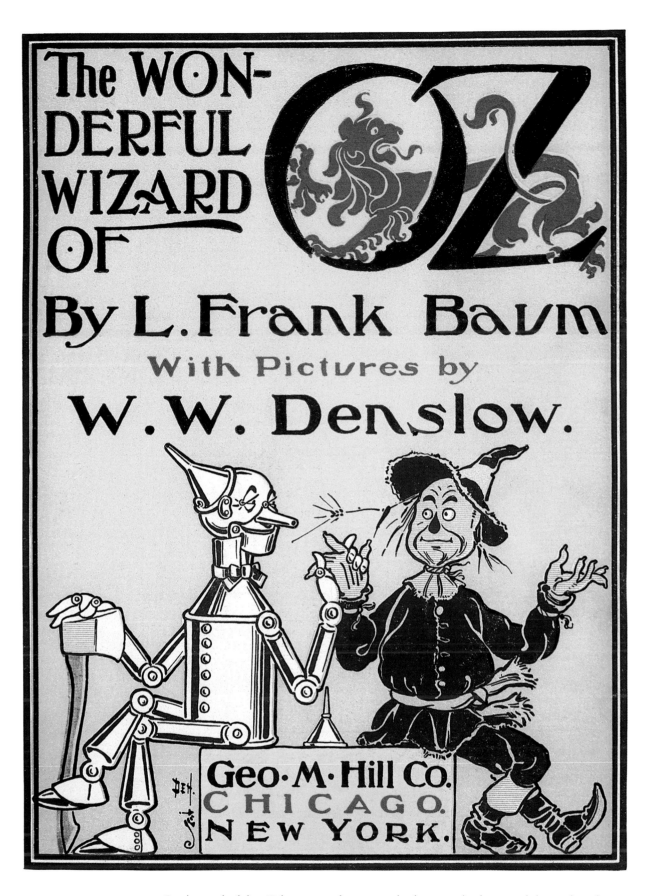

By the end of the 19th century fantasy and adventure had entered the realm of children's books, including this 1899 classic *The Wonderful Wizard of Oz*. For all its thrills, however, this story still offered some serious moral lessons.

the younger members of the family. When increased production costs and competition from paperback books and mass media entertainment spelled the end of the "pulps," they were almost immediately replaced by comic books. Aimed directly at children, these paperbound books basically united pulp-magazine stories with newspaper comic-strip techniques to create feature-length stories with full-color illustrations. Although collections of newspaper comic strips had been published earlier, the comic book as a distinct literary form first made its appearance in 1937. Fantasy and science fiction were the most common themes in comic books, reflecting the new appeal of science-fiction stories among adults. By the early 1950s, 100 million copies of these cheap, easy-to-understand, colorful, and readily available books had been printed.

Despite the increased number of ways in which people can spend their leisure time—including such home pastimes as listening to the radio, watching television, and pursuing various hobbies—reading has remained extremely popular. This has been due, in part, to the portability of reading materials, the large choice of topics available, and, often, the higher quality of information accessible in printed form compared to what can be obtained from the radio and television. Reading expanded tremendously as increasing numbers of people began to commute to work on trains and buses and as public libraries multiplied in number and size.

Left: *As comic books flooded off the presses, the stories they told became increasingly lurid and violent. Parents, educators, and clergymen tried to replace these sensational comics with more educational ones like this 1941 issue of* Real Heroes *with only modest success. Finally the industry itself organized a Comics Code Authority in 1954, with the power to have comic books boycotted if their contents did not comply with the Code's restrictions. Above: Introduced in 1938, Superman comics' blend of action and fantasy made them highly popular and widely imitated. This 1942 photograph of a German youngster at a New York City school for refugee children reading a Superman comic was probably posed to convey the message that he was being rapidly "Americanized." The photograph was taken by Marjory Collins.*

Family Members' Pastimes

The ways in which women spent their leisure time during the later decades of the 19th century reflected their role as the bearers of culture and gentility with primary responsibility for the appearance and activities of their households.

Doing "fancy work" became one of the more fashionable ways for women to employ their leisure time. Most of what they produced with their needlework, painting, leatherwork, and waxwork (to give just a few examples) was for use in the home. It was thought that these handcrafted items would endow the home with culture and refinement. Instructions for fashioning "tasteful" home accessories abounded in books and periodicals. The significance attached to this kind of activity is evident in the introduction to *Fancy Work for Pleasure and Profit,* by Addie Heron, published in 1905:

> *We have tried in the following pages to inculcate a love for home beautifying; to show how every home in this broad land can be rendered beautiful, according to surrounding circumstances and the financial ability of the owners*

Top: *Having the leisure to do fancy work with which to decorate one's home was considered a mark of prosperity and refinement among middle-class women in the late 19th century. This 1890s photograph of a Mrs. E. C. Parsons so engaged in her home also displays the products of her skill.* Above: *An example of popular fancy work is this 1870s wreath woven of human hair. Such objects were prized for their decorative value as well as for their sentimental association with the loved one whose hair was used.*

. . . . In a word, we have tried to give instructions in all things pertaining to the home beautiful so clear and simple that no household, however humble, need be without the refining influences of dainty environments.

Gardening also came into vogue as a leisure activity for middle-class women. Cultivating flowers and plants, both inside and outside the home, was considered a morally uplifting, healthful, and lady-like activity. The popularity of ornamental gardens helped establish the yard as an outdoor center of family life and recreation, a trend that would become even more marked after World War I.

For children, the home was the first and most natural place for play activities. When the use of space in the home became more specialized in the late 19th century, particular areas or entire rooms were designated as play areas for the children of the household. As they grew older and joined peer groups, most of their outdoor play moved to porches and back yards, as well as to sidewalks and streets, parks, school yards, vacant lots, and open fields.

Some of the earliest and most enduring play activities, including tag, jumprope, leapfrog, stilts, hoops, and kites, were brought to America from other countries. Some games were traditionally associated with certain times of the year. Marbles and kites, for example, were linked to spring, and ball games were reportedly played on Fast-day (the first Thursday of April) and on Thanksgiving day in New England (according to William Wells Newell, in his pioneering work *Games and Songs of American Children,* published in 1883).

Left: China painting was one of the handicrafts recommended for ladies during the late 19th century because it required the cultivation of skill and also produced something useful. These plates were hand painted in 1891 by Nellie Bonham Foreman of Charlotte, Michigan. Below: The fashioning of decorative hooked rugs that could serve as home furnishings was another leisure pastime for women during the late 19th century. This rug, hooked in the late 1860s, commemorates the life of Abraham Lincoln. Facing page: Ornamental gardening was considered a genteel and inherently virtuous leisure activity for women. This cover for the first issue of a periodical devoted to floriculture both inside and outside the home makes that clear.

Home Comforts and Pleasures.

Many outdoor games had been around for centuries before being taken up by children in America. Above: Kite-flying and hoop-rolling as depicted on this mid-19th-century child's plate were especially popular during the early spring months. Left: Other traditional children's pastimes included leap-frog, jumprope, and bat-and-ball games, as depicted on this 1871 sheet music cover.

Above: *The decades around the turn of the century saw the development of the playground movement, which encouraged outdoor activities that would help children develop play skills within adult-controlled spaces. Sand trays or boxes like the one set up in this yard were highly favored by advocates of this movement.* Left: *A child's first play place was usually at home. The infant in this photolithograph from around 1900 has been playing with various toys while confined to his Glascock Baby Jumper, made in Detroit, Michigan.* Below: *By the 1950s children could keep themselves occupied at home with a host of toys and amusement devices. In this snapshot the author, aged three, is playing records on a portable phonograph while a spring-operated rocking horse beckons nearby.*

Boys and girls tended to develop different kinds of play activities, as is evident from these illustrations. Facing page top: *The game of marbles was played chiefly by boys. This engraving from* Harper's Weekly, *December 11, 1869, is entitled* Negro Boys Playing Marbles—A Street Scene in Richmond, Virginia. Facing page bottom: *Photojournalist Jenny Chandler captured this scene for the* New York Herald *around 1900. Contemporary investigators of children's play were fascinated by the seemingly endless number of rhymes and songs associated with jumping rope.* Right: *Girls played jacks, as shown on this jacks set container from the 1940s.* Below: *Feathered headdresses and bows and arrows helped give a touch of realism to the game of Cowboys and Indians caught by this turn-of-the-century photograph.*

Playing with dolls and tea sets was thought to prepare girls for their future roles as young ladies and mothers. This photogravure of a make-believe tea party comes from an 1891 children's book entitled Afternoon Tea.

Well into the early 19th century, toys were primarily imported, and were purchased by only the most wealthy families. The children of the less well-to-do had homemade toys, if any. American-made toys and games began to be manufactured in the 1830s, and throughout the 19th century an increasing quantity and variety of toys became available.

The 19th-century concern with the education and moral instruction of the young influenced the kinds of toys and games available for play. Parents and teachers saw it as their responsibility to channel the children's play in directions that would give them useful skills on the one hand and would help shape their future conduct on the other.

As the toy industry expanded, what was produced had less to do with seasonal activities and more with the annual cycle of product development and sales. By the mid-19th century, Christmas had become a major marketing period for toys. After the Civil War, technological innovations and an increase in expendable income accounted for the production and purchase of more toys than ever before. By the turn of the century, the mass production of toys had rendered the debates of clergy and parents concerning their moral value irrelevant.

After World War I, new ideas about child psychology as well as technological advances and the availability of new materials expanded the choice of

playthings. Among postwar developments was, first, a new emphasis on adult participation in children's play, and, second, the designation of certain types of toys and play as appropriate for particular ages. The value of toys and play as means to enjoyment and self-realization came to be appreciated. Other trends included the representation of popular themes and stars—first of the movies and, later, of radio and television—in a variety of toys. The popularity of television in the post-World War II era led to the marketing of toys through commercials and cartoons.

Left: *Throughout the 19th century toys were meant to be educational as well as entertaining, as is clearly signified by this advertisement in the August 6, 1878, issue of* American Agriculturist. *The use of such toys was meant both to instill virtue and to teach skills that would be useful in later life.* Below: *Noah's Arks like this one from the late 19th century were a popular means for teaching Bible lessons to the young. Whether or not this objective was achieved, the children undoubtedly delighted in the dozens of exotic animals that inevitably accompanied the ark.*

Facing page: *Many toys were intended to teach children adult roles. This advertisement from the* Saturday Evening Post, *December 6, 1902, suggests to parents that they should give their sons Stevens rifles to teach them how to handle a firearm should they be called upon to defend their country. A quotation from Theodore Roosevelt to the effect that "good marksmen are scarce," was undoubtedly meant to evoke memories of the Spanish-American War of 1898.* Above: *The notion that children's play can be significant preparation for adulthood did not die with the 19th century. These early 20th-century "Championship Racer Silver Skates" promised to teach children balance, grace, and poise — skills they would undoubtedly need in later life.* Below: *The origin of the rocking horse goes back to the 18th-century hobby horse, which consisted of a stick with a horse's head carved at the top. At the time that rocking horses first became popular, horseback riding was still a primary means of transportation for adults. However, by the 1940s, when this rocking horse was produced, its association was with the Old West as portrayed in comic books and movies.*

Above: *This advertisement from* Life *magazine, February 14, 1949, reflects the mid-20th-century notion that parents should play with their children. Right: The Erector set, first patented in 1913, was an educational toy that taught the elementary principles of mechanics. Erector sets were continually updated with the introduction of new parts and instructions for building a wide range of structures and mechanical toys. This set dates from about 1940.*

Above: *In America's consumerist culture of the mid-20th century, toy manufacturers and the media both profited by combining marketing strategies. This mechanical toy of ''Li'l Abner and His Dogpatch Band,'' issued in 1945, was produced in conjunction with Al Capp's comic strip, which had enjoyed immediate success after its introduction in 1934.* Above left: *This Charlie McCarthy doll, with an additional set of clothing and personal carrying case, was probably manufactured in the 1940s, when ventriloquist Edgar Bergen and his dummy were highly popular. Their renown was due, in part, to national exposure through radio, movie, and television appearances.* Left: *The 1970 Schwinn ''Lemon Peeler,'' shown here, boasted five speeds, hand brakes, a shock-absorbing front wheel, and a ''banana'' seat. The popularity of this type of vehicle, originally introduced merely as a toy, reached such fad proportions by the late 1970s that riding it became a highly competitive sport.*

Left: As the drum of this 1870s zoetrope turned, it created the illusion of picture animation. Several people could view the picture strips through slits in the side as the cylinder revolved. Above: After the Civil War, improvements in projectors and slides transformed magic lanterns from adjuncts to educational lectures into a means for providing entertainment at home, particularly on special occasions. Magic lanterns, like this oil-burning model from 1885, beamed pictures onto a screen from transparent slides. These devices were produced in a variety of sizes and shapes during the late 19th century. Below: This engraving from Godey's Lady's Book, January 1866, shows a magic-lantern show in progress.

The board game of chess, played in Asia since at least the 6th century and first picked up in America by wealthy intellectuals during the 18th century, achieved widespread exposure in this country with the staging of a national championship in 1857. This stereograph depiction of a mid-1860s chess game is unusual, since these dual-imaged picture cards tended to portray exotic scenes from foreign lands, religious spectacles, or news events of national import rather than scenes of domestic life.

Family members often participated together in games and other home pastimes. Among the popular parlor amusements of the late 19th century were charades, theatricals, "tableaux vivants" (in which a number of people grouped themselves to imitate a famous statue or painting while the onlookers guessed what was being depicted), fortunetelling, and conjuring (magic tricks). During the last few decades of the 19th century, various mechanical devices—some of them precursors of moving pictures—provided visual family entertainment. These included the zoetrope, a spinning viewer that produced the impression of animation; the magic lantern, which beamed a picture onto a screen from transparent slides (adapted for home entertainment from its original function as a lecture aid); and the hand-held stereoscope. The latter device displayed two photographs taken at slightly different angles, which, when viewed simultaneously, produced a three-dimen-

sional effect. As mechanical printing techniques improved, millions of stereo cards (also called stereographs) were produced and sold for parlor entertainment. Many depicted distant and exotic places.

Numerous card and board games were devised and produced for family amusement. Although board games like backgammon and chess had been played for centuries, manufacturers competed fiercely by continually introducing new games. Games that emphasized moral instruction were superseded by ones centered around subjects like industry, transportation, sports, and current events.

Although many of these amusements initially evoked scorn and disapproval, they had gained a permanent foothold in most homes by 1900, when Frank De Puy wrote in his *New Century Home Book:*

In the best and happiest homes games and pastimes have their place. There can be no doubt

THE GAME OF THE SEASON!
Horsman's Parlor Archery.

Above: *The moralistic "Mansion of Happiness" game from 1843 was meant to teach young Americans the virtues of industry, honesty, and sobriety, as the teetotum, at bottom left, was spun to take the player on a journey through the virtues and vices of life mapped on the board. The 1883 "Growth of a Century" was meant to teach players about the nation's presidents.* Above left: *By 1875, when the plaster sculpture* Checkers Up at the Farm *was produced, the board game of checkers (derived from the English game of draughts) was popular among players of all ages and social levels. The sculpture was one of dozens designed by craftsman John Rogers for mass production.* Left: *As the interest in indoor games grew during the late 1800s, manufacturers tried to bring sporting pastimes into the parlor. An advertisement in the* American Agriculturist, *November 1878, claimed that the bow and arrows of Horsman's Parlor Archery set were "so constructed and guarded that injury to the Walls, Windows, Mirrors, Furniture or Carpets can be entirely avoided."*

that men and women are helped to happier and better lives by home amusements. The children who are permitted and encouraged to enjoy healthful and innocent games at home cling closer to their homes. They are not tempted to go elsewhere for the amusement for which Nature has given them the desire.

In the 20th century, the popularity of certain games reached fad proportions, including contract bridge and mahjong in the 1920s, Monopoly in the 1930s and after World War II, and Scrabble in the 1950s. Thirty years later, electronic and computerized games would enjoy similar popularity. Card playing, although viewed with disapproval by some religious denominations, became a favored way of getting together with family and friends. With increased informality in home entertaining, card games provided a good excuse to spend time together in each other's homes.

During the late 19th and early 20th centuries affluent families began to maintain specialized rooms for leisure activities. Game rooms often boasted one or more gaming tables and were furnished with such masculine accoutrements as hunting trophies. Benjamin van Nostand of New York owned this game room, photographed around 1900.

FAMOUS PARKER GAMES

PING-PONG

Registered U. S. Patent Office

PARKER BROTHERS, INC., Salem, Mass.
Sole Makers

"The most talked of Game in America"

Be sure your stocks are complete. You will have many calls!

POLLYANNA, Flying-Four, Lame-Duck, Lindy-Hop-Off, Sixes-and-Sevens, ROOK, Parkers'-Indoor-Obstacle-Golf, The-Knight's-Journey HOKUM, Pegity, PIT, Peg-Base-Ball, TOURING, Five-Wise-Birds, We, Across-the-Continent, WINGS, Game-of-OZ, and Pastime Picture Puzzles are other Famous PARKER GAMES.

PARKER BROTHERS, INC. : SALEM, MASS. : FLATIRON BLDG., NEW YORK

Above: *The game of Ping-Pong, adapted for indoor play from lawn tennis, represented a trend toward faster, more exciting, and more competitive home games. Variants of the game had been played since the 1890s, but by 1929, when this advertisement appeared in the* Toy Department *trade journal, it had clearly reached a mass audience. Below: Jigsaw puzzles, consisting of small, odd-shaped, interlocking pieces that fitted together to create a coherent picture, date back to the 19th century. They became especially popular during the depression of the 1930s as an inexpensive evening pastime for adults and children.*

Above: *Unlike the distinctly masculine 19th-century game room, the mid-20th-century recreation room was geared to serve the entire family. As this advertisement from* Collier's *magazine, September 11, 1943, shows, it was usually equipped with a phonograph, and often included a hobby corner as well.* Below: *Card games enjoyed great popularity during the mid-20th century, providing a chance for family and friends to socialize while engaging in a formalized activity. This 1942 photograph by Albert Fenn was part of a series on the life of blacks taken for the United States Office of War Information.*

The search for novelty in home amusements produced some unusual items. The wearer of the "parlor game skirt," shown in Life *magazine, October 19, 1953, was supposed to sit on the floor, spread her skirt out around her, and have passersby sit down beside her for a "hemside round" of bingo. Designer Bettie Murrie was planning game skirts for backgammon, chess, and parcheesi at the time this article appeared.*

As shorter working hours brought more leisure time in the post-World War I era, hobbies became popular in America. The term "hobby" originally derived from the idea of the hobbyhorse, a children's toy. Hobbies were at first confined to the very young and the very old. They were perceived as having moral value and as fostering serenity. The pursuit of certain hobbies gained mass appeal during the Great Depression, when unemployed people had endless time on their hands and when attempts to economize laid the groundwork for a "do-it-yourself" mania that persists to the present. For many, the desire to master or excel in a hobby reflected a similar striving for achievement in their work.

Having a hobby was not limited by gender or age, but was considered important for everyone.

According to Ruth Lampland, the author of *Hobbies for Everybody* (1934), it was not merely a way of using free time, but also served as a vital outlet for self-expression. In contrast to work, which generally offered little freedom of choice, hobbies were there to be fully pursued during the hours in which individuals were "completely their own masters." Earnest Elmo Calkins, an important figure in advertising and author of *Care and Feeding of Hobby Horses,* published in 1934, asserted that in order to be well-rounded, mentally healthy, and spiritually happy individuals, people should choose hobbies that were as different as possible from their daily occupations.

Calkins divided hobbies into four categories: making things, acquiring things, learning things, and doing things. Making things offered an outlet long

Above: *Both educators and child psychologists agreed that a hobby—even if a kit was used—served a beneficial purpose. This kit instructed youngsters on the making of leather novelties.* Above right: *Stamp collecting was a hobby enjoyed by children as well as adults. A Washington, D.C., high school student explains some features of his stamp collection to his nine-year-old brother in this photograph taken by Esther Bubley.* Right: *The man interested in "do-it-yourself" projects was likely to own a home workshop where he could tinker, build furniture, or refinish antiques. Appealing to the home hobbyists, this advertisement in Collier's magazine, October 1, 1954, likens the satisfaction of mixing a Corby's drink to that of making furniture.*

Above: *This kit for making felt doll hats and purses taught girls skills that they would find useful in pursuing adult hobbies.* Above right: *For women, a "do-it-yourself" hobby usually involved sewing, needlework, or some aspect of home decorating. As quilts became less of a household necessity, quilt-making acquired the status of a hobby. This crib quilt was designed as a sampler of traditional patterns by noted quilt authority Florence Peto around 1950.*
Below: *During the 1930s and even more so after World War II, the manufacture and sale of hobby products became highly profitable. This Hobby Hut, pictured in a souvenir booklet from the late 1940s, was located in a newly designed shopping center in Los Angeles, California, called the "Farmers' Market."*

denied by industrialization—that of achieving personal satisfaction through hand-craftsmanship. This included the practice of diverse arts and crafts and the execution of do-it-yourself projects. To supply the demand for these types of hobbies, models and kits of all sorts were produced in tremendous numbers, allowing the assembler to satisfy the desire to create something attractive and worthwhile in a relatively short time.

Acquiring things involved becoming a collector of groupings of objects. These turned out to encompass items associated with a broad range of interests, from nature, history, and arts and crafts to popular culture; from rocks, letters, paintings, stamps, and coins, to comic books and bottle tops. Learning things entailed pursuing a course of study in some branch of knowledge such as a science, a specific period of history, or a new language, or acquiring a special skill. Adult education classes sprang up in the hundreds to foster these hobbies.

The category of doing things was extremely broad and often touched on other aspects of leisure, such as games and sports. Included in this category were amateur photography and gardening. Amateur photography first became popular in the second half of the 19th century as methods of taking and developing photographs were simplified. Because nature was a favored subject, photography became identified with its virtues and this hobby came to be seen as healthful, exhilarating exercise. In the 1880s, when

The interest in home gardening, which had provided supplementary food during the Great Depression and World War II years, carried over into the postwar era, especially in the burgeoning suburbs. This advertisement from Collier's magazine, May 19, 1951, plays to the popularity of gardening as a hobby for men.

it became possible to use preloaded rolls of film in the box camera, amateur photography was permanently launched as a pastime for large numbers of people. The outdoors remained a popular subject.

As more compact, easy to operate, and accurate cameras were developed in the 20th century, all members of the family could participate in photography. Camera manufacturers in Germany (before World War II) and Japan (after World War II) introduced high-quality cameras for serious picture-takers, but the American-made Kodak, with its various innovations, generally remained the family favorite. The development of motion-picture cameras for home use (compact models were available by the 1930s), the introduction of color film (1935), and the invention of the Polaroid Land camera (1948) greatly expanded enthusiasm for photography as a hobby.

Gardening, a leisure pursuit for ladies since the late 19th century, became a popular hobby after World War I. During the Great Depression many men became involved in gardening as a hobby for the more practical reason of supplementing the family diet with home-grown vegetables and fruit.

Specialized hobbies spurred the growth of a variety of industries, retail shops, and special sections in department stores catering to hobby enthusiasts. Features in newspapers and magazines, and on radio and television shows, as well as special exhibits helped promote many of the hobbies that caught the public's interest. Hobby-oriented spaces in and around the home, including sewing rooms, workshops, so-called recreation rooms, and photographic darkrooms, became common in many American households during the 1950s.

Home Music

Music has long been an important part of a variety of home amusements, from entertaining friends to pursuing hobbies. Singing was the most traditional and universal form of music in the home, but instrumental accompaniment was not uncommon when families could afford to own instruments and when religious restrictions did not prohibit them. Until the early decades of the 19th century, wealthy and even middle-class families, especially those living in cities, might own such instruments as violins, flutes, oboes, recorders, or guitars. Playing the harpsichord or spinet was a highly esteemed accomplishment for females until those instruments were replaced by reed organs and pianos in the mid- and late 19th century.

Piano fortes had been imported from Europe since the late 18th century, but it was not until American production began in the 1830s that the square piano took over as the most popular instrument for home entertainment. In July 1867, an article by James Parton in the *Atlantic Monthly* claimed that "almost every couple that sets up housekeeping on a respectable scale considers a piano only less indispensable than a kitchen range." Keen competition was offered by the reed organ, also known as a melodeon, which was not only less expensive (in 1880, a piano cost $200 compared to $20 for a melodeon), but also carried the aura of virtue by its association with religious music and churchgoing.

Smaller instruments, such as accordians and harmonicas, as well as instruments that had been

Facing page: *Playing the piano was considered a highly desirable accomplishment and sign of refinement for young ladies. This lithograph from* Demorest's Family Magazine, *August 1866, depicts a tranquil scene, linking the playing of the piano with the coziness, warmth, and harmony of family life. Above:* The engraving from Our Boys and Girls, *October 1871, however, suggests that the task of teaching one's daughter the art of piano-playing was not always easy.*

popular earlier (for example, guitars and flutes), offered less expensive alternatives for creating music at home. Mary Elizabeth Sherwood addressed the "transcendent powers" of home music in *Home Amusements,* which appeared in 1881:

> *The family circle which has learned three or four instruments, the brothers who can sing part songs, are to be envied. They can never suffer from a dull evening.*

However, she added:

> *The only deep shadow to the musical picture is the necessity of practicing, which is* not *a Home Amusement; it is a home torture. If only a person could learn to play or sing without those dreadful first noises and those hideous shrieks!*

During the 19th century, a mounting tide of printed music became available to the public, including dozens of simple, easy-to-follow "parlor songs" for families. By mid-century, sentimental, nostalgic, and melancholy ballads, like some of the pieces composed by Stephen Foster, were proving highly pleasing to the public taste. Popular music on domestic and moralistic themes retained its appeal into the later decades of the 19th century, although published sheet music also included songs made popular by performers in concerts, clubs, and theaters.

By the 1890s, mass production had brought pianos within the reach of large numbers of middle-class families. Requiring fewer materials and using more standardized parts, upright pianos began to replace the bulkier square pianos. Singing to piano accompaniment became a favored form of entertainment as ownership of a piano came to symbolize prosperity and refinement for middle-class families.

Mass-production methods also were applied to the manufacture of smaller, less expensive instruments like dulcimers and autoharps, and other instruments associated with specific types of ethnic and regional music.

In the 20th century, the phonograph and radio and various forms of mechanical music almost wiped out the sheet music industry and musical performances in the home. The playing of musical instruments was, for the most part, relegated to the school curriculum. Some instruments became popular once more as new styles of music caught the public fancy. This was true of ukeleles in the 1920s, brass band instruments in the 1940s, and guitars in the 1960s and 1970s. On the whole, pianos remained the most popular home instruments, but by now they had lost their 19th-century role as social status symbols. Arthur Loesser noted in *Men, Women, and Pianos: A Social History* (1954):

In the family, the piano competes manfully with the washing machine and the station wagon for the installment dollar, and rather more weakly with gardening, photography, and canasta for hobby time. As a source of passive musical enjoyment, it has been all but snuffed out by the phonograph, the radio, and the television set....

Mechanical music devices presented an easy way for unskilled people to feel creative and artistic. Cylinder-operated music boxes imported from Switzerland in the second half of the 19th century were among the earliest mechanical instruments to provide home entertainment. These devices were expensive, however, and were limited to playing only a few tunes. The more popular disc-operated music boxes, mass produced in the United States from the 1890s to around the 1920s, enjoyed wider popularity. They were less expensive to manufacture and the discs could be changed more easily than the cylinders, although the sound was never as good as that produced by the cylinder boxes.

Other small, inexpensive, and easy-to-use mechanical instruments gained some popularity between the 1880s and World War I. Among these were organettes (handcranked reed organs operated by paper

Above: *This portable reed organ, made by J. Foster between 1829 and 1835, would have been held in the lap and played with both hands while one forearm worked the bellows. These lap organs were cheaper than the cabinet models.* Below: *Popular instruments like this mandolin from around 1910 encouraged increasing numbers of people to make their own music. The appeal of these smaller instruments also stimulated sheet music sales.*

rolls or pinned cylinders), and automatic reed organs (constructed with built-in playing mechanisms).

Player pianos, activated by foot pedals or electricity and using perforated paper music rolls, enjoyed enormous success from the 1890s through the 1920s. As Cleveland, Ohio, manufacturer J. T. Wamelink proclaimed in an advertisement, the performer on one of these pianos could achieve "Perfection without Practice." Apparently, the American public did not need much convincing. By 1919, player pianos far outnumbered standard models! The mechanical principle underlying the working of the automatic paper-roll in player pianos was applied to

create other player instruments as well, including violins, banjos, and mandolins.

A mechanical "reproducing piano," developed in the teens and 1920s, produced a higher quality of music than regular player pianos. Controlling not just the notes, but also conveying the subtlety and nuance of a particular artist's performance, these pianos appealed to discriminating listeners to classical music. However, their price was approximately four times that of player pianos.

It was the phonograph that not only succeeded in replacing most other forms of home music, but also made more music accessible to a larger group of people than ever before. Thomas Alva Edison's "talking machine" of 1877 was first developed for commercial uses, but its entertainment value was quickly recognized. By the 1890s, these machines—using wax cylinders—were making local and national performers known to a large home audience. New, improved cylinder machines were introduced during

Above: *Reed organs or melodeons presented a more modest alternative to pianos, and were especially popular in nonurban areas. This reed organ was manufactured in 1858 by S. D. and H. W. Smith of Boston, Massachusetts.* Below: *Between 1870 and 1890 the number of Americans who owned pianos almost doubled, primarily due to the introduction of the less expensive upright piano. Advertisements associated the upright piano with the warmth of home and family, as does this photographic postcard from around 1895.*

Disc music boxes, less expensive to manufacture and simpler to operate than cylinder machines, were particularly popular between the 1890s and World War I. With occasional winding, this Regina music box from around 1915 would automatically raise each disc to playing position, play it, and return it to the storage rack.

the first decade of the 20th century, but it was the disc phonograph that became the standard for home entertainment.

Introduced in the 1890s, disc records did not provide as high a quality of sound as wax cylinders, but they were cheaper, could play louder, and were more convenient to store and handle than cylinders. Disc records began to determine the course of popular music, as tunes were adapted to fit the three-minute playing time of the new records. Newly released disc recordings could rapidly make a song successful or condemn it to failure. Intricate dance music, ragtime, and Latin rhythms that were difficult to play on the piano could now be recorded by the finest musicians and could be enjoyed at home by proud phonograph owners.

Phonograph and record sales mushroomed. In 1919, some 200 phonograph companies were producing two million phonographs. The recording industry continued to expand in scope to meet specialized interests and also helped to nationalize regional music. Soon Americans were spending more money on phonographs and records than on musical instruments, books, and periodicals combined.

The popularity of phonographs reached a peak in the 1920s. The introduction of electrical recording methods in 1925 significantly altered the nature of phonograph records. Whereas the earlier mechanical recording methods had been successful primarily with loud voices and rhythmic music, electric recording produced a more natural sound that effectively conveyed the complex instrumentation of large orchestras and bands.

Record and phonograph sales plummeted in the early 1930s when the comparatively free entertainment provided by radio took over. Although some predicted that the demise of the phonograph was imminent, greatly improved phonographs and records were introduced by the middle of the 1930s, and the idea of combining radios with phonographs expanded the market tremendously. The reduced price of records and new marketing campaigns, reflected in the slogan of Decca records, "Hear them *when* you want—as *often* as you want—right in your own home," ensured a lasting home audience for phonograph records. With phonograph records home listeners could decide what they wanted to hear. As with the more publicly used record machine of the 1930s and 1940s—the jukebox—phonographs allowed fans of popular dance music and song hits to listen to their favorites over and over again. All they had to do was buy the record and replay it whenever they wanted to hear it.

Contributing to the revived popularity of phonographs and records was the development of high-fidelity sound reproduction and the introduction of 33⅓-rpm, long-playing (LP) records. The experiments that led to both of these advances date back to the 1930s, but the results did not become available to the public until the late 1940s and early 1950s. High-fidelity sound reproduction, made possible by combining amplifiers, speakers, and other components into a unified system, produced a loud, brilliant, full-bodied sound. The growing fascination with high fidelity among discerning record listeners reached the level of a national obsession following the introduction of LPs. These provided the acoustic potential for the best quality of music available on records. The 45-rpm records, introduced in 1949, did not offer the sound quality of LPs, but did provide an inexpensive, convenient format for enjoying

Between 1900 and 1930, some two-and-a-half million American homes acquired player pianos. Because they reduced playing to a mechanical process, these instruments contributed greatly to the demise of the piano as a symbol of accomplishment. This advertisement for a Beckwith Player Piano appeared in a 1915 Sears Roebuck catalog.

A Beautiful Piece of Furniture — A Great Entertainer for Yourself and Friends—A Great Educator for Your Children—Sing, Dance and Be Happy, All in Your Own Home.

Size: 4 feet 9 inches high, 2 feet 4 inches wide and 5 feet 3 inches long. Weight, boxed for shipment, about 950 pounds.

Try It in Your Own Home for Thirty Days before deciding definitely to buy. Read all about our free thirty days' trial offer below.

Left: *By the early 20th century, several different types of phonographs had become available in a variety of price ranges. Wax cylinders like the ones used on this Edison phonograph from around 1908, proved to have a limited range and sound quality and were soon replaced by flat discs on most phonographs. The large horn was needed to amplify the sound of the cylinder recordings.* Below: *The Victor talking machine pictured in this advertisement from the Saturday Evening Post, September 24, 1904, was one of the earliest devices to use the flat discs that eventually became the standard in the industry. Discs were not only more portable and easier to operate than the cylinders, but also had the technical capability to record more complex dance music in addition to the standard repertoire of talking and singing numbers.*

the latest popular music. Phonographs were redesigned to handle the newer types of records, and the heavy and easily scratched 78-rpms of earlier days were gradually phased out.

By the mid-20th century, the phonograph had become a focal point for entertainment in even the most modest American homes. Throughout the 1950s, the sale of phonograph records was heavily influenced by radio disc jockeys, whose choice of records for broadcast helped determine the top sellers. Youth-oriented rock-and-roll music, which became popular at this time, accounted for huge sales of records among affluent teenagers. Technical improvements in the recording industry continued to play an important role in their appeal to home listeners. Such developments later in the 20th century included stereophonic sound (feasible by the late 1950s and widely accepted in the early 1960s), home tape recording (perfected in the 1970s with improvements and new developments in cartridge and cassette tapes and tape players), and, soon after, compact-disc players.

Radio and Television

Even more than the phonograph, radio and television brought standardized entertainment to American homes across the country. These two forms of mass media appealed to people of all ages, tastes, and levels of education and sophistication.

Experiments with the wireless transmission of sound in the late 19th and early 20th centuries had led to a growing realization of radio's vast potential to provide public entertainment. The American gov-

Above left: *During the 1920s dust gathered on home melodeons and pianos as families opted for the highly appealing entertainment offered by phonograph recordings. This 1922 puzzle advertised the Victor Talking Machine Company's "Victrola," a name that had become synonymous with phonographs by that time.* Left: *Beginning in the late 1930s, manufacturers introduced combination radio-phonographs in an attempt to improve the sales of both of these home entertainment devices. As is evident from this Philco radio-phonograph, great attention was paid to the design of the cabinet, which by now had assumed a highly visible place in American living rooms.*

During the 1920s "listening in" on a radio set was considered a hobby appropriate to the enthusiast with a technical bent. This box cover of a "Radio Game," from around 1930, reflects both that early view and the growing acceptance of radio as a part of daily life.

ernment's development of a national communications system, especially as a result of World War I, played an important role in the medium's technological growth. By 1920, experimental stations broadcasting news, music, and market reports encouraged hobbyists by the thousands to construct or purchase receiving sets. In November of that year, KDKA became the first permanent broadcasting station, inspiring even more enthusiasts. In an article in the *American Review of Reviews,* January 1923, entitled "'Listening In,' Our New National Pastime," one observer noted that "the rapidity with which the thing has spread has possibly not been equalled in all the centuries of human progress."

By 1924, families in five million homes owned radio receivers for the primary purpose of entertainment. Through the 1920s and 1930s, radio presented a varied program of music, drama, and comedy. Classical music programs helped meet a growing

public demand for music appealing to a more cultivated level of taste, while radio acquainted the public with popular music so quickly that the orchestras and vocalists could create almost instantaneous hits. Radio theater, including both dramatic and comedy performances, attracted large audiences as vaudeville and stage stars began to perform for the new medium. Situation comedy was defined and popularized, while serial dramas were produced according to standard formulas borrowed and adapted from the theater, fiction, and the movies.

Various programs were geared toward special audiences at different times of the day. Women's shows, especially "soap operas" (so called because their sponsors were often soap manufacturers), and children's programs were scheduled during the daytime, while programs for family members in general dominated the evening hours.

A number of factors accounted for the unique

appeal of radio. Above all, this medium gave listeners the sense that things were happening precisely when they heard them. Neither film, records, nor reading materials could convey this sense of simultaneity and up-to-the-minute accuracy. Radio also conveyed a sense of intimacy, giving the illusion of personal, face-to-face communication. Though the audience for a program might number in the millions, each listener could feel that he or she was being addressed individually. Lacking visual images, the medium allowed listeners to construct whatever mental picture they wished to accompany the sound.

By the late 1920s, radio programs began to be financed by businesses seeking to advertise over the air. The introduction of commercial sponsorship changed forever the nature of radio programming. In connection with the developing network of radio stations that spanned the country, it led to a nationalizing of programs and a standardizing of the entertainment they offered. By allowing programs to be aired free to the public, it set the course for a similar role by commercial advertisers in television a few decades later.

By providing entertainment to be enjoyed in the comfort of the family living room, radios encouraged family togetherness at a time when Americans were becoming highly mobile. During the Great Depression, "listening in" became a favorite and inexpensive home amusement. L. B. Wilson, manager of a chain of theaters in Kentucky, commented on this in an article that appeared in *Broadcasting Magazine* in 1933:

> *Radio is successfully competing with the theatre. Hard times have added millions of persons to the radio audience. You can get Eddie Cantor on the air for nothing. It costs you 50 cents or more to get him at the theatre.*

During the decade of the 1930s, the number of radios in American homes increased from 12 million to 40 million—a clear demonstration of both the wide-reaching popularity of this medium and of the declining cost of radios.

The programming format set in the 1930s proved so successful that it remained much the same

By the late 1940s radio listening had become an integral part of family life, as this 1948 photograph shows. Offering thousands of diverse daily programs that appealed to every age group and level of sophistication, radio enjoyed great prestige and power. Within a few years, however, its preeminent role in American life would be usurped by television.

throughout the next decade. In 1949, radio stations broadcast a national total of 22,000 programs daily and seven-and-a-half million programs a year. However, not everyone approved of the programming. During the 1940s, an increasing amount of criticism was directed at the medium, similar to the attacks that would be mounted against television a few years later. For example, Lee DeForest, who in 1906 had invented the audion tube that helped make radio possible, lamented in 1947 that what could have been "a potent instrumentality for culture, fine music, and the uplifting of America's mass intelligence," had instead become "a laughing stock, that resolutely kept the average intelligence of 13 years." More reflective of public sentiment, however, was a CBS vice president's rebuttal of DeForest's outburst, which appeared in Russel Nye's *Unembarrassed Muse* (1970): "The masses like comic books, Betty Grable, broad comedy, simple drama—it's fast, vulgar, simple, fundamental."

In the 1950s, the success of television, with its imitation of radio programming and usurpation of the public's attention in the evening, forced a significant change in radio. Most radio programs shifted almost completely to music and news, to be heard mainly during the daytime hours. Radio stations became more community-oriented, announcing local events, sponsoring local talk shows, and featuring local disc jockeys who played popular hits. Certain stations specialized in broadcasting particular styles of recorded music so as to attract specific groups of listeners.

Both portable and automobile radios had been on the market for some time but became especially popular after World War II. Home radios became smaller, yielding their once prominent position to the ever-enlarging television set. "Frequency modulation," better known as FM, had been first developed in the 1930s but came into general use in the mid-1960s. With its fuller frequency range and generally improved reception, the FM stations attracted both lovers of serious music and afficionados of the increasingly complex popular music.

Television reached more people every day in their own homes than any previous communication medium had ever done. Combining sights, sounds, and motion available in the home through no other

Above: *Between 1949 and 1952 American consumers purchased some quarter of a million television sets each month. This Zenith Radio Corporation's 1949 television set was one of the first post-World War II models aimed at the home market. It was advertised as offering "full screen" viewing and a unique "black" picture tube designed to reduce glare and eye strain.*

medium, it presented popular entertainment in a form far beyond anything the American public had ever imagined. In a *Harper's Magazine* article published in May 1950, actor-producer John Houseman wrote:

Television is not just the latest and most miraculous of these media. It is a synthesis of them all. It is radio with eyes; it is the press without the travail of printing; it is movies without the physical limitations of mechanical reproduction and projection.

Television remained highly experimental in the 1920s and 1930s, as progressive technical refinements added to its viability as a public communication medium. Experimental broadcasts of major news and sports events in the late 1930s expanded public awareness of its tremendous potential.

After World War II, television rapidly appeared

The Howdy Doody *show, introduced in 1947, was one of television's first full-fledged hits for children; it also won the approval of parents. This board game was an early example of the way in which television and manufacturers of toys and other products could collaborate for mutual benefit.*

on the scene as a viable form of home entertainment. Although television sets were not cheap (in 1947, with average income around $3,000, a black-and-white set cost about $280 while one of the new automatic washing machines cost a somewhat more modest $200), families purchased them with the same enthusiasm as they did dozens of other consumer goods during the postwar economic boom. The one million sets owned by American families in 1948 had increased to a phenomenal 21 million five years later. The *Encyclopedia Americana Annual* for 1956 declared that television could now be regarded "somewhat in the same light as indoor plumbing . . . indisputably a fixture of the household but no longer a novelty."

Once installed in the home, television immediately replaced radio as the chief source of family entertainment. As Michael Lauletta wrote in *TV Book* (edited by Judy Fireman, 1977):

Once that television arrived, my whole life changed. I don't think I ever listened to The Lone Ranger *or* Straight Arrow *on the radio ever again. They just didn't stand a chance against the likes of* Six-Gun Playhouse, Howdy Doody, *or* Beat the Clock. *Suddenly, I hated to go to my grandmother's house because it no longer made a difference that the kid across the street from her had a television set. I had my own.*

Television generally followed the same programming format as radio. The dramas, quiz shows,

detective stories, serials, comedies, and variety shows that families had listened to on the radio could now be watched on the screen. In the same way as radio, it provided entertainment for family members at the times of day they were most likely to be watching television.

Through the 1950s, most television programming shifted from live, theater-like drama to fast-moving, movie-like action and adventure shows. Westerns, which had not proven particularly popular on the radio, turned out to be much more successful on television with the addition of a scenic background to the action.

Several technological advances in the 1950s greatly expanded the scope of television. These included the development of coaxial telephone cables, which made national television stations and broadcasting possible (completed across the country in 1951); the introduction of color television (first announced in 1948, but not available until 1953); the development of ultra-high frequency, which facilitated the establishment of many new channels and stations (beginning in 1952); and the introduction of videotaping, which permitted the recording of high quality sound and pictures that could be replayed whenever desired (starting in 1956).

From the outset, the effects of television on the American public provided a rich source of commentary for critics. Writing in the *New York Herald Tribune,* June 9, 1948, media critic John Crosby noted these effects at a fairly early stage of the new medium's popularity:

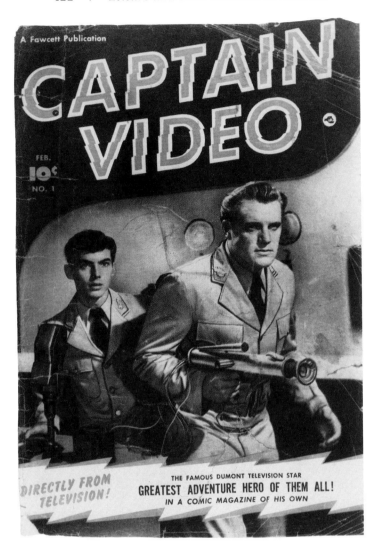

Television has the power to create immediate fantasy heroes like Captain Video, featured in this spin-off comic book from 1951.

The most obvious and dire effect, one that strikes everyone who has seen more than two television broadcasts, is on conversation. There isn't any. The moment the set goes on, conversation dies. I don't mean it languishes. It dies. Messages are transmitted back and forth by means of eye-rolling, eyebrow lifting and frantic wig-wagging of the hands. (Only high priority messages are permitted: You're wanted on the telephone. Could I have another drink. That sort of thing.) People who will venture an occasional whisper in church remain awed and silent in front of a television set.

As television became an indispensable addition to the home during the 1950s, some critics suggested that watching it discouraged other activities in the home. Other commentators maintained that the desire to watch television encouraged people to get their work done faster or made them more productive by motivating them to engage in additional activities while watching television. Few comments on the impact of television during this decade put the matter as succinctly as a November 1957 report from the *Christian Science Monitor,* which concluded:

Television has had its effects on the innermost core of personal habit. The presence of a piece of electronic furniture in the living room has changed how much people eat (more) and how much they sleep (less). It has transformed the pattern of day-by-day living more than any invention since the automobile . . . . It has fascinated people, exasperated people, and bored people; but it has reached them and, on the whole, held them. Few people who now have a television set will ever be without one again.

Whether for better or worse, television has significantly altered the use of leisure time within the home. Since the 1960s, television has offered a proliferation of choices to home viewers, including not-for-profit educational channels, a growing range of subscription cable channels, and the development of VCRs (videocassette recorders). In *A Pictorial History of Television* (1969), authors Irving Settel and William Laas remarked that, whereas people might see one movie a week, attend one play a month, and read one novel in a year, they are known to settle down in front of the television on an average of five hours every day. No wonder television has come to be referred to as America's "modern fireside!"

Home leisure pursuits have changed dramatically, from the informal neighborly visits characteristic of life in preindustrial America to the highly commercial "visitations" and entertainment provided by television in the mid-20th century. Technological developments and mass production have widened the scope of home amusements tremendously, as well as helping to standardize them.

As home leisure products have become more commercialized and as the roles of the home and the family have changed, home amusements have become progressively less instructional and more entertaining, until entertainment appears to have become their chief aim. Active pursuits such as hobbies and games continue to offset the relatively passive forms of entertainment offered by playing records, listening to the radio, or watching television.

An article in the *Pittsburgh Press,* September 27, 1987, entitled "Are We Becoming a Stay-at-Home Society?" quoted sociologist Eviatar Zerubavel on a recent American trend toward "cocooning" as follows:

Despite ebb and flow due to the size of a particular age group, we've been cocooning since the Industrial Revolution at the end of the 18th century and the rise of the modern bureaucracy in the 19th.

An artisan who worked in his cottage or a farmer who tilled his fields did not make a sharp distinction between home and work, between public and private self.

Not so for the modern worker. We feel when we close the front door and take off our tie is when the real life begins. We tend to think of the part when we are at home as more real, as more genuine. A homebody with a VCR and Orville Redenbacher [popcorn] is just a modern manifestation of a much longer trend.

By the 1950s television was the dominant form of home entertainment. As this Motorola advertisement from Woman's Home Companion, *March 1951, shows, manufacturers stressed the role of television in fostering family togetherness.*

GOING OUT:
Public Entertainment

*G*oing out for entertainment has a long history in America. Over the centuries, the number of choices in entertainment has vastly increased, and these choices have come to be accessible to an ever-broadening public.

Among the first entertainers to draw people from their homes were traveling performers, who played to Colonial audiences at fairs and other community gatherings. However, in the beginning, it was primarily the well-to-do who both encouraged and could afford to attend the staged "entertainments" that occasionally passed through town. As cities grew during the decades before the Civil War, urban dwellers became particularly eager for diversions from their everyday lives. This inspired entrepreneurs and showmen to devise inexpensive, crowd-pleasing entertainment and, as a result, many new types of formalized shows evolved. Often the promoters marketed the performances as educational and moral to appeal to middle-class members of society, who disapproved of many existing forms of public amusement.

After the Civil War, entertainment choices multiplied for audiences across the country, especially for those living in urban areas. Traveling shows reached the height of their popularity, entertaining residents of numerous small towns and rural communities and introducing formalized programs to some Americans for the first time. By the early 20th century, public censure of many forms of entertainment relaxed, as new diversions like ragtime music and dancing, amusement parks, and movies drew even the most conservative members of the middle class.

Since World War I, automobile travel and the development of the mass media have led to a standardization of public entertainment, particularly with the growing domination of movies and the subsequent decline of live performances. But the same technological changes also have made a wide range of entertainment choices accessible to the general public, making it possible for almost anyone to consider spending the day, the evening, or simply a few hours "going out."

Facing page: *From the outset movies offered their audiences the excitement and adventure lacking in their daily lives. The Edison Company produced dozens of moving pictures from the 1890s into the early 20th century, including the short subjects listed on this turn-of-the-century poster. Such movies were viewed together at a kinetoscope parlor, penny arcade, or seen as part of a variety show.*

STEP RIGHT UP: BEGINNINGS

Some of the early colonists objected to theatrical performances as being conducive to idleness and immorality. As late as 1750, the Massachusetts General Court banned "public stage-plays, interludes, and other theatrical entertainments" because they:

[N]ot only occasion great and unnecessary expenses, and discourage industry and frugality, but likewise tend generally to increase immorality, impiety, and a contempt for religion.

Nevertheless, by the middle of the 18th century, traveling theatrical companies were performing to small audiences in taverns, assembly halls, and private homes. Their earliest following was among the wealthy families of the large East Coast towns like New York, Philadelphia, and Boston, and in the South, where exposure to troupers encouraged the establishment of local amateur theatrical societies. New York, an early center for public entertainment, boasted its first permanent theater in 1767.

Also by the 1760s, subscription concerts had become regular entries on the social calendars of upper-class families. This interest in music led to the formation of amateur choral and instrumental groups, which performed the newest and most fashionable European music. Often, these amateur groups were organized and guided by professional musicians who had emigrated from Europe. The first, and perhaps most famous, of these groups was Boston's Handel and Haydn Society, founded in 1815.

The New City Audience

In the period from the 1820s to the Civil War, public entertainment was invigorated by the growth of cities, especially in the Northeast, and by the increasing numbers of the urban working class eager for diversion. By the mid-19th century, hundreds of performers were entertaining urban audiences in popular theater and variety entertainments like minstrel shows, as well as at circuses, popular museums, and public concerts. Throughout this period, the regional distribution and the quality of entertainment remained very uneven.

Like urban spectator sports of the time, and in contrast to the customary rural pastimes, these forms of live entertainment transformed people into watchers rather than participants. However, the audiences were far from passive, responding boisterously and vociferously to what happened on the stage.

During the 1820s and 1830s, large cities and small towns alike experienced a boom in theater construction, while many companies continued to perform in tents, taverns, ballrooms, and barns. The new theaters in major cities accommodated large audiences of all classes. New York City boasted some of the most spacious of these. For example, the second Park Theater, built in 1821, accommodated 2,500 patrons, and a decade later, the Broadway Theater advertised seating for 4,000.

At the larger theaters, the social status of the playgoers usually determined which of three distinctive seating areas they occupied: the boxes for the wealthy; the "pit" directly in front of the stage for the middle and working classes; and the top gallery

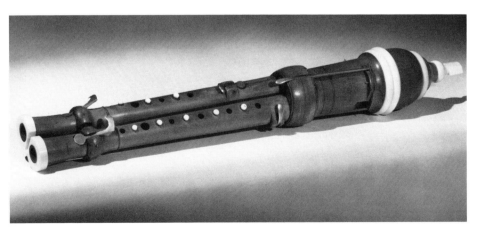

Double flageolets like this instrument from around 1827, made by Firth & Hall of New York, consisted of two tubes and a single mouthpiece. Because a player could master it relatively easily, this instrument was popular among amateur musicians.

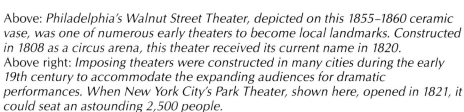

Above: *Philadelphia's Walnut Street Theater, depicted on this 1855–1860 ceramic vase, was one of numerous early theaters to become local landmarks. Constructed in 1808 as a circus arena, this theater received its current name in 1820.*
Above right: *Imposing theaters were constructed in many cities during the early 19th century to accommodate the expanding audiences for dramatic performances. When New York City's Park Theater, shown here, opened in 1821, it could seat an astounding 2,500 people.*

above the boxes for those considered of the lowest rank, including blacks and prostitutes. In contrast to the genteel Colonial audiences, the new audiences drawn from the "middle and humbler ranks" were unruly and ill-mannered. Spitting, eating, and drinking beer were not uncommon, and many people moved about during the performances.

Because theatrical companies tried to appeal to a wide-ranging audience, theater bills were likely to include a little of everything. A single theater might feature more than 100 different plays in one season, and even performances of Shakespeare were often interspersed between the acts with such entertainment as specialty dances, music, jugglers, and trained animals.

When attending a dramatic performance, the popular audience wished to be uplifted as well as entertained. Thus plays with moral messages attracted large numbers of people. The popularity of two such plays, in particular, led to the custom of presenting an unchanging bill over a long period of time. The first of these, a temperance play called *The Drunkard, or the Fallen Saved,* was performed 130 times in its initial run in 1844.

Left: *Throughout the 19th century, performers in popular dramas and variety shows had to endure all manner of insults from rowdy audiences, as can be seen in this 1878 engraving.* Facing page: *The tremendous popularity of the dramatic adaptation of* Uncle Tom's Cabin *helped overcome religious objections to playgoing and made numerous converts to the theater. This 1880s poster advertises a particularly lavish production of the play.*

But it was *Uncle Tom's Cabin,* a "moral, religious, instructive play" based on the novel by abolitionist Harriet Beecher Stowe, that set the record. From the time this play was introduced in the 1850s, it was staged an estimated four times per day for the next 75 years. As early as 1854, some theatrical companies were performing nothing but *Uncle Tom's Cabin.* This play helped make new converts to the theater, overcoming earlier prejudices against theatrical entertainment. After attending a performance of the play in October 1853, a reviewer for the *New York Atlas* noted that seated in the pit were:

> *[M]any people who have been taught to look on the stage with horror and contempt, . . . Methodists, Presbyterians, and Congregationalists of the strait-laced school . . . .*

These new audiences, drawn increasingly from the middle class, lent major support to the theater throughout the remainder of the 19th century.

Until the middle of the 19th century, the majority of plays were geared toward middle- and working-class audiences. So-called "legitimate drama," staged more for its artistic merit than its entertainment value, was largely overpowered by popular plays and between-acts variety performances. The tension between serious and popular drama and the different classes to which they appealed came to a head with the violent Astor Place riot in 1849. This unseemly event occurred because the American public elevated a bitter personal feud between Charles Macready, an aristocratic English tragedian, and American stage favorite Edwin Forrest into a nationalistic contest. By the time the bloody riot ended, 30 people had been killed and 150 more had been injured. Before long, the legitimate stage and the popular theater went separate ways, offering distinctive attractions to their particular audiences.

At the same time, between-acts variety performances also were evolving into new and distinctive forms of theatrical entertainment. From the start, minstrel shows, variety shows, and burlesque acts consciously avoided gaining the elitist reputation of legitimate drama and committed themselves to popular audiences.

GRISWOLD OPERA HOUSE, TWO NIGHTS & MATINEE, **FRIDAY & SATURDAY, DEC. 16 & 17**

RESCUE OF EVA.

THE SLAVE MARKET.

MRS. G. C. HOWARD

PLANTATION SCENE.

THE ORIGINAL, TOPSY

THE SEPARATION.

DEATH OF EVA.

H.A. THOMAS, LITH STUDIO, 112 FOURTH AVE N.Y.

UNCLE TOM'S CABIN.

The Christy Minstrels, organized in 1846, combined the elements of earlier blackface dialogue, music, and variety performance into a standardized minstrel show. This group became so famous that it performed nightly for close to a decade in New York City's Mechanics Hall. Here the Christy Minstrels appear on the cover of the sheet music for Oh! Susanna *by the famous minstrel-song composer Stephen Foster. The song was published in 1848.*

Minstrel shows were the first distinctive form of popular entertainment to emerge from this division. During the 1840s and 1850s, this uniquely American entertainment form rapidly achieved popularity in Northeastern cities and then spread across the country. At one point as many as 10 minstrel shows were being staged simultaneously in New York City. Even the gold prospectors in faraway California enjoyed entertainment by minstrels. Although elements of these shows had appeared earlier (most notably the blackface Jim Crow act of comedian Thomas Rice), Dan Emmett's Virginia Minstrels introduced the first staged minstrel show in 1843. A few years later, the famous Christy Minstrels established the standard

pattern for these shows. Edwin Christy not only assigned distinctive characters to the blackface performers, but also evolved the three-part format of the shows—a portion of song-and-dance numbers, a variety section, and a one-act skit.

Minstrel shows owed little or nothing to real life, clearly presenting a mixture of racial stereotypes. They were primarily a stage creation of white performers directed at white audiences. Though clearly offensive to modern sensibilities, they presented what was then perceived as easily understandable humor in a clean, moral setting. The chief legacy of the minstrel shows was musical, as the shows became major disseminators of both traditional and newly written popular songs (most notably those written by Stephen Foster). The comic elements and dance numbers in the shows also became important features in later forms of public entertainment.

When formal variety shows first evolved as separate offshoots of popular theater in the mid-19th century, they were strongly associated with urban and frontier saloons and their unsophisticated, largely male, audiences. These so-called "concert saloons," similar to English music halls, were well established in New York by the late 1850s, and by the mid-1860s numerous cities and towns across the country boasted at least one such establishment. The ones that did not charge admission but depended on the proceeds from gambling and the sale of food and drink were referred to as "free concert saloons," "honky-tonks," or "free-and-easies." The origin of the latter term can be found in the remarks of a *New York Evening Post* writer in 1862, who noted that these establishments were:

From the 1840s into the early 20th century, concert saloons or "free-and-easies" presented lowbrow (and often suggestive) entertainment to a predominantly male audience. Such establishments continued to thrive in New York City even after most variety entertainment had moved to legitimate theaters. This Harper's Weekly *engraving from October 8, 1859, suggests one writer's rather dubious opinion of the performances at this theater.*

A BROADWAY SUNDAY SACRED CONCERT IN NEW YORK.

Left: "Opera dancing," later known as ballet, was introduced in America along with various forms of European opera during the early 19th century. Although dancer Fanny Elssler helped to popularize ballet in the 1840s, it remained an essentially highbrow form of entertainment. This fashion engraving from Graham's Magazine, November 1849, depicts the type of audience that might have attended a ballet or operatic performance. Below: The spectacular success of the American tour by Swedish operatic singer Jenny Lind, promoted and organized by P. T. Barnum, paved the way for similar tours by many other performers. This engraving from Gleason's Pictorial, May 17, 1851, depicts a capacity crowd, "composed of many of the city's elite," attending her concert in New York City's Castle Garden. The huge auditorium was said to hold 10,000 persons (at a time when the population of New York numbered around 696,000).

The Germania Musical Society, composed of musicians who had emigrated from Germany, toured the settled portions of America between 1848 and 1854. Its members are memorialized on this sheet music cover published in 1855, the year after the organization was dissolved.

[E]xtensively patronized by the public, especially on Saturday nights, when all parts of the house are crowded by male visitors . . . [who] wear their hats and caps at pleasure, smoke cigars and pipes, and conduct themselves generally in accordance with the popular song of "We'll be free and easy still."

The shows themselves were light, amusing, suggestive and, most important, varied. Increasingly, they came to include a "corps de ballet," in this case a performing chorus line of shapely young ladies.

A more specific form of variety entertainment was the burlesque. Prior to the Civil War, a burlesque was a parody or musical travesty adapted from an older English tradition of low comedy. Popular as an entertainment offered during minstrel shows and between and after dramatic performances, burlesque put-ons of popular plays and novels appealed to both upper- and working-class audiences.

During the first half of the 19th century, a wide range of vocal and instrumental musicians received support through public performances. Audiences at these shows were usually boisterous and aggressive, much like those who attended theatrical performances.

A colorful performance was generally valued more highly than the musical quality of the composition or arrangement. The result was public adulation of an assortment of virtuosi, including Norwegian violinist Ole Bull, Viennese ballet dancer Fanny Elssler, and Swedish singer Jenny Lind, as well as a number of musical families who toured the country at this time. Many of these performers were part of variety shows rather than strictly musical programs.

In the mid-19th century, audiences welcomed an increasing number of emigrant musicians from Germany. These brought a style of music considered more refined and "scientific" than the British-derived music that had been mostly performed until then. A group of them formed the Germania Musical Society in Germany in 1848, and traveled through America for the next six years, where their performances of symphonic music were enthusiastically received. Since all of its members became American citizens during this period, the Society could be considered the first full-time orchestra in America to devote itself exclusively to the performance of symphonic music. After the group disbanded in 1854, individual members of the Society played significant roles in later efforts to organize orchestras and choral societies.

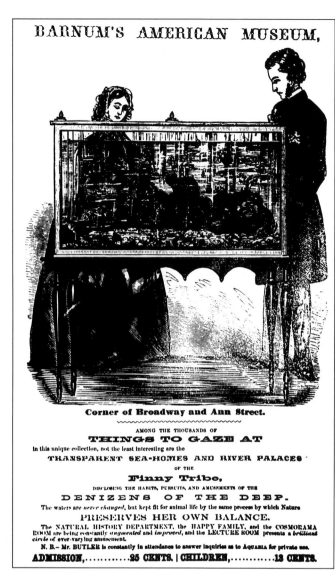

Above: *During the second quarter of the 19th century, public speakers traveled across the country to hold forth on every conceivable issue of the day. This depiction of a lecture on women's rights is from an 1850s parlor game card.* Left: *More than anyone else Phineas T. Barnum popularized museums by providing the public with the types of features he thought they wanted. Among the attractions of his New York City museum were thousands of curiosities as promised in this 1858 advertisement.*

"Strictly Moral" Entertainment

During the early and mid-19th century, education was considered a primary responsibility of all citizens. The enthusiasm for learning and self-improvement was manifested not only in the growth of subscription libraries (which tripled between 1825 and 1850), but also in the tremendous popularity of lyceums.

The lyceum movement brought public speakers to many towns, providing a diversion considered less frivolous than the more lighthearted entertainments. Deriving its name from the site close to ancient Athens where Aristotle taught his students, the American lyceum movement was started in 1826 by scientific lecturer Josiah Holbrook of Derby, Connecticut. To elevate the cultural level of American communities and to help draw young people away from such unwholesome amusements as dancing schools and balls, Holbrook proposed subscription lecture series on literary, scientific, and moral subjects.

By 1828, the lyceum movement had spread to more than 100 towns, especially in the Northeast. Some towns even built auditoriums intended specifically for the staging of oratorical presentations by the traveling speakers. By the mid-19th century, some 3,000 lyceums could be found throughout the country; indeed, towns were considered "backward," if not downright "barbarous," if they did not support one. In the Midwest and West, especially, lyceums came to serve as a major form of recreation, combining the appreciation for learning with the pleasures of getting together with friends and acquaintances. Although educational purpose and entertainment value were occasionally hard to distinguish in lyceum presentations, they received full support from those who believed that other public amusements were sinful.

The urge for self-improvement also manifested

itself in the emergence of public museums. Attempts to accumulate and display objects of scientific interest had been under way in major Eastern cities since the late 18th century. One of the best known of these was the collection of the American Philosophical Society, which came to be housed with Charles Willson Peale's portraits and natural history collection in Philadelphia in 1794. However, these types of "museums" often were not accessible to the public. Moreover, it seemed that they did not satisfy the entertainment needs of the urban public nearly as well as did the displays of human and animal freaks, mechanical and scientific oddities, wax figures, and peep shows that showmen had begun to organize into "cabinets of curiosity" during the early 19th century. Among these more popular establishments was Rembrandt Peale's museum in Baltimore, established in 1814, which contained a mastodon skeleton unearthed a few years earlier.

P. T. Barnum emerged as the key figure in developing, promoting, and popularizing museums. In 1841, he purchased the American Museum in New York (which had been established in 1830 by John Scudder), and transformed what had been considered an unimpressive collection of historical and scientific curiosities into an entertaining diversion that was patronized by viewers of all classes and ages.

At a time when the theater was still widely regarded as somewhat disreputable, Barnum marketed his Grand Colossal Museum and Menagerie as highly educational and strictly moral. In the 3,000-seat "lecture room," for example, dramatic performances and variety acts were staged under the guise of "chaste scenic entertainments" for "all those who disapprove of the dissipations, debaucheries, profanity, vulgarity, and other abominations which characterize our modern theaters." By 1850, Barnum claimed to have amassed more than 600,000 curiosities in his museum, including living serpents, waxwork figures, models of new machines and Niagara Falls, and fortune tellers. He also sent major exhibitions out on the road, and promoted such personalities as General Tom Thumb and singer Jenny Lind to the status of national (and sometimes international) celebrities.

The success of Barnum's museum and related stage entertainments spawned hundreds of imita-

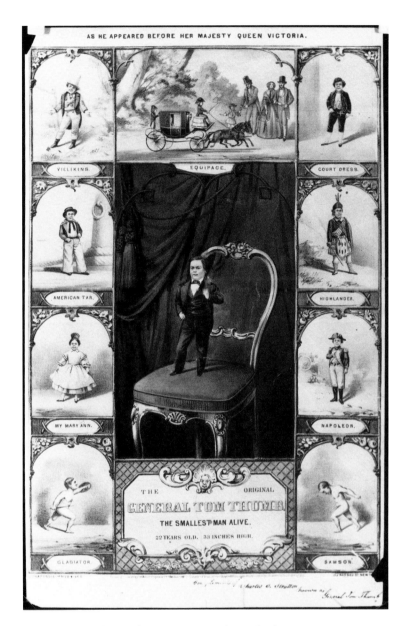

Beginning in the mid-1840s Barnum brought five-year-old midget Charles Stratton to international stardom as General Tom Thumb. For several years Thumb toured America and Europe, and remained a popular favorite as one of Barnum's museum curiosities. This Currier & Ives lithograph from 1860 shows the various ways in which this performer would delight audiences wherever he toured.

tions. By the 1850s, almost every city boasted a museum offering a jumbled collection of curiosities and variety acts. (These later came to be called dime museums because of their modest admission charges and the correspondingly modest entertainment they offered.) At the same time, the serious scientific museums added more sensational features to their displays and lecture programs.

Traveling Shows Emerge

Since Colonial times, traveling performers had put on informal shows or exhibited animals, freaks, or mechanical and scientific oddities in taverns and other public buildings, as well as at community celebrations. During the 19th century, such activities evolved into more formalized traveling shows. Among the first of these were medicine shows, panorama displays, and circuses.

Although roving, performing quack doctors had touted tonics and elixirs earlier, the development of formalized medicine shows coincided with the phenomenal growth of the patent medicine industry in the 19th century. Traveling performers borrowed many of their techniques from the popular theater of the time. Often smaller shows were presented free of charge to attract customers for the products. (In a way, medicine shows might be viewed as precursors of the commercially sponsored radio and television programs of our own time.)

Historic panoramas and cycloramas often constituted their own traveling shows, being displayed in special buildings or in museums along a designated route. At first imported from Europe, they reached the peak of their popularity between 1840 and 1860, when hundreds of them traveled across the country.

Panoramas, in their numerous variations, generally consisted of immense murals that were turned in sequential order in front of an audience. With cycloramas, this procedure was reversed and the seated audience was rotated in front of the murals to achieve a similar effect. The subjects of the murals included depictions of cities, beautiful scenery, trips on lakes and rivers, historic and religious scenes,

---

Panoramas traveled to hundreds of cities and towns during the mid- and late 19th century, combining instruction with entertainment in a way that foreshadowed the movie newsreels of the 20th century. This 1870s advertisement announces the exhibition of a 1,200-square-foot panorama depicting Jerusalem and the Holy Land at the Georama, located on Broadway in New York City. This grand painting was said to include "myriads" of life-size figures as well as all the important natural features, holy shrines, and sacred localities mentioned in the Bible and in the history of the Crusades.

Wonders of Nature Displayed.

EXTRAORDINARY NOVELTY.

TO be seen at the Pennsylvania Farmer, in Third, between Vine and Callowhill streets, for a few nights only.

The ELEPHANT HAHEEM MAHEEM ALLA KHAN, formerly belonging to the Prime Minister to the King of Oube, of the same name, and probably the most sagacious, docile, and the largest ever brought to the United States, and one that was held in high estimation by its former owner, and cost much to procure him.

The Elephant Alla Khan is 20 years old, 8 feet 9 inches high, and 25 feet long—has 2 beautiful tusks, about 30 inches long, which, with his ears, are ornamented—and has the Mahote, who accompanied him from Calcutta, to attend him.

Alla Khan is in good health, and his sagacity is wonderful. He extricated and saved himself by his trunk, after having fallen overboard, when landing at Perot's dock, in Philadelphia.   oct 5—6t

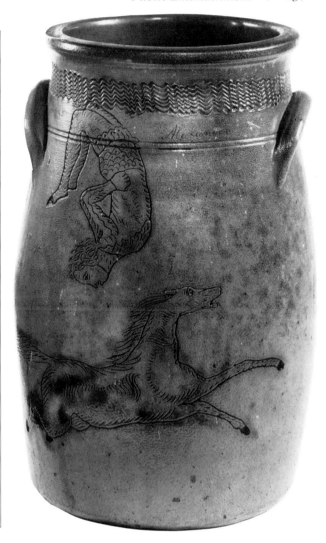

Above: *Acrobats and equestrian performers eventually joined forces with animal exhibitors to form the basic features of the American circus. This mid-19th-century stoneware churn depicts one such performer executing stunts on horseback.* Above left: *The promoters of traveling animal shows lavished extravagant praise on their subjects, as can be seen from this 1833 advertisement. It claimed that, upon landing in Philadelphia, this "sagacious, docile" elephant had "extricated and saved himself by his trunk after having fallen overboard."*

famous battles, and current news events. Serving an educational as well as an entertainment purpose, they offered knowledge of a larger world to audiences from every walk of life.

The formal circus, which evolved into a distinct entertainment form in the mid-19th century, combined three different types of traveling performances: staged equestrian shows, animal displays, and acrobatic performances. Equestrian shows, usually enacted within a ring on a stage, first became popular in America during the 1790s. Based on similar shows in England, they combined trick horseback riding with acrobatic feats and clown acts.

Traveling animal menageries were highly popular in the early 19th century as "great moral and educational exhibitions." In the 1820s, some 30 or more animal shows traversed the Eastern United States, traveling as far west as Detroit by 1830. During the 1830s and 1840s, acrobatic troupes and animal menageries often teamed up to travel together. The portable canvas walls or tents they brought, and the clowns and parades some used to announce their coming, later became standard circus features. Side shows, featuring freaks and other oddities, also were incorporated into the performances at this time.

Around the middle of the 19th century, all three types of traveling shows finally merged. The more prominent troupes set up large tents that provided seating for their audiences and used specially constructed wagons for transportation and parades. Circuses would continue to grow in number and scope during succeeding decades, along with a host of other traveling shows that were developing.

THE GREATEST SHOWS ON EARTH: CIVIL WAR TO WORLD WAR I

Between the Civil War and World War I, opportunities to enjoy live entertainment in all forms of theater, music, dancing, lectures, and exhibitions expanded tremendously, especially in urban areas. By the end of the 19th century, public entertainment had become extremely specialized and was taking on the characteristics of big business. Expanded railroad networks, better roads, increased availability of printed materials, and invention of the phonograph greatly affected the nature of entertainment.

All Manner of Variety

Variety entertainment continued to broaden both its scope and audience. From the 1860s to the 1890s, variety shows struggled to escape the stigma of the saloons and tried to earn a seal of approval from family audiences. Only when they evolved into vaudeville shows in the 1880s and 1890s did they succeed in doing so. During these two decades, a new generation of managers and producers elevated and refined variety entertainment to "a high plane of respectability and moral cleanliness." Vaudeville experienced its greatest popularity between 1890 and 1920, appealing especially to a broad middle-class audience.

Lavish vaudeville palaces and traveling circuits sprang up across the country, presenting short acts by all manner of variety entertainers and borrowing materials from all other forms of show business. An average bill included 20 to 30 short acts, each lasting about 15 minutes. Robert Toll's book *On With the Show* (1976) quoted comedian George Burns's reflections on what was required for success in vaudeville:

You know, all you needed in vaudeville was seventeen good minutes. If you had seventeen good minutes, you could work for seventeen years. There were so many theaters, you wouldn't come back to the same one for four years and who would remember what you did the last time you were there?

In addition to comics like Burns, other acts on a vaudeville bill might include singers, dancers, theat-

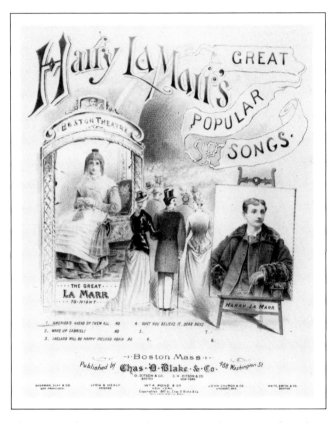

Above: *By the 1880s such variety performers as female impersonator Harry La Marr were appearing at respectable theaters like the one on this 1887 sheet music cover. The performers included child prodigies, acrobats, dancers, and magicians.* Facing page top: *Families of musicians offered programs designed to appeal to heterogeneous audiences but also tried to introduce their listeners to serious music. This is an 1880s photograph.* Facing page bottom: *Vaudeville shows consisted of a series of short, rapid, self-contained acts, including animal acts and comic, musical, and other variety performances. Lavishly decorated vaudeville theaters like this New York City one, were designed to attract middle-class audiences.*

rical performers, impersonators, magicians, trained animals, and even trick cyclists and fancy roller skaters.

The blackface minstrel show in its antebellum form did not survive the Civil War; changes in the society and culture forced changes in the form of this type of entertainment. By the turn of the century the core of the minstrel show—the blackface dialect act—had been absorbed by other forms of entertainment. However, minstrel shows continued to serve as one of the chief vehicles for disseminating music to a large, unsophisticated audience.

After the Civil War, burlesque became quite different from what it had been before, increasingly focusing on the attractions of the female form.

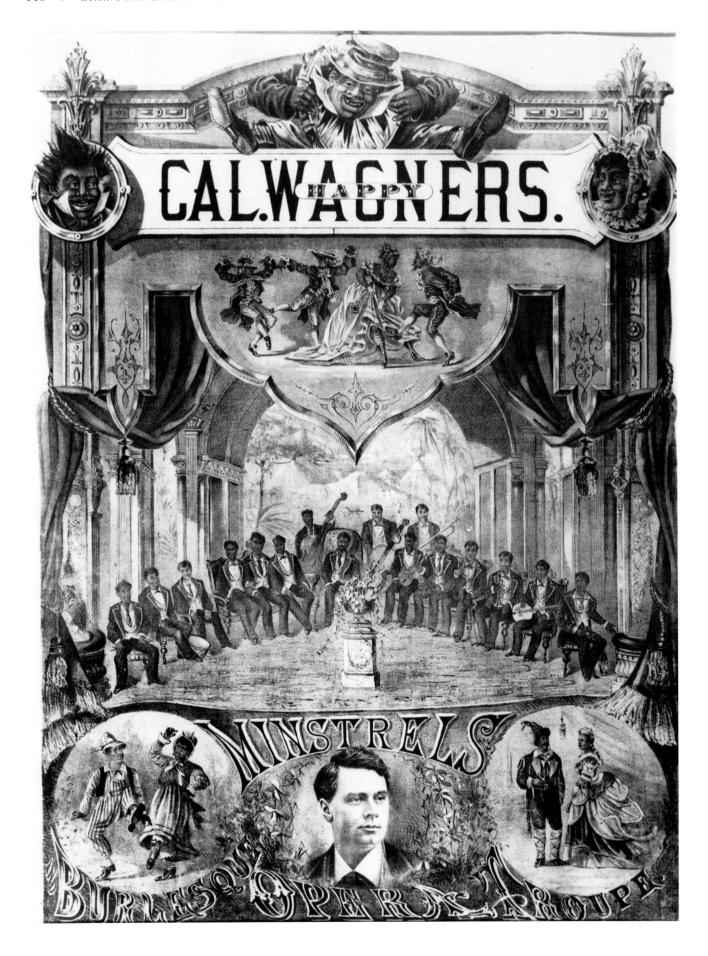

"THE BLACK CROOK"

Facing page: *After the Civil War the tightly-knit minstrel show format was revised to enable such shows to compete with other types of popular entertainment. As this 1880s poster indicates, touring troupes became larger, performed lavish production numbers, and incorporated many variety features into the new types of minstrel shows.* Above: The Black Crook, *first presented in 1866, helped shape the basic structure both of burlesque shows and musical comedies. As this 1880s poster suggests, this musical extravaganza featured a large ballet corps (100 women) in ''form-fitting'' silk tights.* Right: *Musical comedy flourished during the early years of the 20th century, as its disparate elements blended. In no small part, this was due to the energy and talent of George M. Cohan, creator of, and performer in, fast-moving, highly appealing shows for popular audiences. ''Yankee Doodle Boy,'' from Cohan's 1904 play* Little Johnny Jones, *became a classic of the American musical stage.*

"Girlie shows," featuring females in skin-tight clothes, flourished during the late 19th century in variety halls, concert saloons, beer gardens, and lower-class theaters. Burlesque gained even wider public exposure through the vehicle of lavish musical extravaganzas and variety shows, in which troupes of women performed parodies in tights or in revealing men's clothing. The popularity of the belly dancer billed as "Little Egypt" at the 1893 World's Columbian Exposition in Chicago introduced yet another element into burlesque, namely, the "exotic dance."

Musical comedy evolved as a specialized theatrical form in the post-Civil War years. It generally combined a rudimentary plot, a vernacular style of language and music, and a somewhat elaborate production to become what one critic described in 1894 as "an indefinable melange of music and drama." It was given a particular boost by the popularity of operettas—especially those of Gilbert and Sullivan and Victor Herbert—during the closing decades of the 19th and the early decades of the 20th centuries.

The musical revue, as exemplified by the Ziegfeld Follies, combined the opulence of extravaganzas and musical comedy, the variety and fast pace of vaudeville, and a refined form of burlesque. Its direct antecedent was the spicy Paris revue, which Florenz Ziegfeld adapted to American taste in a series of annual productions that made their debut in 1907. Ziegfeld was a true showman, promoting the revues with promises of glamour and sensual appeal.

The Proliferation of Traveling Shows

Expanding modes of transportation and greater interest in diverse entertainments helped traveling shows become highly successful in the decades from the 1870s to the outbreak of World War I. Traveling theatrical companies and circuses continued to offer their special brands of entertainment, while new types of traveling shows, such as Wild West Exhibitions and tent Chautauquas, also appeared on the scene. These shows frequently borrowed techniques, performers, and themes from one another.

With the growth of railroad networks after the Civil War, small towns became important and profitable stops for touring theatrical companies. Many of the towns constructed so-called "opera houses" or "academies of music" to accommodate the traveling shows that formerly had staged their offerings in courthouses, schools, town halls, and churches.

During their heyday, these opera houses provided the setting for highly varied programs with broad audience appeal. Melodrama was especially popular. However, the quality of dramatic performances being offered by the touring companies was very uneven, as the supply of first-rate shows simply could not equal the demand. In an *Atlantic Monthly* article dated August 1897, one jaded commentator complained: "Doubtless there are worse theatrical companies than those that visit Kansas, but no one has ever described them."

Traveling tent shows emerged during the late

In contrast to the negative associations evoked in the minds of many small-town Americans by the notion of theater, an opera house or academy of music was thought to lend an air of refinement and respectability to a community. This turn-of-the-century photograph shows a parade passing by the Opera House in Marquette, Michigan.

19th century. Their numbers were augmented when more and more small performing companies moved their shows to portable tents after the turn of the century. Presenting some form of dramatic performance or variety entertainment, these shows were marketed as family entertainment, described by one tent manager as a decent alternative to the "epics, orgies, sex, and horror of the movies."

During the late 19th century, medicine shows traversed the country, appealing especially to rural

After the Civil War entertainment superseded moral instruction as the major feature of lecture series. Increasingly, lecture bureaus booked performers who promised novelty and amusement, as in this 1889 promotion piece.

Americans in the Midwest and South, where entertainment and medical care were both lacking. By the end of the century, some companies employed as many as 35 or 40 performers. The players traveled in their own railroad cars, performed in tents, and drew paying crowds in the thousands.

After the Civil War, traveling lyceum programs gradually became more commercial as large booking agencies took over their management. As a result, local citizens, especially in communities in the West, stopped feeling a strong obligation to support them. To compete with other forms of popular amusement, the surviving lecture programs increased the ratio of entertainment to instruction, thus watering down the original intention of the lyceum movement. By the end of the century, most of the lyceums' functions had been absorbed by the Chautauqua movement, although lecture bureaus continued to book speaking tours for prominent literary figures and celebrities in other fields, especially on the college circuit.

The name Chautauqua derived from a lake in upstate New York, near which an assembly for Sunday School teachers had been established in the summer of 1874. Before long, the offerings at the assembly expanded from religious instruction to include such subjects as history, music, the natural sciences, and foreign languages, and Chautauqua became a form of adult summer school.

By 1900, more than 200 communities had established permanent Chautauqua-like pavilions by lakes or in parks to serve as centers of cultural activity during the summer months. Moreover, numerous local groups had organized what were known as Chautauqua Literary and Scientific circles, to pursue assigned courses of study at home year round.

Recognizing the public interest in this type of program and the profit to be derived from it, several entrepreneurs organized traveling or circuit Chautauquas. Booking and routing lecturers, musicians, and performers according to a regular schedule and standardized program, these circuits used the techniques of the traveling theatrical companies of the time to offer their unique brand of "culture under a tent." Like the earlier lyceums, they depended upon the involvement of community members.

The traveling Chautauquas, combining elements

The Chautauqua movement evolved from instructional Sunday School assemblies held on the northwestern bank of Lake Chautauqua, New York, from the 1870s on. After the turn of the century tent Chautauqua circuits were organized and visited numerous towns and cities, including Racine, Wisconsin, where this 1906 photograph was taken.

of vaudeville, dramatic "entertainments," lectures, and musical performance, provided an acceptable and highly anticipated diversion for many Americans living in small towns and rural areas. Usually a week in duration, these shows subtly combined the highly moral and religious atmosphere of a camp meeting, and elements of the lyceum lectures, with the entertainment aspects of a county fair. (*See "Getting Together" for camp meetings and fairs.*)

Circuses reached their peak in number and popularity during the last quarter of the 19th and first decade of the 20th centuries, when at least 40 large shows and numerous smaller ones toured the United States. They held a special appeal for rural crowds, providing some of the splendor and excitement associated with the amusements of city life. Hamlin Garland summed up this feeling in his reminiscences of life in Iowa in the 1870s, entitled *Boy Life on the Prairie* (1899):

No one but a country boy can rightly measure the majesty and allurement of a circus. To go from the lonely prairie or the dusty corn-field and come face to face with the "amazing aggregation of world-wide wonders" was like enduring the visions of the Apocalypse.

Facing page: *This 1896 Barnum & Bailey poster played on the identification of children with circuses, depicting the circus's diverse acts as they might crowd into a child's dream.* Right: *This ornate cast-iron toy circus wagon from around 1875 gives some idea of the splendor of circus parades.* Below: *Circuses incorporated elements from many other forms of popular entertainment, including the dime museums' side shows, which usually included freaks. Borrowing heavily from the types of amusements offered in Barnum's earlier museum, the Barnum & Bailey circus developed its shows into major attractions like those pictured in this 1898 poster.*

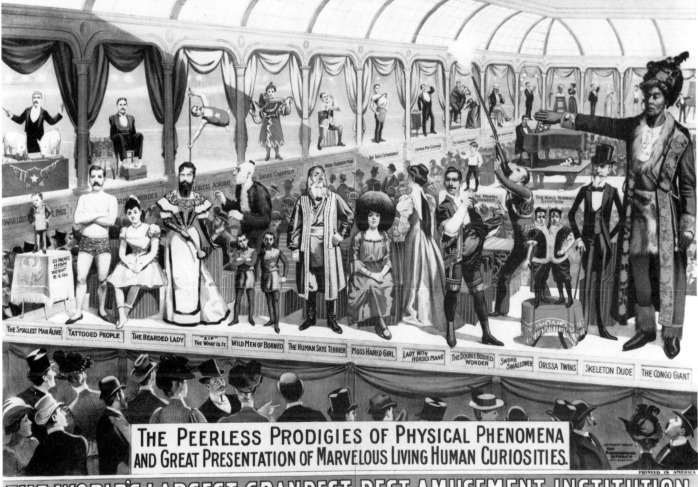

Left: The "steam organ" or calliope, which made its first appearance in American circuses in the 1850s, attracted tremendous crowds to circus parades with its colorful appearance and resounding musical productions. This calliope was produced in 1917 by the Bode Wagon Works of Cincinnati, Ohio, for Mugivan and Bowers's American Circus, Peru, Indiana. The keyboard and whistles at the top were originally inside the vehicle. Below: Traveling circuses brought exotic animals to many a remote American town. In this 1890s photograph visitors to Clyde Wixom's circus meet the King of the Jungle face to face.

As larger circuses began to bypass the more isolated towns and villages, smaller traveling shows took their place. This early 1920s photograph depicts an outdoor one-ring circus act typical of these kinds of shows.

Competition among the traveling circuses was fierce, with smaller ones trying to imitate the glamour of the larger ones as far as possible. Before long, the larger circuses discovered that it was not worth their while to travel to the more isolated areas. By the 1890s, therefore, most rural audiences were being entertained by smaller circuses called "dog and pony shows," so named because those were the staple of the entertainment they could afford to offer.

Wild West shows trace their origins to the competitive cowboy stunts and contests featured at roundups and community celebrations in Western states like Colorado, Arizona, and Wyoming. The Wild West shows, however, featured salaried performers and borrowed heavily from the spectacular pageantry of circuses. Although P. T. Barnum had brought such Western curiosities as Indians and buffalo to the East before the Civil War, the credit for consolidating and popularizing this form of entertainment is usually given to frontiersman William F. "Buffalo Bill" Cody. Some say that Cody conceived

the idea for his shows while watching a Wild West extravaganza that concluded a Barnum circus performance in New York City in 1874. However, it is known that he was particularly impressed by the enthusiastic crowd that attended a rodeo he helped to organize in North Platte, Nebraska, in 1882. Soon after, he began to take companies of cowboys, Indians, horses, and buffalo on tour.

Becoming successively larger and more spectacular, his so-called "Wild West Exhibitions" drew tremendous crowds. On its opening day in St. Louis in 1884, Cody's show attracted 35,000 customers, while the show he pitched outside the World's Columbian Exposition in Chicago in 1893 reportedly drew six million patrons.

By the turn of the century, more than 100 Wild West shows were touring the country. Small shows of varying quality, produced with limited capital, flourished at county fairs and carnivals. During their heyday, Wild West shows were phenomenally successful throughout the country, appealing especially to urban audiences and recent immigrants. In a greatly romanticized way, they addressed the prevailing popular curiosity about the West.

After 1910, other forms of entertainment—especially cowboy movies in which the illusions and scenery were more believable than in the live shows—largely replaced the Wild West shows. Changing attitudes toward the West also made the romantic extravaganzas less appealing, while rodeo competitions became generally popular as professional spectator sports.

Carnivals evolved during the 1890s, spurred on by the success of the Midway Plaisance, the amusement strip of the 1893 World's Columbian Exposition in Chicago. (*See "Getting Away" for world's fairs.*) By 1895, some 15 traveling carnival companies had been established, combining three distinctive

features: side shows or exhibits, concessions, and mechanical thrill rides.

Carnivals were transported to and set up wherever crowds of people gathered and were likely to spend money. Often they accompanied trade-promotion activities in the centers of towns, helping to stimulate local business by attracting a crowd. At other times they were set up on vacant lots or on the outskirts of cities and towns under the sponsorship of local civic organizations.

Soon after their emergence in the 1890s, traveling carnivals began to appear at agricultural fairs, as the more modest fairs desperately tried to match the larger fairs' increasing emphasis on entertainment. Hundreds of fair midways began to feature such carnival side show attractions as dancing girls, lady boxers, baby shows, and freaks.

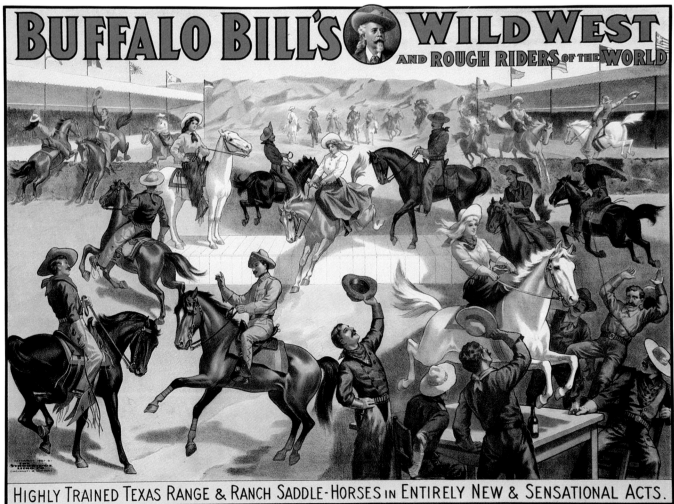

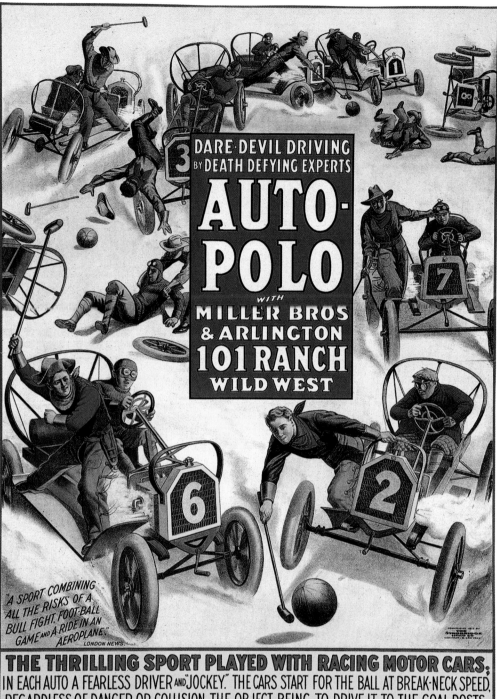

Facing page: *Buffalo Bill Cody's Wild West shows were greeted with enthusiasm from their inception in the 1880s through the early years of the 20th century. In the 1890s Cody added to his shows a "Congress of Rough Riders of the World," who incorporated various kinds of specialized riding from countries outside the United States. This 1907 poster depicts the characteristic combination of rodeo and variety features that made up these shows. Above left: The aim of the concession owners at amusement parks, fairs, and carnivals was to entice their customers to spend money freely, often by participating in games of chance. This Wheel of Fortune from around 1900 commonly found at such places, is remarkably similar to the one featured on the 1980s television game show of the same name. Above: Wild West shows made little effort to achieve authenticity, often presenting entertainment that was not related to the West in any way. One such act, an auto polo match, was featured on this 1913 poster for the Arlington 101 Ranch Wild West show.*

Arbiters of Taste

During the waning decades of the 19th and early decades of the 20th centuries, an increasing number of entertainment forms attracted response and support from middle- and upper-class patrons, both for their own enjoyment and in an attempt to bring "appropriate" culture and refinement to those they considered beneath them. These "refinements" included legitimate theater, symphony orchestras, and serious museums.

Wealthy supporters of legitimate theater might pay one to three dollars to attend a performance in a small, quiet, luxuriously appointed playhouse. The performances at these theaters did not so much mirror the tastes of the audience as seek to mold them by borrowing and adapting what were considered the most cultivated and civilized offerings from the European theater of the time.

The performance of classical music in America departed from the European tradition during the second half of the 19th century as symphony orchestras and operas went their separate ways. Needing sponsorship, such organizations as the Boston Symphony (1881) and the Chicago Symphony (1891) courted the support of the financial and social elites of their cities. Like the legitimate theater, orchestras tended to direct their performances toward raising and molding the tastes of their audiences rather than to simply entertaining them. The rising importance of the conductor in shaping programs, in striving to achieve polished orchestral performances, and in setting new standards of professional training, further removed the so-called "cultivated" musical experience from the popular audience.

Growing centers in the Midwest and West followed the lead of East Coast cities by establishing a

Left: *The stylish Rialto section of Broadway (probably named after the famous bridge in Venice) was lined with fashionable playhouses. The Herald Square Theater, shown on this 1895 sheet music cover, had been remodeled the previous year.* Above: *For children toy panoramas simulated the excitement of live theatrical performances. Made of cardboard mounted on wood, this 1890s panorama shows characteristic orchestra pit and box seats. Two vertical wooden rollers concealed behind the screen support a painted roll of paper which, when revolved by metal cranks, displays 12 scenes from the story of Cinderella.*

variety of musical organizations, including choral societies and amateur orchestras. These performed in the same facilities—the academies of music and opera houses—used by theatrical troupes. Local music clubs, church choirs, and touring musicians and concert singers also helped maintain some popular interest in classical music.

During the second half of the 19th century, European opera and what was known as "opera dancing," or ballet, became somewhat specialized. These performances primarily attracted the patronage of the elite, although less well-to-do music lovers also attended, especially if the music being performed was by composers from their homelands. Although light opera and ballet often were incorporated into popular theater in this era, grand opera continued as one of the most exclusive and fashionable of all diversions. It was only through phonograph recordings—beginning with the notable early recordings of legendary opera singer Enrico Caruso —that a wider, more general audience was exposed to grand opera.

Dancing among the middle and upper classes became increasingly refined, in contrast to the more informal dances characteristic of rural community gatherings. Specific dances were circumscribed by rigorous rules of etiquette and often required special training for mastery of intricate steps. Dance manuals proliferated and professional dancing instructors found themselves in great demand.

Above: *As early as the first decades of the 20th century, summer festivals and outdoor concerts helped bring classical and operatic music to a broad audience. Conductor Walter Damrosch, shown here at a rehearsal with the New York Symphony in the theater at the Ravinia Amusement Park outside Chicago, was a strong advocate for making this kind of music more accessible. Between 1905 and 1910, his orchestra presented lengthy programs at Ravinia seven days a week for six weeks during the summer. Meanwhile, elsewhere on the grounds visitors could watch a game of baseball, enjoy refreshments, or have their fortunes told by gypsies.* Right: *This violin was reputedly made around 1860 by the celebrated George Gemunder of Astoria, New York. It was played by Maud Powell, an outstanding American soloist, during her concert tours of Europe and America. In 1904, Powell, who had made her American debut with the New York Philharmonic in 1885, became one of the first violinists to make phonograph recordings.*

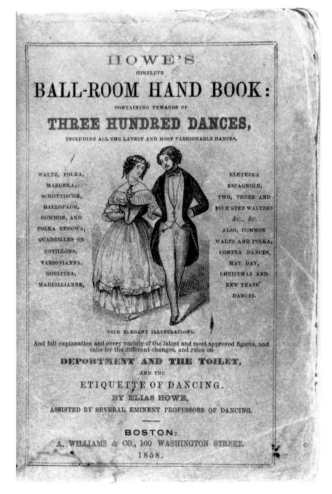

Above: *Most of the operas performed in America during the 19th century were by the established European operatic composers. The audience in this* Harper's Weekly *engraving from February 3, 1883, for example, is watching a performance of Richard Wagner's* Lohengrin *at the Cincinnati Opera Festival.* Left: *Learning social dancing required more than mastery of the actual steps, as the cover of this 1848 handbook clearly indicates.*

Formal balls and assemblies organized by families and social clubs were private and barred outsiders. The favored forms of dance called for control, regularity, and patterned movement. Most important, they strengthened group cohesion, since individual pleasure was almost completely dependent upon the enjoyment of the entire social group. Nowhere were these social obligations more visible than in the institution of the dance card, which generally prevented a dancer from holding onto the same partner all evening.

Many new museums were founded in major cities, sponsored by financial and social elites but intended for general public enlightenment. These museums were more specialized in their subject matter, more selective in their collections, and less sensational in their displays than were the disreputable dime museums that were to be found in all fair-sized American cities.

Above: *In contrast to the lowbrow appeal of the dime museums were the "legitimate" museums, financed by the social elite. The contents of one such museum and its elegantly attired patrons are depicted in this fashion engraving from* Frank Leslie's Lady's Magazine, *January 1875.* Below: *As public interest in museums grew, these institutions increased their emphasis on education. This turn-of-the-century photograph, taken for the* New York Herald *by photojournalist Jenny Chandler, depicts a "children's museum" inside a New York City library.*

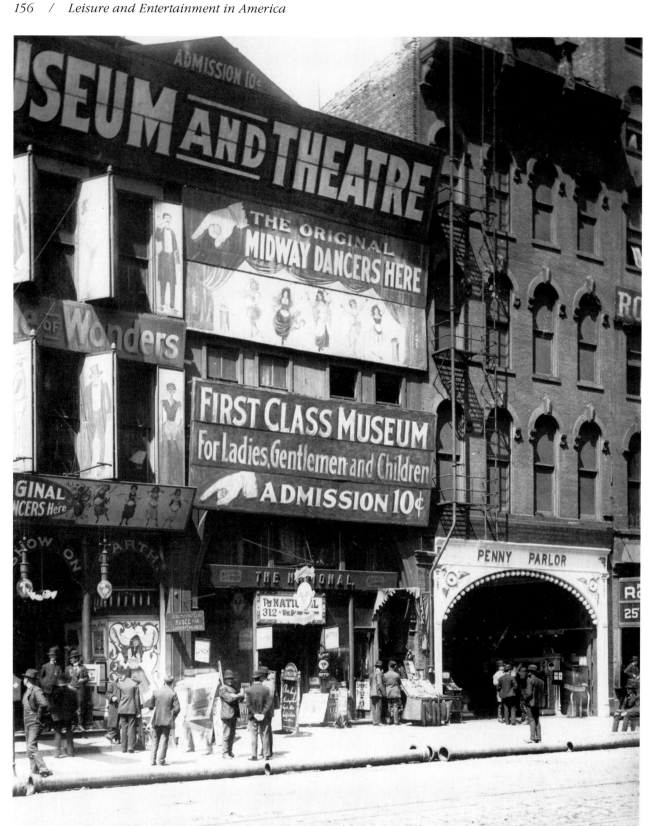

By the time this photograph was taken in Chicago in 1912, dime museums had acquired a somewhat seedy reputation because of their association with dance halls, drinking, and gambling. They did not survive much longer in the face of competition from vaudeville and moving pictures shown in penny parlors like the one above. The sign for the "Original Midway Dancers" refers to the exotic dancers who had performed on the Midway at Chicago's Columbian Exposition in 1893.

By the mid-19th century, when tattooed "freaks" began to appear in circuses and dime museums, tattooing had become an established profession in America and Europe. The development of electrical tattooing instruments revolutionized the art in the 1880s, making it faster, less painful, and more artistic. Tattooing often attracted customers among ordinary citizens as well as circus and carnival performers, and was associated with the lowbrow amusements of penny arcades and gambling parlors. This tattoo kit, including a complete set of instruments and colors, several original designs, and instructions, was used by Detroit tattoo artist Percy Waters from around 1900 to 1918.

Embracing New Forms of Entertainment

By the end of the 19th century, Progressive-era reformers were scrutinizing many of the cheaper amusements enjoyed by the working classes, and denouncing places like dance halls, penny arcades, and the new moving picture theaters as wicked and immoral. Goaded by disapproving members of the middle class, they attempted to ban or control these so-called vices of urban life. However, by the early 20th century, constrained by fewer cultural and moral restrictions, even members of the middle class found themselves eagerly turning to such new entertainment forms as amusement parks, ragtime music and dancing, and, eventually, the movies.

The impact of amusement parks on the American public during the late 19th and early 20th centuries was considerable. The first area to incorporate the modern concept of an amusement park as an autonomous, independent entity was the seaside resort of Coney Island adjacent to New York City. In an attempt to counteract the increasing shabbiness of this resort, railway companies and resort entrepreneurs rebuilt it in the late 1890s, creating a series of new, separate amusement parks.

For nearly two decades, the overwhelming size and scope of Coney Island dominated the amusement park industry. Its bathing facilities, dance halls, and vaudeville theaters never failed to entertain visitors; but it was the novelty of the exotic settings and the mechanical amusements that most attracted them. The success of Coney Island inspired countless other amusement parks, creating a veritable building boom in cities and towns across the country.

Crowds attended these parks by the millions, enjoying unadulterated amusement on a scale unheard of before. While the parks were accessible to

The modern concept of the amusement park was created at the Brooklyn, New York, beach resort of Coney Island. This turn-of-the-century photograph of Luna Park (created in 1903 from the earlier Sea Lion Park) shows both the exotic architecture and the types of rides (this one was called the "Helter Skelter") that thrilled urban crowds at these parks.

To many people the syncopated rhythms of ragtime music presented a welcome change from the sentimental ballads of the 19th century. As Tin Pan Alley joined in the production of this musical form, popular songwriters like Irving Berlin adapted the earlier rhythms into new melodies geared to a broad general public. This sheet music was published in 1914.

the working classes and immigrant groups, advertisements reassured potential middle-class customers as to the respectable, "wholesome" character of the entertainment offered there. The promoters succeeded in drawing a heterogeneous audience hungry for sensory experiences and emotional release. Offering diversion from their daily lives, the amusement parks also provided visitors with a temporary respite from customary social restraints.

From the 1890s to World War I, the songs emanating from New York City's Tin Pan Alley (the portion of 28th Street around Broadway, where the major songwriters and sheet music publishers concentrated) dominated the musical taste of most of the country. Live entertainers of all sorts created a great demand for this music and became the chief means for popularizing it. During this period, instrumental ragtime music, which had been introduced by urban

blacks, was "refined" by white songwriters and publishers on Tin Pan Alley. The latter made this music accessible to a large public, which found it a welcome relief from the overwhelming number of sentimental ballads and parlor songs then current. Intended to be listened to rather than sung, ragtime pieces like the ones created by black composer Scott Joplin increased the public interest in performances by piano players and small dance bands.

The music of this period achieved even wider exposure through phonographs and mechanical music machines. Purchased for home use and installed at numerous public gathering spots, these devices made the new music available to people who would not or could not attend a live performance by a ragtime musician. Music recordings also increased the exposure of musicians to these new compositions, thus inspiring further innovations.

During the early 20th century new songs and dance tunes became popular with the help of mechanical, coin-operated music machines installed in public gathering places. Above: Coin-operated pianos reached the peak of their popularity during the years immediately preceding World War I, when the demand for music in public places seemed insatiable. This "automatic piano" was produced by the J. P. Seeburg Piano Company of Chicago around 1915. Left: This Regina Hexaphone from around 1912 was equipped with six cylindrical records, each of which could be played by dropping a nickel in the slot.

The great popularity of ragtime music, and the increasing exposure of white Americans to black dance traditions in minstrel and vaudeville shows and musical comedies during the 1880s and 1890s, led to an unprecedented interest in dance by the end of the century. For the first time, rhythm became more important than lyrics in popular music, and sheet music originally published for vocal performers began to reappear with dance orchestrations. Such dances as the cakewalk, introduced by black stage performers, became popular in high society in the 1890s, while the two-step and even the waltz became freer and quicker when adapted to the new syncopated rhythms. The new dances not only encouraged free interpretation of broadly prescribed steps, but, above all, emphasized the importance of the individual dancing couple rather than that of the entire social group.

Although upper-class enthusiasm for the new dances for the most part filtered down the social scale, many people attacked them as crude, and accused participants of lacking good deportment and ignoring etiquette. It was largely through the efforts of professional ballroom dancers, especially the team of Vernon and Irene Castle, that the new dances eventually gained respectability and glamour. The Castles turned what was considered "blatant eroticism" in many of the new dances into graceful, refined forms considered suitable for Americans from all social classes. During the second decade of the 20th century, more than 100 dances (including the turkey trot, bunny hug, fox trot, and tango) were introduced for the first time, and thousands of new converts were drawn to the dance floor.

This dance craze led to a proliferation of municipal dance halls, as reformers sought to separate dancing from the vices associated with concert saloons. Many public dancing places, however, had trouble combating the tendency for people to identify them with saloons, especially since they often

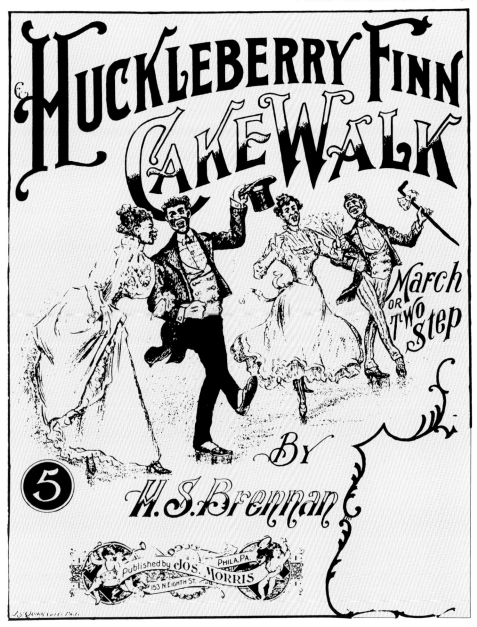

The cakewalk, consisting of prancing kick-steps, bows back and forward, and salutes to the audience, was popularized by black minstrel-show and musical-comedy performers in the 1890s, as shown on this sheet music cover from 1900. Although the cakewalk was primarily an exhibition rather than a social dance, it paved the way for a wider public interest in, and often a preference for, the steps and the inventiveness of vernacular black dances over the more formal European dances favored earlier.

continued to sell liquor. Managers worked tirelessly to present a respectable image, instituting dance contests, free dance lessons, and special holiday dances. Young people were attracted to the dance halls not only by a desire to dance but also because they were places where they could socialize and enjoy some freedom from the restrictions of home.

A more specialized kind of dance place, the "taxi-dance" hall, surfaced at this time. The taxi-dance was so called because a dance partner, like a taxi, was hired for the occasion. Combining the concept of the dancing school with that of the public dance hall, taxi-dance halls employed young women to teach male patrons the popular dances. Some restaurants also added dance floors, and cabarets offered a combination of refreshments, dancing, and musical entertainment. An article in the October 1913

issue of *Current Opinion* noted the new enthusiasm for dancing at these spots:

> [P]eople who have not danced before in twenty years have been dancing, during the past summer, afternoons, as well as evenings. Up-to-date restaurants provide a dancing floor so that patrons may lose no time while the waiter is changing the plates. Cabaret artists are disappearing except as interludes while people recover their breaths for the following number.

By the second decade of the 20th century, popular music had become so closely associated with dancing that songs were considered successful only if they could be danced to. From that time on, popular music and dance would remain intimately linked.

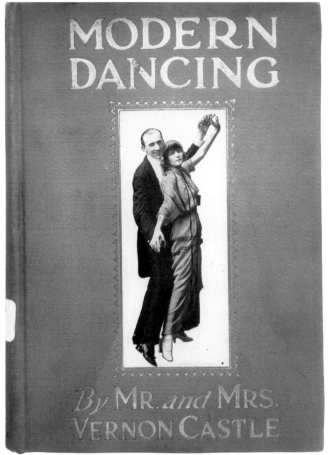

Above: *During the first decade of the 20th century the social dance repertoire of earlier days expanded to include less formal and faster dances like the two-step, reflecting the influence of black dance traditions. This sheet music cover from 1907 points up the change by using the device of the dance card.* Above right: *The grace and elegance exhibited by the dance team of Vernon and Irene Castle attracted thousands to the art of ballroom dancing. During the height of their popularity, the Castles produced numerous records and instruction books, including this 1914 publication copyrighted by Harper & Brothers.*

Of all forms of public entertainment, the movies probably have had the greatest impact on the American public. In contrast to live performances, they could be reproduced cheaply and in quantity, and could be viewed by millions of people simultaneously. The movies affected all other forms of public entertainment, altering some, completely eliminating others, and surpassing them all in popularity.

The earliest moving pictures in the United States were displayed in the 1890s as curious novelties in penny arcades, phonograph parlors, and billiard-rooms. By 1895, projectors were being developed that enabled large groups of people to view films simultaneously. Soon, these jerky, flickering "living pictures" were featured on vaudeville programs and in variety halls. Middle-class audiences, however, tended to look down on such shows as being merely a novelty that would never be able to compete with live performances.

From the beginning, moving pictures appealed most to the urban working classes and immigrants who could not afford more expensive live entertainment. The silent, visual method of communication by film made movies particularly appealing to non-English-speaking audiences. In *The Spirit of Youth and the City Streets,* published in 1909, Jane Addams commented upon the communal nature of the movie houses she observed in Chicago:

The five-cent theater is . . . fast becoming the general social center and club house in many crowded neighborhoods . . . . The room which contains the . . . stage is small and cozy, and less formal than the regular theater, and there is much more gossip and social life as if the foyer and pit were mingled.

Realizing the potential profits to be made from moving pictures, exhibitors hastily set up projectors in dozens of penny arcades and storefronts in working-class neighborhoods.

Audiences in the West also maintained an avid interest in movies, which were introduced to them through Chautauquas, carnivals, and other traveling road shows. The nickel admission price was particularly appealing.

Theaters exclusively devoted to showing movies were being built by 1905, and before long thousands more sprang up across the country. In August 1907, a *Harper's Weekly* article entitled "Nickel Madness" claimed that nearly a quarter of a million people—men, women, and children—were flocking daily "through the gaudy blatant entrances" of these so-called nickelodeons.

The short skits and bits of action shown in the early kinetoscope films soon gave way to longer films with more developed plots and characterization, produced specifically to be shown on a big screen. The phenomenal success of one of these films, *The Great Train Robbery,* in 1903, led to the production of numerous similar one-reel thrillers. Aimed at a large popular audience from the beginning, movies were produced cheaply, with an emphasis on quantity rather than quality. By 1910, about 10,000 movie houses were drawing a national audience of some 25 million people a week—a greater volume of business than all legitimate dramatic performances, variety shows, dime museums, lecture programs, concerts, circuses, and street carnivals combined.

From the outset, spokesmen for morality and propriety tried to regulate and gain more control of films, attacking them as silly, time-wasting, and immoral. An article in the August 1910 issue of *Good Housekeeping* denounced movies as "a primary school for criminals" and remarked that "the motto of the moving-picture companies might easily read: A red-light district in easy reach of every home. See the murders and the debauchery while you wait. It is only a nickel." Some movies were censored, and many storefront movie houses were criticized as a waste of time. Indignant citizens pressed for municipal codes to regulate movie theaters. Realizing the potential profits to be made by attracting the more conventional middle-class audience, many filmmakers began to gear their movies to this group with encouragement from the exhibitors.

During the second decade of the 20th century, moviemaking developed into a full-scale industry and the enthusiasm and demands of the middle-class audience influenced their contents strongly. By 1912, filmmakers were producing feature films of five or more reels. Their complex plots and sophisticated subjects called forth an assemblage of skilled actors, directors, and technicians. D. W. Griffith's 1915 film, *The Birth of a Nation,* was an early example of a feature length motion picture. Although his movie

Thomas Edison's first experiments with moving pictures date back to 1889. By 1894 he had produced about 60 subjects on film and the following year he fabricated this prototype of the kinetoscope, a machine for viewing moving pictures. During the 1890s, amusement parlors and penny arcades would have been stocked with such devices.

From 1905 on special theaters known as nickelodeons were designed to show moving pictures. Within a few years there were some 10,000 of these furnished with up-to-date equipment, a piano for the musical accompaniment, and permanent seating. New York City alone boasted more than 600 of these movie houses, including the Comet Theatre shown in this photograph from around 1910.

drew criticism for its racial bias from the outset, it was hailed as a pioneering achievement in film.

As a result of the more diverse audience, two distinctive types of movies began to be produced. The first featured top actors and complicated plots calculated to attract sophisticated audiences; the second offered lesser-known actors and more predictable, melodramatic plots, geared to the mass trade. The latter became known as grade "B" movies.

The increased demand for films at movie houses across the country spurred the development of the film industry. After 1910, several smaller film companies moved from New York City to Hollywood, California. They wanted to escape harassment from the 10 major companies that had pooled their patents in 1908 and had virtually monopolized the motion-

picture industry. But they also were drawn by the cheap labor and land, good year-round climate, and diverse scenery to be found on the West Coast. By 1916, about one-half of all American movies were made in California. (That figure rose to 90 percent a few years later.) For the first time, New York's preeminent place as the center of American popular entertainment was challenged. Before long Hollywood came to symbolize the appeal and glamour of motion pictures not only for the United States but for the world at large.

Hollywood's movie producers capitalized on the audience's desire to see stars. A "star" system similar to the traditional billing in theatrical and vaudeville performances was instituted, and became even more firmly fixed than it had been in the theater. By 1914,

Above: *Edwin S. Porter's* The Great Train Robbery *(1903), a one-reel thriller, was generally considered the first moving picture to tell a story. Its rudimentary plot, rapid action, and outdoor scenery conveyed a sense of realism lacking in theatrical Westerns and Wild West shows.* Right: *D. W. Griffith's epic film* The Birth of a Nation *(1915) admittedly presented a biased view of American history, but established the feature-length motion picture as a respectable art form. This wall of movie posters, from a building in Peoria, Illinois, illustrates several scenes from Griffith's film.*

THE NEW FOX TROT SONG

CHARLIE CHAPLIN WALK

Words by W^mA. DOWNS
Music by ROY BARTON

Essanay

HAROLD ROSSITER MUSIC COMPANY
Chicago — New York — U.S.A.

Left: *Actor Charlie Chaplin developed silent-film comedy into a major genre, and became one of the first stars to sell feature films on the basis of his name alone. In the course of 1915, when this sheet music was produced, Chaplin directed and acted in 14 films and developed the depth of his "tramp" character.* Facing page: *By the time this sheet music was published in 1919, the movies had begun to eclipse all other forms of popular entertainment. The anonymity offered by the darkened theater proved a great boon to romance.*

almost all feature films were sold on the basis of the personalities acting in them rather than on their plots. Comedian Charlie Chaplin and "America's sweetheart" Mary Pickford led the way to a great talent hunt for new stars that continues to the present day. The stars encouraged consumerism and the pursuit of leisure activities, and audiences eagerly imitated their appearance and extravagant lifestyles.

The new audience affected both the kinds of movies produced and the places at which they were shown. Like their influence on the earlier vaudeville palaces, affluent audiences demanded, and were willing to pay for, comfortable surroundings in which to view feature-length films. In 1914, New York City's Strand Theater pointed the way to opu-

lent "movie palaces." The Strand featured a pipe-organ and 30-piece orchestra (instead of the piano used in more modest movie houses), 3,000 seats, lavish furnishings, and a corps of ushers trained like military cadets. By 1916, more than 21,000 theaters had been constructed or remodeled, some with seating capacities in the thousands and ticket prices as high as $1.50. Many of the theaters instituted scheduled features and different pricing structures. These new, more elaborate movie theaters were located on main thoroughfares rather than on side streets. The fact that most of them were copied or converted from live theaters enhanced their dignity and that of their patrons, while lending respectability to the motion pictures shown there.

THE SHOW MUST GO ON: SINCE WORLD WAR I

Increased use of the automobile after World War I led to a decline in some forms of entertainment and changed the character of others. While the mass media, including recordings, movies, radio, and television, also contributed to a general decrease in live entertainment, they simultaneously helped attract new audiences to the live performances by giving them widespread national exposure.

The Decline of Live Performance

Some types of live performances continued to enjoy a following for a time before dying out; others adapted in order to survive. After World War I, major theatrical productions were concentrated around the Broadway area of New York City and in similar though smaller theater districts in major cities across the country. In competition with movies and, later, with television, plays generally became more sophisticated and serious, often attracting affluent audiences of the middle and upper classes. Musicals maintained the widest appeal of any types of theatrical performances.

An important trend in the post-World War I years was the development of the community theater movement, in which local citizens served as actors, directors, and set designers in the production of amateur theatricals. Since its inception in the 1920s, community theater has remained especially popular in rural and suburban communities. It offers opportunities for theater enthusiasts to take part in actual productions and provides affordable and convenient entertainment for local audiences.

In the 1920s, the Ziegfeld and other musical revues became extremely elaborate, complex, and costly, and served as an important means to popularize new songs and showcase individual performers. On a smaller scale, they also became important features at cabarets and nightclubs—especially the standard chorus line of beautiful and seductive women. High production and ticket costs of revues during the Great Depression and the proliferation of inexpensive sound movies in the 1930s led to their rapid decline during that decade.

Blackface variety entertainment persisted into

Above: *During the 1920s fierce competition forced managers of musical revues to continually expand and enhance their acts. This 1921 Follies' sheet music cover reflects the sensual and sultry image that the chorus girls who performed in the revues were expected to convey.* Facing page: *During the 1910s and 1920s the musical comedies of the late 19th century evolved into more coherent musical plays, marked by strong character development and tightly knit plots linked to the musical scores. This poster depicts a scene from the 1922 musical play* Up in the Clouds, *starring Grace Moore as the ''ambitious heroine'' aspiring to motion picture stardom and Hal Van Rensselaer as her ''devoted swain'' who risked all to save her from ruin.*

the 20th century through musical comedy, film, and radio, and helped pave the way for professional black entertainers. However, all the outgrowths of the original minstrel show disappeared swiftly after World War II.

As the variety entertainment aspects of burlesque shows became progressively more respectable, the "quick-change" acts assumed greater prominence, and by the second decade of the 20th century had evolved into striptease. In 1923, *Variety* magazine referred to burlesque as "99% strip with the other just to pad out the show." Burlesque thrived during the depression years of the 1930s thanks to the special brand of escapism it offered. Although city ordinances forced the closing of most burlesque houses in the late 1930s and early 1940s, the burlesque tradition, with its emphasis on female sensuality, continued to influence show business.

"Love Lights the Way"

A
NEW MUSICAL PLAY
OF YOUTH · HUMOR · BEAUTY AND ROMANCE

UP IN THE CLOUDS

BOOK BY WILL B. JOHNSTONE, AUTHOR of "TAKE IT FROM ME"
LYRICS AND MUSIC BY TOM JOHNSTONE
ENTIRE PRODUCTION UNDER PERSONAL DIRECTION
JOS. M. GAITES

Left: *A few minstrel shows continued to travel, though primarily to rural areas, through the first decades of the 20th century. Often they provided an outlet for black entertainers, as can be seen in this photograph by John Collier, taken in July 1942 at a Farm Security Administration agricultural workers' camp in Bridgeton, New Jersey. Below: In contrast to their 19th-century form, post-World War I burlesque shows almost exclusively presented striptease. Despite public disapproval the shows thrived during the early years of the Great Depression, but by 1937, when John Vachon took this photograph for the Farm Security Administration, many burlesque houses were being forced to close.*

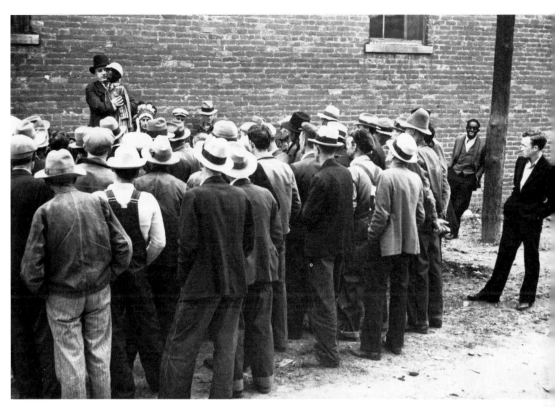

Right: *Medicine shows offered audiences novel entertainment combined with cures and tonics. Although the number of medicine shows declined after World War I, some continued to travel the rural South and Midwest for many years. This photograph, taken in 1935 by artist Ben Shahn for the Farm Security Administration, depicts a medicine show in Huntington, Tennessee, complete with a ventriloquist, an Indian, and blackface performers.* Below: *More than 4,000 magicians toured the country on vaudeville circuits or in their own shows between the 1890s and the 1930s. Among them was Master Magician Thurston, some of whose feats are depicted on this poster from around 1928.*

From Overseas
to You
Hear her Story at
CHAUTAUQUA

While the programs of traveling Chautauquas varied widely, the format of the original "Assembly" at Lake Chautauqua remained highly structured, lasting for 50 days each summer. The afternoons were filled with lectures and discussions on serious subjects, as can be seen from this poster dating from around 1918. The evenings were given over to a varied program of concerts and entertainment.

Many of the features associated with variety shows survived. Comedians and magicians continued to provide entertainment for small, intimate audiences at hotels, restaurants, bars, nightclubs, and even on city streets. Elements of earlier variety entertainment could be discerned in ice shows, circuses, rodeos, and the kinds of elaborate revues staged in entertainment centers like Las Vegas, Nevada.

Competition from better and more affordable entertainment alternatives, especially radio and movies, forced a decline in traveling theatrical shows,

from several hundred around the turn of the century to fewer than 50 by 1920. The demand for modest tent shows continued through the 1920s but they, too, declined soon after. These shows would, however, survive in the guise of permanent, open-air "musical tents," in which traveling summer stock companies and occasional star performers appeared.

The Chautauqua movement continued to flourish after World War I. At its peak, in the early 1920s, an estimated one in every three Americans attended a Chautauqua. The rapid demise of the traveling

Above: *By the mid-20th century most circuses were playing for large urban crowds in indoor arenas. Many were staged for promotional reasons by civic or charitable organizations. Shown here is a 1950 circus performance in Detroit held under the aegis of the Shriners, who became well known for this type of sponsorship.* Right: *In 1919 Barnum & Bailey and Ringling Brothers merged to become the largest circus of their time. This 1940s peanut bag recalls Barnum & Bailey's chief 19th-century attraction, the highly popular Jumbo the elephant.*

Chautauqua after that is attributable to several factors. In general, rural communities were becoming more cosmopolitan, and a new, more sophisticated generation bypassed Chautauqua in favor of entertainment with less moralistic overtones, especially radio programs. (*See "Staying In" for the development of radio.*) The original, permanently sited Chautauqua Institution, however, has continued to offer its summer programs to enthusiastic audiences.

Attendance at circuses dwindled after World War I as other forms of entertainment like movies, phonograph records, and radio usurped their place as sources of exotic escapism, and as automobiles enabled people to travel greater distances for their entertainment. The handful of circuses that survived moved to sports arenas, ball parks, county fairgrounds, and ultimately to permanent indoor arenas. Ironically, interest in circuses would be revived again through the very media forms that almost rendered them obsolete—television and the movies.

Above: *Disneyland, founded in 1955, was America's first theme park. Four of its attractions—designed to provide a romantic yet wholesome escape from the real world—are shown on this 1975 postcard: the Sleeping Beauty Castle, the Mark Twain steamboat, the jungle cruise, and Tomorrowland. By the 1980s theme parks in varying sizes and degrees of complexity could be found throughout the country.* Left: *Mechanical rides were popular and characteristic features of fairs, amusement parks, and traveling carnivals. One of the oldest and most beloved of these rides was the carousel, as depicted on the outside of this 1940s sand pail.*

Entertainment for All

Automobile travel and the mass media have helped make accessible to the average citizen a vast range of public entertainment, from amusement park rides to live concerts and dance performances to the movies.

Amusement Parks. A National Association of Amusement Parks was organized after World War I, and by 1919 some 1,500 amusement parks were operating across the country. However, within a few years these parks faced competition from other forms of mass entertainment, especially the movies, where convincing illusions could be obtained at a lesser cost.

During the Great Depression, many small parks were forced to close, while numerous others were plagued by lack of maintenance, public boredom with aging rides, and vandalism. As older rides lost their appeal, newer, more exciting ones were introduced. One such ride, devoted to "the sadistic sport of motor-car collision," provoked the following reflections, cited in the book *Leisure: A Suburban Study,* which focused on life in Westchester County, New York (1934):

At first glance, this would appear to be one of the strangest recreational pursuits ever heard of. Still, when we reflect that here one may drive a car without rules or reason, and collide with other cars with impunity and without fear of legal retribution, perhaps the phenomenon should be regarded as only another outlet for the repressions of the motor age.

By the early 1980s, fewer than 100 of the "traditional" amusement parks were still in operation.

A more recent trend in amusement parks has been the so-called "theme park," which originated with Disneyland in Anaheim, California, in 1955. Operated not by professional showmen, as in earlier days, but by businessmen and large corporations, these parks feature organized amusement areas centered around particular themes. Traditional showmanship, gaming operations, pitchmen, and the somewhat seedy attractions of penny arcades, shooting galleries, and side shows, have been replaced by a homogenized, hygienic atmosphere. In 1984, a total of 34 theme parks attracted more than 70 million visitors.

Museums. After World War I, the numerous art, science, and history museums throughout the country expanded their educational and community functions to attract and instruct a growing number of visitors. Conducted tours, lectures, and support groups became popular features of many of these institutions. Following examples set by department stores and world's fairs in the 1920s and 1930s, museum displays became more selective in their presentations, grouping objects into contextual environments like period rooms and dioramas.

Widespread automobile travel encouraged the

The Metropolitan Museum of Art, founded in New York City in 1870, has become one of the most celebrated repositories of art in the world.

proliferation of an astounding number of museums located outside urban centers. It also led to a great increase in the number of historic houses and other historic structures, either standing by themselves or grouped together at such places as Greenfield Village (Dearborn, Michigan, 1929) and Colonial Williamsburg (Virginia, 1934). Trailside museums also proliferated, displaying scientific or archaeological items of interest relating to the areas in which they were located. Increasing automobile travel also lent great impetus to the development of local and state historical societies.

In the post-World War II era, museums have multiplied tremendously in both number and scope. Public programs have come to emphasize even more strongly the museums' functions as learning centers for people of all ages and walks of life. Similarly, exhibit techniques have changed to encourage more active participation by visitors and to focus on the interpretation, rather than just the display, of the museums' collections.

While the latter decades of the 19th century saw the establishment of major museums of art and natural history, a variety of museums aimed at educating and diverting the local populace have proliferated in the course of the 20th century. Top: An early installation in the Dinosaur Hall of The Carnegie Museum of Natural History, Pittsburgh, Pennsylvania. Above: A parade passes the imposing exterior (right) of The Art Institute of Chicago. Right: This museum was promoted as being "free to all" and "as accessible as your neighborhood store."

Scattered in natural settings across the American continent, internationally prominent summer music festivals range from large ones like those in Tanglewood, Massachusetts, and Aspen, Colorado, to more intimate ones like the chamber music festival at Marlboro, Vermont. Pictured above is the Ravinia Festival, Illinois.

Music and Dance. The audience for choral, orchestral, and operatic music, as well as ballet, has grown tremendously since World War I. Radio, records, movies, and television have created a vast new potential audience for the performance of classical music and dance. As early as the 1920s, Walter Damrosch, who was then conducting weekly radio concerts with the New York Symphony Orchestra, was astounded to learn that the audience during the run of his program totaled 340 million. In *My Musical Life,* published in 1935, he recounted:

As the majority of these people, living far away from the centres of musical culture, had never heard the kind of music which I gave them, and as even the names of Mozart, Beethoven, and Wagner were unknown to them, it was a joy to cultivate such a virgin field and to find out how easy it was to make willing converts of my listeners.

Other developments also have helped to popularize these types of performances. Orchestral music, for example, has become more available to the public through free concerts in public parks. Ballet and modern dance are frequently offered as college courses and several dance companies perform regularly. Open-air music and dance festivals, accessible by automobile, draw faithful and enthusiastic audiences of all ages. Although the most significant purveyors of orchestral music remain the permanent, professional symphony orchestras, orchestral and choral music also are now widely performed by community, college, school, and youth groups.

The massive migration of blacks from the South in search of employment opportunities in the North and Midwest during and after World War I, led to the introduction of jazz to new, highly receptive urban audiences. Live performances in nightclubs and cabarets helped popularize the "Dixieland" jazz of such black musicians as Kid Ory, King Oliver, and Jelly Roll Morton. Once purged of what were considered raucous and crude elements by white music producers and bandleaders, jazz, like ragtime before it, turned out to have tremendous appeal for mass audiences. Records and radio helped give it a nationwide following during the 1920s.

In the 1930s, jazz was again "refined" into what became known as the "big band" sound, characterized by a new rhythmic style called "swing." The enthusiasm for this kind of music reached its peak between the mid-1930s and the early 1940s, when some 300 bands—including those of Benny Goodman and Glenn Miller—performed around the country, and about 70 percent of all recordings made featured this music.

Left: *Jazz became the most popular musical style of the 1920s, especially in the urban areas to which black Americans had migrated in large numbers during World War I. The energy and exuberance of this music is reflected in the images on the early 1930s punchbowl, created by Viktor Schreckengost for the Cowan Pottery. Below: New Orleans jazz bands placed great importance on improvisation while incorporating vocal and rhythmic elements from other styles of music. Edward "Kid" Ory, who first led a band in New Orleans in 1911, moved to Los Angeles in 1919, and to Chicago in 1924, played with and influenced many musicians of this "Dixieland" jazz style.*

Right: *Paul Whiteman was one of the first bandleaders to bring a popular version of jazz to a white audience, transforming what some considered as "raucous" and "crude" music into smooth, harmonious production numbers. This 1921 sheet music boasting that "Wang-Wang Blues" was the "most popular dance melody written in years," pictured Whiteman's orchestra on its cover. Below: Pianist and bandleader James Fletcher Henderson is sometimes credited with originating "swing" and the "big band" that performed this kind of music. Although he was a successful dance-band leader in the 1920s, Henderson is now best known for arranging many of the songs popularized by bandleader Benny Goodman.*

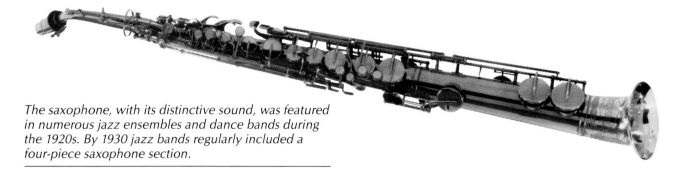

The saxophone, with its distinctive sound, was featured in numerous jazz ensembles and dance bands during the 1920s. By 1930 jazz bands regularly included a four-piece saxophone section.

From the 1920s to the early 1940s, public dancing reached unprecedented heights of popularity, as the new music inspired the invention of new dances. Hundreds of dance bands and orchestras traversed the countryside, performing nightly at dance halls and ballrooms, while so-called "dance palaces" attracted millions of patrons in cities and towns.

Variations of the ever-changing popular dances were taught by dance instructors through studio and home courses. The best known of the dance instructors was Arthur Murray, who developed techniques that drew millions of Americans to his nationwide studios. Meanwhile, interpretations of the latest dances also could be seen at the movies. No dancers were more avidly followed than the team of Fred Astaire and Ginger Rogers, who probably inspired more people to rush to the dance studios than anyone or anything else.

Coin-operated music machines and phonographs gave new tunes rapid and broad exposure. The spread of mechanical jukeboxes in the 1930s and 1940s became as crucial to molding popular

Between the 1920s and 1940s hundreds of dance orchestras and big bands played popular dance music at public ballrooms. Among these were the bands led by pianist Edward Kennedy "Duke" Ellington. This photograph by Gordon Parks shows Ellington playing at the Hurricane Ballroom in New York City in April 1943. Beginning in the 1920s, and throughout his extensive career, Ellington continually expanded and varied the conventional forms of jazz.

musical tastes as radio disc jockeys would become after World War II. By 1942, approximately 400,000 jukeboxes had been installed in public places nationwide, where they proved especially attractive to teenagers. Critic Francis Chase wrote about the importance of jukeboxes to popular music in his 1942 book on broadcasting, *Sound and Fury:*

> *One tremendous hit on a jukebox, most band-leaders now agree, will do as much for a dance band as six solid weeks of broadcasting, and many of the great dance bands which have come to the front in recent years have done so on the basis of a jukebox hit.*

One of the most influential types of music popularized through radio and record exposure was a style of black vocal music that came to be known as "rhythm and blues." A distillation of diverse influences, this music of the late 1940s and 1950s appealed especially to teenagers. But once again, black performers were generally denied the chance to reach white audiences because record producers felt it necessary to have their songs "smoothed out" or "covered" by white singers. Rhythm-and-blues music encouraged new styles of dancing, as did its 1950s offshoot—rock and roll.

From the 1950s on, rock-and-roll music increased its popularity through recordings, radio, the movies, and the new medium of television. (*See the impact of television in "Staying In."*) Soon after its introduction in 1956, the television show devoted to rock-and-roll music, *American Bandstand* (with Dick Clark officiating), boasted an estimated audience of 20 million. Recordings and radio also helped provide wider audiences for previously regional music, including blues and so-called hillbilly (or country) and cowboy (or Western) music.

Public dance halls and ballrooms declined after World War II in favor of bars and nightclubs, where people could dance and listen to music in a more intimate and less formal setting. As the character of popular music and dancing changed so did the dance places. Recorded music began to replace live performances, although relatively unknown local bands continued to appear at bars and roadhouses. The popularity of jukeboxes declined as more so-

phisticated sound equipment became available for the transmission of recorded music. Live performances of popular music by major stars survived only through a limited number of live concerts, music festivals, and media appearances. Music and dancing continue to rank among the most popular forms of entertainment in America.

At studios and through home instruction courses, the enterprising Arthur Murray taught millions of people the latest dance steps. In this 1937 booklet he assured his customers "I do not teach people to merely 'get by' on the dance floor—I teach them to dance so well that their dancing is a source of keen enjoyment to them."

Left: *Between 1934 and 1939 Fred Astaire joined partner Ginger Rogers in eight musical films that featured their dancing. Scenes like this one from the 1936 movie* Swing Time, *inspired countless viewers to sign up for dance lessons.* Below: *"Juke joints," popular among blacks in the rural South, were some of the earliest places to feature recorded music for dancing, since records were convenient to play and were less expensive than live bands. This photo of a juke joint was taken on a Saturday evening in November 1939, outside Clarksdale, Mississippi, by photographer Marion Post Wolcott.*

Above: *The powerful stage presence and driving rhythm-and-blues style of Chuck Berry endeared this singer-guitarist to a large youthful audience in the 1950s, while the originality of his music had an enormous impact on later rock-and-roll musicians. Berry enjoyed a comeback in the late 1960s, as shown in this photograph, when a new interest in the origins of rock-and-roll music led to the revived popularity of his earlier songs.* Right: *During the late 1950s and early 1960s no rock-and-roll singer approached Elvis Presley in popularity. His succession of hits, combining rhythm and blues with a country-western music influence, and his charismatic performing style influenced a whole generation of rock-and-roll singers. This photograph shows Presley performing in 1956 at a fair and dairy show in his hometown of Tupelo, Mississippi.*

Above: *As rock-and-roll music attracted growing audiences, the television show* American Bandstand *became a forum for stars to mouth the words of their latest hit records, which were being played offstage. Meanwhile youthful fans executed the latest dances on stage, as in this 1960s photograph in which a couple performs the Slop.* Left: *No other group influenced rock-and-roll music and American culture more than those imports from Liverpool, England, the Beatles. From 1964 until their breakup in 1970, this group enjoyed fantastic popularity, continually expanding the stylistic range of rock-and-roll music while gaining wider exposure through an array of merchandise, including this "Official Fan Club" jigsaw puzzle. Their popularity has continued into the 1980s.*

The Movies. After World War I, moving pictures came to overshadow all other forms of public entertainment until they themselves were displaced by yet another form of transmitted performance, namely, home television. In the 1920s, Hollywood and the movie industry reached new heights of popularity. Tremendous sums of money were spent on elaborate productions and on the salaries of major stars. By the mid-1920s, the major studios were producing 700 to 800 feature films per year, each studio finishing one or two per week! A worshipful public devoured movie magazines filled with gossip about the stars. In 1926, movies in America attracted a daily audience of about 7 million. New York City's Roxy Theater, built in 1927 and advertised as a "cathedral of motion pictures," represented the ultimate both in comfort and in the splendor of its design.

Although a score of second-rate films that exploited the relatively relaxed moral climate of the decade led to a new outcry for censorship, most people accepted the movies as a permanent part of the national scene and a powerful influence on life in the United States. Films affected American culture at all levels, from manners and morals, to speech, fashions, and social and ethical values. Movies provided the escape, excitement, and adventure that most people lacked in their daily lives. As a 1929 *Saturday Evening Post* advertisement put it:

By the 1920s the "star" system had taken firm hold, as celebrated film actors "sold" the movies to an adoring public. This postcard was pasted into a scrapbook kept by Mildred Cramer during a cross-country trip she took with her husband in 1931. The popular movie stars of the time are depicted alongside Grauman's legendary Chinese Theatre in Hollywood, California. Opened in 1927, it was probably the most famous movie palace in the world when it was built.

A star of the silent movie era, Rudolph Valentino attracted the adulation of millions of women with his dashing, romantic roles. This poster, advertising the last movie he made before his death in 1926, was produced for a mid-1930s revival of the film.

Go to a motion picture . . . and let yourself go. Before you know it you are living the story— laughing, loving, hating, struggling, winning! All the adventure, all the romance, all the excitement you lack in your daily life are in—Pictures. They take you completely out of yourself into a wonderful new world . . . . Out of the cage of everyday existence! If only for an afternoon or an evening—escape!

The desire for heightened realism led to the development of new technology which made possible the synchronization of recorded sound with the action being captured on film. While this had become commercially feasible by 1926, movie companies had such a large investment in silent films— including stars and equipment—that they did not rush to use the new synchronization techniques. Instead, they continued to lure audiences to the movies by adding live vaudeville, variety, and musical performers to their bills.

It was finally the small, failing studio of Warner Brothers that gave national prominence to the "talkies" when it added songs and 250 words of dialogue to *The Jazz Singer,* which it produced in 1927. The gamble paid off. As profits shot up and the public demand for sound increased, other studios frantically inserted sound effects and vocal numbers into their films wherever possible. By 1929, the first all-talking motion pictures were being made. Numerous theaters were wired for sound, and weekly attendance at movies almost doubled from what it had been just two years earlier.

Audiences wholeheartedly welcomed sound in the movies. Having grown used to the sound entertainment of recordings and radio, the public soon found silent movies artificial and incomplete compared to those with sound. Resistance continued in the film industry, especially among those who lost their jobs because their voices did not accord with the images they had projected on the silent screen. Others, like D. W. Griffith, complained that "these chattering horrors will destroy all we have achieved in twenty years of hard work," while one contemporary film critic summed up the achievements of the new technique as "All-Talking, All-Singing, All-Nothing!" However, the victory of sound movies over silent films was swift and complete. Only two silent movies were produced in 1931. But sound movies did not merely replace silent films; they dealt the final blow to many forms of live entertainment as well, including vaudeville, burlesque shows, and musical revues.

The addition of sound influenced both the tone and the subject matter of movies. Musicals became a popular genre. Fast-moving dialogue influenced other genres, especially verbal comedy (in contrast to the slapstick comedy of the silent films), crime films, and animated films (those made by Walt Disney were particularly notable). The sound engineer became an important new member of the film crew, as actors moved less and talked more and as a full range of sound effects became possible. While sound

Right: *The tremendous success of* The Jazz Singer *(1927), in which this scene appears, led to the rapid conversion of silent movie houses into sound theaters. Most of this film, which starred Al Jolson, was actually silent, but the vitality of the four musical sequences and the excitement of hearing the 250-word dialogue contributed significantly to the movie's success. Below: With the advent of sound, musicals became the rage. MGM's* Broadway Melody *(1929), like other films of that genre, blended a simple plot with stunning production numbers to highlight glamorous stars and popular dances.*

forced live musicians out of the movie theaters, it expanded the recording and sheet music market immeasurably. By 1929, *Photoplay* reported that within a month of a film's release, the average motion picture song sold a combined total of close to 100,000 records and copies of sheet music.

Movie attendance declined during the early years of the Great Depression. In an attempt to regain audiences, many movie theaters offered double features and other enticements like free giveaways and bingo nights. By the late 1930s, however, the movie industry was solidly back on its feet. Sweeping historical romances and well-known classics were given big-budget treatment, epitomized by the 1939 blockbuster *Gone With the Wind.* Color films became highly popular at this time, although Technicolor had been introduced more than 20 years earlier.

Between 1936 and 1949, the average weekly attendance at movie theaters in the United States never dropped below 80 million. Hollywood and motion pictures had become firmly rooted in the habits and consciousness of the nation.

The stability of the movie industry and its dom-inance of popular visual entertainment might have continued had it not been for the introduction of a formidable new competitor—television. As television caught the imagination of the American public, providing continual free entertainment in people's own homes, movie attendance declined dramatically. By the mid-1950s, it had dwindled to about half of its peak 1946 levels. By 1969, movies commanded a mere 3 percent of the country's total recreation dollars, as opposed to 23 percent in the early 1940s.

Although thousands of people were staying home to watch television by the late 1940s, the movie industry at first shrugged off the threat and tried to prevent its stars and films from entering the new medium. However, as television became an ever more powerful competitor, and as the major studios faced antitrust suits brought by the government against their monopolistic ownership of movie theaters, they were forced to relinquish much of their earlier control. By 1956, movie studios had sold the rights to telecast more than 2,000 pre-1948 feature films, and were beginning to film serials especially created for television. Within a few years, Hollywood

Fast-moving gangster films became especially popular in the early 1930s, offering distraction from the sad realities of the Great Depression. Among the most successful of these films was Scarface (1932), recounting the exploits of notorious gangster Al Capone.

With the addition of sound and color, animated cartoons became a popular and profitable form of entertainment. Walt Disney dominated this genre through the 1930s and 1940s, captivating both mass and highbrow audiences. It took 600 artists, two million drawings, and four years to complete Disney's first feature-length cartoon, Snow White and the Seven Dwarfs, *released in 1937.*

would become known as a television town. Many more films were sold to television, and movies became staple programming fare for a major portion of the television schedule.

In an effort to combat the growing dominance of television in people's lives, the movie industry resorted to various techniques to distinguish the two media from one another as much as possible. These included greater use of Technicolor, wide screens, dramatic special effects, the illusion of three-dimensional pictures, and, later, the introduction of stereo and quadrophonic sound and holographic images. However, none of these innovations would prove as dramatic a catalyst for arousing public interest as the introduction of sound had been in the 1920s.

Film subjects also changed. In order to create a contrast with television programming, movie makers departed from what had become traditional in film and began to depict sex and violence more explicitly. Movies featuring young stars, rock-and-roll music, and plots centering around adolescent problems increased in number as Hollywood set out to tap into the growing youth market.

Other efforts to lure audiences away from television included the construction of more informal and intimate types of movie theaters. Among these were drive-in movie theaters, which enjoyed their greatest popularity in the 1950s and 1960s. Built in the suburbs and on the outskirts of towns and cities, their fare of some high-standard and numerous grade-B

Left: *The 1939 historical epic* Gone With the Wind *epitomized the lush, big-budget Hollywood blockbusters of the time and established the use of Technicolor as the industry standard. This souvenir program was available at theaters where this movie was screened.* Above: *This Scarlett O'Hara doll, produced by Madame Alexander of New York, was promoted by special advertising and store displays following the release of* Gone With the Wind. *Different versions of this doll sold in department stores and other retail outlets for between $2.95 and $6.95.*

double features proved especially appealing to families and teenagers. In 1958, there were almost 5,000 drive-ins in the United States; by the 1960s they comprised about one-third of all movie theaters. The establishment of what became known as "art theaters," devoted to foreign and risqué films, signaled another attempt to revive moviegoing in the era following World War II.

In recent decades, movie audiences have become increasingly fragmented and specialized. A major trend since the 1960s has been to convert the large movie palaces into smaller, more intimate neighborhood theaters, as well as to construct multiple-theater and cinema complexes in suburban shopping centers and malls. The multiple theater has been designed to accommodate more specialized

audiences by simultaneously showing several different types of movies in the same complex. Current-day audiences tend to be younger, better educated, and more affluent than previous generations of moviegoers. As a consequence of these changes, they are more knowledgeable about the movies they attend, more selective, and more willing to pay high prices for what they have chosen to see.

The interest in motion pictures as artistic and historical documents has reached new heights in recent years, reinforced by college courses and the efforts of film societies to show old movies to new audiences. Films are analyzed, written about, and discussed in serious fashion. Film festivals, televised awards presentations, live and media appearances by stars and directors, and the increased presence of film

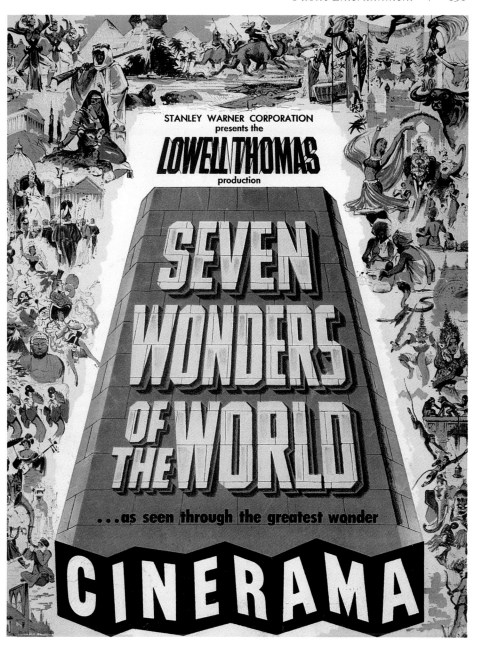

STANLEY WARNER CORPORATION
presents the
LOWELL THOMAS
production

SEVEN WONDERS OF THE WORLD

...as seen through the greatest wonder

CINERAMA

To contrast the grandeur of movies with the small scale of television, producers experimented with a variety of wide screens during the 1950s. Cinerama, first available in 1952, claimed to "put you in the picture and excite you with the emotional impact of the real thing." This mid-1950s movie program, reminiscent of the traveling panoramas of the previous century, accompanied a Cinerama film that "sent" the audience on a "round-the-world adventure" under the guidance of celebrated travel journalist Lowell Thomas.

crews in the streets of towns and cities throughout the country have combined to give the public great familiarity with many aspects of filmmaking.

Moviegoing is far from obsolete. New film theaters are being incorporated into large urban civic and cultural centers, while the institution of bargain-price "dollar nights" and reduced daytime rates at suburban theaters have made moviegoing an increasingly casual experience. As Leo Bogart prophesied in *The Age of Television* (1956):

The heroic-sized figures on a theater screen create a mood and convey an effect which is very different from that of the intimate atmosphere of the living room. The movie-house will remain as a focus of interest for those who are bored with their familiar surroundings, as a refuge for lovers, and as an answer to the need for "going out" as a form of sociability.

Despite the impact of television, movies have remained a permanent fixture on the American scene. Americans see a larger number of motion pictures today than ever, but paradoxically they see many of them on television. Regular feature films and special made-for-television movies comprise a significant segment of the total programming watched on television; top films are featured as special television attractions. Cable television and videocassette recorders have multiplied the number of films viewed on television many times over and further link the two entertainment forms.

Drive-in movies were yet another effort to draw audiences away from their television sets and back to the large screen. The giant drive-in screen proved particularly suitable to Westerns, with their panoramic scenery and larger-than-life heroes. This photograph was taken at the El Cerrito theater near Oakland, California, during a showing of Red River *(1948) starring John Wayne.*

Public entertainment evolved in America from a number of small, informal traveling shows, largely performed in front of elite audiences. In the course of the 19th century, the forms of entertainment available to the public expanded immensely, especially in urban areas. Promoters and showmen aggressively marketed diverse entertainment forms, which increasingly gained acceptance by a wider public. In time these amusements became more structured and lost many of their moralistic trappings. Live performance reached the peak of its popularity between the 1890s and World War I, although the choices of entertainment varied widely between rural and urban areas, as well as between social classes.

Within a decade, however, automobile travel and the mass media had greatly affected all aspects of public entertainment. These technological advances not only replaced or altered certain entertainment forms, but also encouraged standardization of format and content as producers found themselves able to reach a national audience. This homogenizing trend has been countered to some degree by the development of specialized performances targeting smaller audiences.

Whether "going out" takes the form of a movie or a Broadway play, a circus performance or a rock concert, the American public continues to be enticed by the promises of excitement, escape, sociability, and occasional instruction that are offered. Most people would probably still agree with the viewpoint, expressed in *Struggles and Triumphs, or Forty Years' Recollections of P. T. Barnum* (1869):

> *This is a trading world, and men, women, and children, who cannot live on gravity alone, need something to satisfy their gayer, lighter moods and hours, and he who ministers to their want is in a business established by the Author of our nature. If he worthily fulfills his mission, and amuses without corrupting, he need never feel that he has lived in vain.*

In a continuing effort to overcome the competition posed by television, moviemakers increased the amount of explicit sex and violence in films for commercial theaters. This 1964 poster advertised a film that exemplified this trend as well as the popularity of a new genre, the spy thriller.

PRICE 10 CENTS.

SPALDING'S OFFICIAL

BASE BALL GUIDE.

1886.

PUBLISHED BY

A. G. SPALDING & BROS.,

108 Madison St., Chicago. 241 Broadway, New York.

COMPETING:
Sports to 1915

Sports in some form or other have been part of American life since Colonial times. The sports in which the American colonists engaged were largely the same as those they had enjoyed in their homelands, with English traditions exerting the strongest overall influence. As the population became more diversified, regional, ethnic, religious, and class differences played a part in determining the popularity of various sports. Growing urbanization and the progressive expansion of railroad networks, particularly after the 1860s, also influenced the development of various athletic activities, stimulating the formation and increasing organization of a number of distinctive sports.

In response to America's accelerating industrialization in the post-Civil War era, many people began to view sports as a necessary and safe outlet from the pressures of work. At the same time, the organization and conduct of sports began to reflect the structure and methods of other business ventures. Inevitably, sports also were affected by technological advances, especially by improvements in transportation and communication, which gave many sports national scope and status.

Facing page: *Albert Spalding, a shrewd entrepreneur, became a nationally recognized leader in the sporting goods industry by the end of the 19th century. His popular baseball guide, advertised in this 1886 price list for sports equipment, reflected a growing interest in the rules and statistical records of organized sports.*

PREINDUSTRIAL SPORTS

The rules and formats of sporting pastimes in Colonial America were largely unwritten and informal. They were often revised to fit particular circumstances, and consequently evolved into regional variants. Five groups of colonists and settlers exerted a significant influence on the evolution of sports in the New World: the New England Puritans, the Southern aristocracy, the upper class in the early towns and cities of the East Coast, the Dutch immigrants in New York, and settlers on the frontier.

Much has been written about the Puritan "detestation of idleness." Most games brought from England were banned at one time or another in Colonial New England as having no place in the "ordering, and preservation and furtherance" of Puritan theocracy. But many of these laws were ignored or not enforced. In fact, as early as 1700, few local prohibitions remained in force, except those banning the playing of games on Sundays. However, for several decades the general disapproval of frivolous play that had been inculcated in the minds of many New Englanders inhibited the growth and acceptance of sports, especially in that region.

In contrast, the fashionable standards and sporting traditions established by wealthy Southern planters influenced the future acceptance and organization of American sports. Of the wide variety of sporting diversions in which these people engaged, horse racing was the most popular. Subscription races were held in larger towns, while quarter-races (informal quarter-mile matches) were a universal feature of Southern country life at the time.

Like the members of the English gentry, Southern planters engaged in fashionable hunting expeditions and leisurely horseback riding to display gallantry, polished manners, and gentle breeding. They also arranged and attended boxing matches between their slaves, and played billiards and bowls in their homes to avoid mingling with the common people in the public taverns. Most of these diversions involved heavy betting.

An increasing number of wealthy Americans farther north, especially in the larger towns and cities, also sought diversions. Following the example of their Southern counterparts, many took up horseback riding and horse racing, while others became enamored of various forms of boating, especially yachting.

The less well-to-do engaged in other sorts of competitions. Displays of skill, speed, and endurance became appealing aspects of communal celebrations, including military training days, election days, holidays, and frolics. This included such games as quoits (adapted in the New World to the game of horseshoes), bowls or ninepins (in some areas changed to tenpins to bypass a law forbidding this pastime), and various types of ball games. Children were major participants in these early informal games, while competitions of running, wrestling, and shooting held a special appeal for men. Other children's games also were encouraged, although more as vehicles for learning life's lessons than for mere enjoyment.

The enthusiasm for winter sports, especially sleighing, also spread among the general public. As

The Southern planters' enthusiasm for horse racing in the mid-17th century was soon matched by that of the wealthy gentry living along the Eastern seaboard. This racing trophy, made by the New York silversmith Jesse Kip in 1699, is said to have been awarded to a colt for winning a one-mile race in Middletown, New Jersey. The colt was trained and ridden by a slave.

The game of bowling evolved from the European pastimes of ninepins and skittles, depicted in this 1672 painting Skittle Players Outside an Inn by Dutch artist Jan Steen. Religious leaders in New England strongly opposed the game and forbade its being played. As a result some of the early settlers supposedly added an extra pin (thus the name tenpins) to evade the ban against the game.

During the first half of the 19th century, the so-called "sporting halls" frequented by groups of men referred to as the "fancy," featured a regular fare of violent animal baitings. This scene of ratting, from the early 19th century, depicts "the celebrated terrier dog Major performing his wonderful feat of killing 100 rats in 8 minutes, 58 seconds."

early as the 1770s, a Scottish traveler (cited in "Those Were the Days," by Douglas R. Capra, *The Carriage Journal,* Spring 1983) remarked:

> *The young ladies and gentlemen are so fond of this, as a diversion, that whenever the snow gives over falling, tho' it be after sun-set, they will not wait till next day, but have their sleigh yoked directly, and drive out without the least fear of catching cold from the night air.*

Taverns and inns served as social centers for many types of popular pastimes, including bowls, billiards, cockfights, and animal baitings. Tavern owners sometimes even put up prizes and set up marks for shooting matches as a way of stimulating business.

Dutch immigrants maintained fewer strict religious restraints than many of the nearby English settlers. They brought a rich sporting heritage to the New World, including an early form of bowling and a distinctive game similar to golf called "kolven." Taking advantage of the plentiful bodies of water and temperate climate of New York, they engaged enthusiastically in boat races, ice skating, and sleighing.

The diversity of sports and games that developed on the frontier were basically extensions of daily life. Shooting matches and competitive hunts were popular, while the importance attached to physical strength encouraged such competitions as flinging rails, rolling logs, and no-holds-barred wrestling matches. The popularity of horse racing in the East also spread rapidly to the frontier, especially the spontaneous quarter-races between neighboring settlers' horses. By 1788, a circular racetrack had been constructed as far west as Lexington, Kentucky.

Except for the very wealthy, sports and games were relatively minor aspects of people's lives at this time. Indeed, through the first half of the 19th century many travelers pointed out that Americans bypassed amusements in favor of working. This peculiar American trait might have continued had it not been for the increasing movement of population to urban centers. Between 1820 and 1860, urbanization would become a major influence in nurturing American sports.

SPORTS IN ANTEBELLUM AMERICA: 1820s TO THE CIVIL WAR

City Sports

As city life broke up the traditional patterns of communal activity, urban dwellers developed the recreational habit of watching others perform. With few sports organized for mass participation, spectator sports provided the excitement of competition and the thrill of vicarious participation. In fact, at a time when most Americans were being criticized for their lack of interest in amusements, urban dwellers were singled out for their "addiction" to spectator sports. Visiting New York in 1841, Englishman James Silk Buckingham commented in *America, Historical, Statistic, and Descriptive:*

> *Every new attraction gathers its countless throng, as if the people had no other occupation than sight-seeing, though it is well known that they are among the most constantly occupied and busiest people in the world.*

It was the upper and lower levels of society that encouraged, supported, and ultimately laid the groundwork for organized sports in America. Members of the working classes, including the highly mobile and unstable work force of the cities, often were ready for anything that promised amusement and provided a release from the drudgery of their daily lives. As a result, some of them became associated with the so-called sporting fraternities, otherwise known as "the fancy." Patronizing barrooms and gambling dens or sporting halls, they drank and bet on the outcome of cockfights, horse races, and prize fights. Violence was commonplace at these events. Brutality at prize fights was so extreme that frequently they were banned, only to be held secretly on the outskirts of towns.

Promoters of some of these sporting contests soon recognized the need to present them in a more genteel setting to attract spectators from the socially more acceptable segments of society. As a result, sports connected with the urban "rabble," like prize fights and horse racing, moved toward greater

Taverns served as the site for all manner of games, including the disreputable but highly popular pastime of cockfighting. This engraving from the Days' Doings, February 28, 1874, depicts the arrest of 37 cockfighters at John Mulholland's New York City saloon. The date attests to the fact that these activities existed well into the 19th century, and indeed, would continue in some communities through the 20th century.

respectability in the course of the 19th century.

Wealthy urban dwellers continued to participate in the same types of sports they had engaged in or watched earlier, especially horse racing and yachting. The extent to which both the upper and working classes rallied behind sports was to contribute significantly to the eventual enthusiasm of the middle class for these activities later in the century.

Early Spectator Sports

The most popular spectator sports of the early 19th century were horse races, foot races, and regattas, any of which might attract several thousand spectators to a single event. After being prohibited in several areas earlier in the century, horse racing was revived in the 1820s and became extremely popular. Highly organized meets took place in cities, as new courses and larger grandstands were built for paying customers. Rules were standardized, schedules published, and racing times recorded. Early sporting periodicals—including the most popular of this era, *The Spirit of the Times*—spurred the growing enthusiasm. Although betting continued, horse racing had achieved some degree of respectability by the 1850s. Except in New England, it flourished in all parts of the country, especially in the South, the West, and on Long Island in New York State.

Horse racing also became a major feature of agricultural fairs, to the annoyance of those who had supported the earlier, noncommercial character of these events. During these decades, the distinctive American sport of trotting, also called harness racing, largely replaced thoroughbred races at fairs. This sport gained popular support because a trotting horse with a rig was far less expensive to buy, train, and maintain than a thoroughbred racehorse. Moreover, many people considered these types of races to be more respectable than thoroughbred racing since they were not as closely associated with gambling. Writer William Henry Herbert commented on the mass appeal of trotting in *Frank Forester's Horse and Horsemanship of the United States and British Provinces of North America* (1857), as follows:

Now, horse-racing and steeple-chasing can never, from their very nature, become in the true sense of the word, POPULAR. The people may love to be spectators, but can never hope to become participants in them . . . . The trotting-course, on the other hand, is common to all. It is . . . open to every one who keeps a horse for his own driving . . . the butcher, the baker, or the farmer . . . . Trotting, in America, is the people's sport, the people's pastime, and consequently, is, and will be, supported by the people.

Foot (or "ped," from the Latin word for foot) races competed for a time with horse races. Initially, informal five- and ten-mile running races were held in city streets; later they were scheduled at enclosed race courses to which admission was charged. Runners often were paid for their services, placing them among the first professionals in American sports. Popular champions, including several native Indian runners who became known by their conspicuous costumes, as well as by colorful nicknames like "American Deer" and "Boston Buck," were among the earliest sports heroes. Eventually, other contests of individual prowess were added to the foot races, including hurdle races, sprints, and walking contests. These races often were connected with gambling, and the participants' professionalism was regarded unfavorably by more genteel spectators because it was a sign of working-class status not to be able to engage in sports for pure pleasure. Despite their somewhat unsavory reputation, these contests provided the impetus for the track-and-field competitions held later in the century.

Competitive boat races between seamen had taken place earlier, but boat racing first gained nationwide interest as a spectator sport during an international rowing race in 1824. Through the next few decades, rowing and sailing races (known as regattas) excited intense interest among spectators. Wealthy members of amateur boat clubs, as well as collegiate and professional oarsmen, all participated in these events.

The popular enthusiasm for regattas led to a more widespread participation in rowing. Rowing hulls not only were cheaper to purchase and maintain than yachts, but also were easier to master and more adaptable to racing short distances on narrow waterways. Several rowing clubs were formed in the

Above: *From the 1830s to the Civil War, competitions between both amateur and professional oarsmen became extremely popular spectator events, as can be seen in this engraving from* Gleason's Pictorial, August 16, 1851, *depicting a race between two oarsmen around New York Bay. A large amount of money apparently changed hands during this event and the excitement reached such a high pitch that in several instances it "vented itself in heated words and even blows."* Below: *Foot or "ped" races also attracted great interest and were revived for a time after the Civil War. The article accompanying this engraving from* Harper's Weekly, March 29, 1879, *noted that "no sporting event" had caused "so much excitement in New York for many years as the great walking match at Gilmore's Garden between four redoubtable contestants."*

1830s and 1840s, and rowing was to become the most popular college sport of the 19th century. As rowing gained a public following, the wealthy increasingly confined themselves to the more exclusive and expensive sport of yachting. This set up a pattern that would be repeated in other sports as well. The interest in yachting led to the formation of the New York Yacht Club in 1844, and an American victory at the international regatta in Cowes, England, in 1851.

Left: *While its antecedents were the English games of cricket and rounders, baseball had evolved into a uniquely American game by the mid-19th century. This china plate, one in an English-produced series on American sports from around 1840, depicts two key players of the game—the striker (batter) and the catcher.* Below: *The popularity of cricket in America paralleled its revival in Britain as part of the 1830s enthusiasm for athletics. The author of the article accompanying this engraving in* Ballou's Pictorial, *June 4, 1859, was pleased to see Americans engaging in this sort of athletic exercise, which would raise them to the fine physical fettle attained by their English counterparts.*

During the first half of the 19th century fishing became an appealing pastime. Fishing scenes were popular subjects in contemporary illustrations, such as this 1852 Currier & Ives lithograph, entitled The Trout Stream, *which emphasized this sport's tendency to encourage meditation and relaxation.*

Team and Field Sports

On the whole, other games and sports remained largely informal, their character dictated by local custom. Rules were relatively simple and unwritten, and few players were trained in systematic fashion. However, a move toward standardization, formalizing the rules, and organizing players into teams was becoming apparent. Most of the techniques, rules, equipment, and methods of organization for these pastimes were initially borrowed from England, where an interest in team and field sports had developed several decades earlier.

Cricket was one of the most popular team sports in antebellum America. Played wherever English immigrants settled, it became especially popular during and after the 1830s. By 1840, as many as three cricket teams had been organized as far west as Chicago. One commentator declared in 1858 that cricket was "the leading game played out of doors in the United States."

But the quicker pace of baseball soon led to its supplanting the more leisurely game of cricket. In an article for *Atlantic Monthly,* March 1858, prominent Bostonian Thomas Wentworth Higginson voiced the opinion of many Americans when he wrote that the "briskness and unceasing activity" of "our indigenous American game of baseball" was "perhaps more congenial . . . to our national character, than the comparative deliberations of cricket."

Baseball borrowed and adapted rules and techniques from cricket and from popular English ball games like town ball and rounders played by children in the early 19th century. The Knickerbocker Base Ball Club, formed in New York City in 1845, provided the initial impetus for organization, and many amateur teams were established after that. The National Association of Base Ball Players was formed by the 50 or so teams centered around the New York area in 1858. On July 20 of that year, the *Long Island Democrat* remarked that:

By the 1850s wealthy Easterners were traveling to secluded wilderness spots to hunt and fish as well as to seek spiritual regeneration. This 1856 lithograph, entitled Camping Out, depicts a gentleman's camp of that period.

It is only a few years that the game of base ball has been considered of much account; excepting by school boys, who played entirely different from the clubs organized for base ball playing. But now we have daily accounts of spirited contests in this healthy and exhilarating game, from almost every section of the country.

By 1860, baseball teams had been organized in Detroit, Chicago, St. Louis, New Orleans, San Francisco, and St. Paul. As teams from different regions began to compete against each other, regional variations in rules, format, and equipment had to be standardized, a trend that became more pronounced after the Civil War.

The pastimes of game-hunting and marksmanship had been popular in the South and on the frontier since Colonial days, especially among young gentlemen. However, by the mid-19th century, wealthy Easterners took up hunting as a form of sport and organized hunt and rifle clubs. Trapshooting, which involved shooting at a series of flying targets from a fixed position, became a way for gentlemen to practice and compete without traveling to the wilds. By 1840, two trapshooting clubs had been established near New York City. Those who preferred adventure farther afield might journey to the forests and lakes of Maine or the Adirondacks; to the Atlantic seaboard or inland bays and swamps; to forests on the fringes of settlement; or, if they were truly adventurous, to the lands west of the Mississippi River.

Fishing as a sport also came increasingly into vogue at this time. Anglers' clubs were established as early as 1822 in Philadelphia and 1830 in Cincinnati. Groups were organized to go on fishing excursions, while individuals could pursue the meditative benefits of the sport on their own. Anglers sought to satisfy their passion in much the same locations as hunters — in the Adirondacks and harbors, bays, and inlets of the Atlantic Coast, as well as along various inland rivers and lakes. Improvements in railroad travel expanded the scope for hunting and fishing to include northern Maine, New Brunswick, and the Midwest, particularly around the Great Lakes.

The Growing Importance of Exercise

In 1855, English traveler William Baxter noted in his account, *America and the Americans,* that:

The Americans, it appears to me, devote far too little time to innocent amusement, and that recreation which is so conducive to health. Day after day they harass their bodies and minds in the counting-house or the store-room, making business a slavery, and money-making an unnecessary toil.

Other writers, ministers, educators, and statesmen, bent on launching crusades in favor of exercise, all criticized the sedentary nature of city dwellers. For the first time, sports were extolled as a useful means to improve health and provide a respite from work.

They could serve as a "safety valve" from the vices of the city, its supporters urged, as well as helping build character in the young.

While this campaign failed to generate the widespread interest its advocates hoped for, its influence persisted through the end of the 19th century, when it reached vast proportions. The ideal of "muscular Christianity," which had its roots in England, was an important element in this movement. Emphasizing the attainment of spiritual well-being through physical exercise, this philosophy was most dramatically introduced to Americans through a highly popular book for boys published in 1857, *Tom Brown's Schooldays* by British author Thomas Hughes. Focusing heavily on the role of athletics at England's renowned public school Rugby, this work of fiction launched thousands of young men into programs for

A small but vocal group of educators and reformers advocated physical exercise for both men and women during the mid-19th century. The author of an article on home exercise, published in Harper's Weekly, *July 11, 1857, advised that the daily practice of "battle-door and shuttle-cock," as depicted in the accompanying engraving, "will benefit females of every age and condition of health."*

building their physical strength and endurance.

Around the same time, German immigrants introduced formal gymnastics and regularized calisthenics to the American public. Deriving their origin from the "Turnvereine" (gymnastic societies) that had begun in Prussia earlier in the century, the German Turners in America promoted the cultivation of "rational training both physical and intellectual." By 1860, as many as 150 Turner Societies, with a membership of about 10,000, had been organized in America. Thousands of spectators witnessed demonstrations of the Turners' routines on outdoor apparatus, and their societies became highly influential in establishing indoor gymnasiums later in the century.

Enthusiasm for New and Earlier Sports

In addition to the Turner Societies, German immigrants brought a new enthusiasm for lawn bowls as well as the custom of seeking amusement on Sundays. Other newcomers also made contributions to American sports. Scottish settlers introduced the winter sport of curling, as well as a complex series of athletic contests known as the Highland or Caledonian Games, which were enthusiastically attended by American spectators. Swedish and other Scandinavian immigrants maintained an interest in physical education and winter sports. Still other immigrant groups became noted for their participation in sports that were already established by the

---

Interest in the activities of the German immigrants' Turner Society led to the widespread establishment of gymnasiums and regularized calisthenics programs, as reflected in this sheet music cover from 1861.

PUTTING THE HEAVY STONE.

THROWING THE HEAVY HAMMER.

Above: *The Scottish or Caledonian games, first held in America in 1836, combined exercise with entertainment and drew tremendous crowds. As depicted in* Harper's Weekly, *July 20, 1867, the games held at Jones's Woods (a retreat on the outskirts of New York City) were attended by more than 20,000 people. The two competitive events featured in the illustrations—"putting the stone" and "throwing the heavy hammer"—required brute strength and skill. The Highland fling was a Scottish dance "indulged in by a great number, who displayed unusual grace and agility and endurance, and were highly applauded by the audience." Below: The gymnastic events performed at Turner Society meetings attracted large numbers of outside spectators. An account of the 1865 convention at Cincinnati, Ohio, published in the September 30 issue of* Harper's Weekly, *reported that "every body was delighted with the entertainment."*

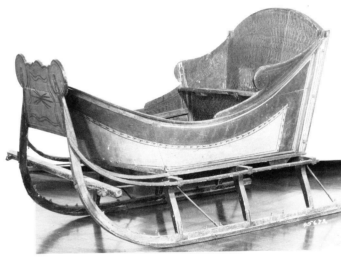

Above: *Ice skating experienced a surge of popularity during the mid-19th century, as eager skaters flocked to country ponds and city rinks during the winter season. This hand-colored lithograph, entitled* American Winter Scenes/Morning, *points to the enthusiasm for this winter diversion in the 1850s.* Left: *If one did not wish to engage in the strenuous exercise of skating, a sleigh ride could provide some of the same exhilaration and fresh air. This sleigh from about 1830 might have carried a group of young people to a party or frolic, ending at a local tavern or private home.*

time of their arrival, as in the case of the Irish, who rose to prominence in prize fighting.

While playing a minor role in everyday life, certain sports from earlier times continued to be enjoyed by large numbers as the 19th century progressed. Billiards and ten-pin bowling, long associated with drinking parlors, came to be considered more respectable. Even women began to participate in games of bowling at fashionable alleys constructed away from saloons. Billiards became the rage in many towns and villages across the country, with matches attracting great spectator interest in the 1850s. This wave of enthusiasm climaxed during the first national championship matches which were held in 1859. As

far west as Nebraska City, the *People's Press* declared in 1860: "No matter how hard the times are people will have their amusement and the fever now is for billiards."

Winter sports, especially sleighing and ice skating, continued to gain in popularity. Skating appears to have reached mania proportions during the mid-19th century, as thousands took to the ice on country ponds and at city rinks when the weather allowed. In *America Learns to Play* (1965), Foster Rhea Dulles talks of a 27-day period of good ice during which an estimated 200,000 enthusiastic skaters visited the frozen lakes of New York's newly opened Central Park. Less adventurous women could be pushed over the ice on sleds or chairs with runners. Some winter sports enthusiasts took up ice boating, which was especially popular along the Hudson River. The major participants in winter sports, of course, were

Children engaged in the pastime of sledding with great enthusiasm, testing their speed and skill against those of their peers. This engraving from Ballou's Pictorial, *November 28, 1857, part of an article on Thanksgiving in New England, shows a hillside "crowded with joyous youngsters gliding down over the smooth surface with the velocity of lightning."*

children. In the journal she published in 1850, Susan Fenimore Cooper, daughter of the famous writer, described sledding and skating in her home town of Cooperstown, New York:

Thursday, [January] 18th.—. . . The children are enjoying their favorite amusement of sliding to their heart's content; boys and girls, mounted on their little sleds, fly swiftly past you at every turn. Wherever there is a slight descent, there you are sure to find the children with their sleds . . . . Tuesday, [January] 23d.—. . . Troops of boys skating. There were no very scientific performers among them; nevertheless . . . their movement was . . . easy and rapid . . . . Some of the little rogues, with the laudable desire of showing off, whirled to and fro about us, rather nearer than was agreeable. "Where's your manners, I'd like to know!" exclaimed an older lad, in an indignant tone.

In addition to winter activities, children and adolescents engaged in other sports and games. Boys were urged to participate in ball games, to swim, hunt, and fish in order to test their speed, strength, and agility, and to develop habits of industry useful for adult life. Writer Richard Henry Dana, Jr., commenting on his childhood years in Boston in the period from 1815 to 1830, wrote in his journal:

I have since heard [my father] say that he frequently gave me leave to go swimming, boating, skating, & fishing, or into the woods, with other boys, when it required great effort in his own mind to get over a sense of the dangers I might be in; for he felt that habits of self reliance & self help, & familiarity with exposure & risks, to a boy not foolhardy, are a greater protection than all the guardings & watching of the most careful parents, beside being a far better preparation for manhood.

Girls did not receive the same kind of encouragement. People generally considered most games and sports—except for tossing a ball, rolling a hoop, or playing the game of battledore and shuttlecock (a precursor of badminton that was played without a net) — as being too rough and demanding for female constitutions.

Sports also flourished on the edges of settlement. Shooting contests continued, with targets often replacing live marks. Fishing and hunting contests; throwing, running, and rail-splitting competitions; and wrestling matches often accompanied festive community gatherings. In regions where religious restraints tended to be less confining than in the settled East, frontier life and attitudes played a significant role in spreading sporting interests during the mid-19th century.

By mid-century, sports and attitudes toward them had taken on many of the characteristics that would determine their future direction. The Civil War provided an impetus to expand and to organize sports on a national level, but it was industrialization that would play the key role in the development of American sports from that time on. As sports became both a product of and an antidote to industrialization, the two became inextricably linked.

On the frontier, the interest in sports developed primarily out of the necessary activities of daily life. Shooting matches like the one depicted in Harper's Weekly, *January 5, 1867, evolved from hunting for sustenance into popular sporting events.*

SPORTS MIRROR INDUSTRIALIZATION: CIVIL WAR TO WORLD WAR I

In an article entitled "America Revisited: The Changes of a Quarter-Century" (*Outlook,* March 25, 1905), Lord James Bryce, the English author, statesman, and commentator on American life, wrote of the American "passion for looking on at and reading about athletic sports":

It occupies the minds not only of the youth at the universities, but also of their parents and of the general public. Baseball matches and football matches excite an interest greater than any other public events except the Presidential election, and that comes only once in four years . . . . [T]he interest in one of the great contests . . . appears to pervade nearly all classes . . . . The American love of excitement and love of competition has seized upon these games.

Between the Civil War and World War I, sports assumed an increasingly important role in American life. Not only did they attract a growing proportion of the general public as a means of recreation and entertainment, but they came to be viewed as an essential emotional and physical release.

Technological Changes

The effects of industrialization, including the contributions of technology, were key factors in the rising importance of sporting activities. The telegraph helped disseminate information about sports, for the first time providing instantaneous reporting of sports activities and scores. General knowledge about sports also became available to millions of people through the publication of woodcuts, lithographs, and photographs depicting sports activities of various kinds.

Numerous new publications made their appearance as magazine and newspaper editors capitalized on the growing national enthusiasm for sports. Early sporting journals, like the *Spirit of the Times,* published results of races and athletic contests. More specialized journals included the periodical *Outing,* begun in 1881, and several field sports magazines. The somewhat lurid *National Police Gazette,* di-

Periodicals were instrumental in popularizing various sports. This engraving from Demorest's Family Magazine, *October 1866, reflects the national enthusiasm for such sports as croquet, ice skating, and baseball.*

rected at the urban man in the street, promoted prize fights and became the best selling sports periodical in the United States in the 1870s. Dozens of new sporting periodicals appeared between the 1890s and World War I, including an abundance of magazines about cycling.

Metropolitan newspapers capitalized on the popular interest in sports. The *New York World* claimed to have established the first newspaper sports department in 1883, although other newspapers had employed sportswriters earlier. By the 1890s, almost all large newspapers in leading cities had "sporting editors" with trained staffs, and were publishing sections devoted entirely to sports. These newspapers introduced the specialized terms and colorful language of the various sports into popular speech. Novels also helped to familiarize the public with outdoor sports, while directories, guidebooks, and rule books helped fans to expand their knowledge of their favorite sports.

Outing magazine, founded in 1881, led the way for a wide variety of sports-related periodicals. During the 1890s this magazine devoted its coverage almost entirely to the cycling craze.

Transportation improvements helped spread the interest in sports across the country. Railroads carried teams and spectators and sportsmen of all kinds across the continent. By the end of the century, mass transit systems provided interurban transportation to sporting events in many parts of the country.

Sports equipment became standardized, aided by mass-production methods and improved materials such as more durable iron, steel, and vulcanized rubber. The invention of electric lighting in 1879 greatly expanded the potential for indoor athletic clubs, gyms, and arenas, and eventually made nighttime outdoor games possible as well. Other inventions, including bicycles, automobiles, and airplanes, also became associated with sporting activities.

Changing Attitudes

Like other activities, sports were highly structured according to the needs, values, and aspirations of the different socio-economic groups. The seeds planted by the upper class in encouraging sports before the Civil War came to flower during the postwar decades. Athletic clubs became popular and such sports as croquet, hunting, riflery, archery, tennis, and golf became fashionable. In 1900, sportswriter Caspar Whitney commented in a periodical called the *Independent:*

We may turn up our noses generally at those who in this country profess to lead fashions, but in the matter of showing the way to healthy, vigorous outdoor play they have set a fine example and one that has taken a firm hold upon the people.

The middle class for the first time began to view sports as an agency for reinforcing rather than undermining prevailing moral standards and values. As they sought to emulate the social elites, they became ardent supporters of athletic clubs and other sporting pastimes. In response, wealthy members of society tended to switch to the kinds of sports that were too expensive, time-consuming, or demanding of space for other classes to follow. These included a variety of equestrian activities like fox hunting, polo, and horseback riding. Because of the enormous cost involved, yachting also remained a preserve of the very rich.

By 1900 sports equipment was mass produced and readily available at retail stores across the country. This postcard depicts an eye-catching window display in a sporting goods store.

For their part, members of the middle class sought to maintain strict barriers between themselves and the nonrespectable sporting fraternity. Boxing and wrestling, for example, retained their raffish aura throughout most of the 19th century. Despite these self-conscious distinctions, however, sports increasingly served to help assimilate immi-

Accessories for field sports were standardized and mass produced by the end of the 19th century. Along with other sports equipment, they often were sold through mail-order catalogs like this one, issued by Montgomery Ward & Company in 1890.

grants into the mainstream, and occasionally provided the means for less privileged members of society to improve their social status. Blacks, for the most part excluded from white sports of any kind, often formed their own teams and competed against each other.

Also in keeping with prevailing social attitudes, gender differences were strictly observed. Although women participated in sports activities to a greater extent than before, they still were kept away from strenuous games, and from physical contact and spectator sports. The sports and games considered respectable for women—croquet, archery, tennis, bowling, golf, skating, and cycling—were to be engaged in for health reasons rather than in search of achievement and prestige. They often took place within socially protected and gender-segregated facilities in YWCAs, colleges, and athletic clubs. Some of these sports ultimately promoted greater freedom in women's dress and behavior. However, the general belief that competition and strenuous athletics impeded the social and physical development of young women hindered active female participation in sports until well into the 20th century.

Above: *The addition of electric lighting enhanced both the capability and appeal of evening sporting events. This St. Louis horse-racing track, for example, drew tremendous crowds only after it was electrified. For, according to the accompanying article in* Harper's Weekly, *August 18, 1894, ''never was a daylight race more exciting than this.''* Right: *Wrestling, with its contaminating influences of professionalism, rowdiness, and gambling, retained its aura of non-respectability through most of the 19th century. This engraving from* Days' Doings, *December 5, 1874, shows a large crowd of ''sporting men'' assembled to witness a typically brutal contest.*

Facing page top: *The California Athletic Club of San Francisco, pictured in this engraving from* Harper's Weekly, *April 5, 1890, was conceded to be the richest club of its kind in the world. It was at clubs like this that boxing became a socially acceptable sport for the first time.* Facing page bottom: *As the middle class became more active in various sporting pursuits, the wealthy clung avidly to more exclusive pastimes that required vast outlays of money. Among these was yachting, depicted in this turn-of-the-century advertisement for whiskey.* Right: *Country clubs evolved from urban athletic and cricket clubs into socially exclusive meeting places for the wealthy. Until surpassed by golf, horsemanship and horse racing were the most popular pastimes engaged in at these clubs, as shown in this scene from* Harper's Weekly, *June 9, 1894.*

The Urge to Organize

In the growing anonymity of America's urban-industrial society, sports clubs and teams helped satisfy a need to be part of a well-defined community. Athletic clubs owed their existence and structure primarily to counterparts in the organized sports movement in England. The athletic clubs that were established at this time were player-centered: the players themselves took the initiative to organize, manage, and often to finance them as well. Members of the clubs perceived their activities as overwhelmingly respectable and, most important, as an indication that they were amateurs, participating for the love of the sport, not for money.

New York City led the way with the organization of the New York Athletic Club in 1866. Popular sports engaged in by these clubs included track-and-field events, polo, lawn tennis, and boating. By the 1870s, some clubs had expanded their scope to offer national amateur championship meets in swimming,

boxing, and wrestling, and many clubs eventually sponsored football and basketball games as well.

The 1880s to early 1890s marked the major period of growth in the number of athletic clubs. In 1887, *The Brooklyn Daily Eagle Almanac* claimed:

Athletic clubs are now springing into existence in the United States in such profusion as to baffle the effort to enumerate them. Scarce a city can be found having a population of more than 30,000 inhabitants, in which there is not at least one club of this class. In the large cities, there are from five to twenty-five; sometimes even more . . . . It would be impracticable to enumerate the athletic clubs of the smaller cities of the United States . . . . The total number is several thousand.

During this time, clubs became more social, featuring fancy clubhouses with gyms, track fields, swimming pools, bowling alleys, rifle ranges, billiard

Rowing became a popular collegiate sport during the 1830s and remained so for the next several decades. Enthusiasm for rowing competitions was particularly strong between the 1860s and the 1890s, when this cast-iron rowing-team pull toy was manufactured.

rooms, dining rooms, and sleeping accommodations. Some clubs even constructed summer clubhouses with tennis courts and bathhouses. As their focus became more social, the clubs employed professional administrators as managers.

When the middle class began to join athletic clubs, the wealthy felt the need to organize more exclusive social clubs for themselves. Following the English model, they began to establish country clubs. The first such club in America was built in Brookline, Massachusetts, in 1882. From the outset, country clubs placed less emphasis on strenuous athletics and more on the types of outdoor pursuits associated with English country estates—horseback riding and hunting. Later in the century, golf became important.

The increasingly sedentary lifestyles of the post-Civil War era led to a mounting concern with health. Health publications, sporting journals, and other periodicals stressed the importance—even the urgency—of exercising to maintain a sound mind and body. Public institutions, particularly churches and schools, played a major role in this movement, especially with the emergence of adult-managed sports programs for youth.

Much rhetoric was devoted to the notion that such play areas as gyms, athletic fields, and playgrounds would steer children and adolescents away from the vices associated with urban life toward the virtues of the lost rural experience. This view reached its fullest development in America at the turn of the century with a new nationwide movement that encouraged as "essential" participation in aggressive, manly sports to maintain "the existence of a strong nation." This movement was spearheaded by Theodore Roosevelt, organizer and commander of the Rough-Riders in the Spanish-American War of 1898, and president of the United States from 1901 to 1909. A passionate outdoorsman and hunter, Roosevelt was reacting against what he considered to be the overwhelming feminization of American culture in the Victorian era.

The Young Men's Christian Association (founded in England in 1844 and first established in the United States in the city of Boston in 1851) emerged as a major public institution promoting these new ideas. This organization went a long way toward persuading American families of the values of physical training. YMCAs had organized classes in physical culture, that is, athletics and gymnastics, since the 1860s, but their programs really captured public interest in the 1890s. On June 21, 1890, *Harper's Weekly* reported that in New York:

> *Almost every well-organized Young Men's Christian Association in the city and neighborhood has now its athletic department, and many of them have gymnasiums. It is the muscular form of Christianity that seems to take best among young men.*

In 1892, membership totaled a quarter of a million, and 384 gyms had been constructed at YMCAs across the country. In fact, both the new sports of basketball and volleyball originated as part of YMCA programs (*see pages 226 and 228*).

College-level sports greatly expanded after the Civil War: baseball was organized at an intercollegiate level and rowing remained in vogue, until football superseded both of these sports in popularity late in the century. Gymnastics and track-and-field competitions had both acquired a following by this time, while other team sports included lacrosse, cricket, and, by 1900, basketball and ice hockey. Dual and individual sports included tennis by the 1880s, and swimming and fencing by the 1890s.

The COLLEGE MAN'S NUMBER

By 1900 sports had become a dominant feature of college life. Athletic clubs and the Olympic games gave particular impetus to collegiate track-and-field contests, like the hammer throw pictured on the cover of the Saturday Evening Post, *June 18, 1904. By this time the "hammer" had evolved into a metal ball attached to a flexible wire handle.*

Above: *Physical education programs filtered down from colleges to secondary schools. This photograph of a boys' physical education class at Puritan Secondary School was taken by the* New York Herald's *special feature writer and photographer Jenny Chandler around 1900.* Right: *Pairs of Indian clubs like these were recommended particularly for exercise programs at schools and YMCAs. These inexpensive exercising tools helped build muscle tone and strength when used in a series of specialized maneuvers.*

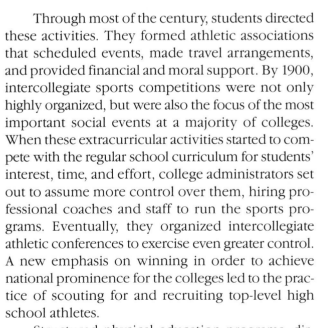

Through most of the century, students directed these activities. They formed athletic associations that scheduled events, made travel arrangements, and provided financial and moral support. By 1900, intercollegiate sports competitions were not only highly organized, but were also the focus of the most important social events at a majority of colleges. When these extracurricular activities started to compete with the regular school curriculum for students' interest, time, and effort, college administrators set out to assume more control over them, hiring professional coaches and staff to run the sports programs. Eventually, they organized intercollegiate athletic conferences to exercise even greater control. A new emphasis on winning in order to achieve national prominence for the colleges led to the practice of scouting for and recruiting top-level high school athletes.

Structured physical education programs, directed by school faculty, also filtered down to secondary schools at this time. In 1903, New York City formed the first organized athletic organization for public schools, and other regional organizations followed. By the outbreak of World War I, most

American schools already required physical education classes—at least for boys.

Among the many Progressive-era reforms of the late 19th and early 20th centuries, the parks and playground movements pointed to a similar interest in structured programming. As organized recreation became more closely linked with parks, planners advocated and provided better and more diverse facilities. Baseball diamonds became especially prevalent, as the enthusiasm for sandlot baseball pervaded nearly every American community. Numerous recreation centers constructed at this time provided access to outdoor and indoor games and sports for both adults and children.

In the second half of the 19th century, reformers promoted playgrounds as outlets for inner-city youth to vent their "animal spirits." Before 1900, however, the only official playgrounds consisted of sandpiles and simple play equipment aimed at pre-adolescent children. The movement for the provision of playgrounds and the corresponding organization of supervised youth recreation programs assumed national proportions in the decade before World War I. The Playground Association of America, formed in 1906, provided training programs for playground directors and recreation specialists and published *Playground Magazine.* Within the next few years, the number of playgrounds increased dramatically. However, the original intention of attracting slum-dwelling and immigrant youth to the playgrounds was not particularly successful; the chief users tended to be middle- and upper-class youngsters.

The construction of New York City's Central Park in 1858 marked the beginning of a movement of national proportions. By the turn of the century such parks often included sport and recreational facilities, like the tennis courts shown here.

Team and Spectator Sports

After the Civil War, baseball emerged as a nationally favored team sport. A writer for the *Spirit of the Times,* May 4, 1867, observed:

Of all out-door sports, base-ball is that in which the greatest number of our people participate, either as players or as spectators . . . it is a pastime that best suits the temperament of our people. The accessories being less costly than those of the turf, the acquatic [sic] course, or the cricket-field, it is an economic game, and within the easy reach of the masses . . . . It has become the rage with all classes and conditions.

Many cities and towns had formed baseball clubs by the late 1860s. According to an 1867 issue of a Minnesota newspaper (cited in "The Rise of Baseball in Minnesota," by Cecil O. Monroe, *Minnesota History,* June 1938):

The game of Base Ball has become so much the style that nearly every village and hamlet has its club, and to be a member of the first nine is now looked upon as being nearly as honorable a position as a seat in the legislature.

During this period, baseball games became major spectator sports, and bitter rivalries often

---

Progressive-era reformers believed that playgrounds would help reduce juvenile delinquency by allowing youths to "vent" their "animal spirits." Depicted in these photographs are two children's playgrounds from the turn of the century. Below: The Girl's Playground on Harriet Island, St. Paul, Minnesota. Facing page: The grounds sponsored by the Brooklyn Playground Society.

developed between the ball clubs of neighboring towns. Although they maintained a public veneer of amateurism, baseball clubs often charged admission to games and recruited talented players. Improved transportation, especially the developing railroad networks, and increased publicity contributed to the popularity of the game.

Some sports historians have associated baseball with a return to America's earlier pastoral way of life. However, in his article "Working at Playing: The Culture of the Workplace and the Rise of Baseball" (*Journal of Social History,* Summer 1983), Steven Gelber has argued that it was more directly related to the emergence of America's urban-industrial society

and the corresponding development of corporate values. Like industry, the game of baseball at this time embodied the characteristics of individual accountability combined with collective success or failure, competitiveness between groups and cooperation within them, as well as increasing levels of structure and organization.

Baseball was also closely associated with national pride. This connection reached a peak in 1904, when a seven-man commission (including two United States senators) was appointed to investigate the origins of baseball. Relying primarily on old-timers' reminiscences, the commission declared that baseball was an indigenous American game invented

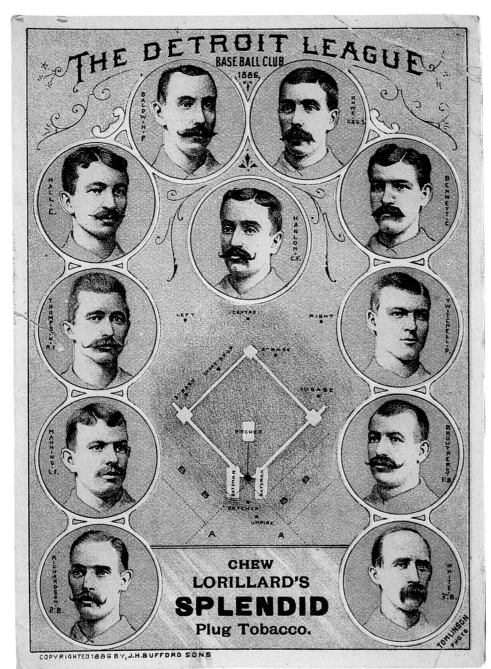

The Detroit League Base Ball Club became part of the National League in 1881, and went on to win the pennant and the forerunner of the World Series in 1887. The team achieved second place in the League in 1886, the date of this trade card, with the aid of star catcher Charley Bennett. Within a few years, however, the popularity of the team had declined to such an extent that it was auctioned off. Detroit remained without another major league team until 1901, when the Tigers were created as part of the newly organized American League.

by General Abner Doubleday in Cooperstown, New York, in 1839. (Later researchers discredited the findings of the commission, tracing the origins of the game to various English ball games.) This need for Americans to rationalize and glorify their enthusiasm for baseball also contributed to the growing cult of sports heroes.

The emergence of professional teams led to a major change in baseball. The Cincinnati Red Stockings, formed in 1869, was the first of these teams. The success of the Red Stockings and the other teams that followed assured that professional baseball would dictate rule changes and the style of play of the game from that time onward. With the organization of the

National League of Professional Base Ball Clubs in 1876, control over regulations, scheduling, and team management visibly shifted from the players to the team owners. The early team owners were instrumental in applying a business framework to sports management, a technique that became standard for all team sports in the 20th century.

Through the end of the century, professional baseball had to fight to achieve respectability because it had acquired an association with gambling, drinking, and rowdiness. The raucousness of a typical game was recounted in James Muirhead's *The Land of Contrasts: A Briton's View of His American Kin,* published in 1898:

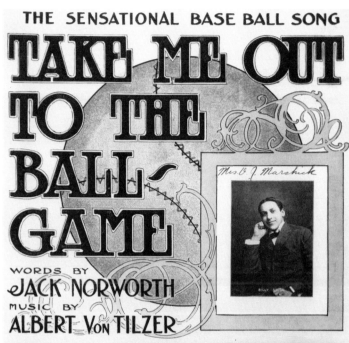

Above: *Organized baseball prospered during the early years of the 20th century. In 1907, after deliberating for three years, a specially convened commission proclaimed baseball to be of unquestionably American origin; two years later the tradition of having the president of the United States throw out the first ball of the season was established. This 1908 sheet music reflects the national enthusiasm for this sport.*
Above right: *From 1907 until after World War I, Detroit Tiger Ty Cobb reigned as the best baseball player in the American League, and was duly accorded the status of hero by his fans. Cobb's fiery temper and untamed ways reflected the rowdiness associated with the game during these years. This scene is from 1918.*

As a rule not much sympathy or courtesy is extended to the visiting team, and the duties of an umpire are sometimes accompanied by real danger. . . . A match played in no less aristocratic a place than Newport on Sept. 2, 1897, between the local team and a club from Brockton, ended in a general scrimmage, in which even women joined in the cry of "Kill the umpire!"

The game's crudeness also was criticized in *Outing* magazine, July 1898:

Our professional baseball, with its paid players and its thousands of smoking, and sometimes umpire-mobbing spectators, is doing more harm than good. The players are devoting their lives, instead of their spare time, to diversion instead of duty; and the spectators are wasting two or three hours of fresh air and sunshine looking at what they ought to be doing.

Eventually, baseball acquired a better reputation, mainly by recruiting college players, issuing positive publicity, and promoting a new style of play that incorporated strategy, signals, and highly integrated team play. To sustain spectator interest, a World Series competition between the best teams in the two existing professional leagues was introduced

In contrast to the overridingly professional character of baseball, football gained popularity as a collegiate sport. By the time this print was made in 1897, college football had become a nationwide commercial spectator sport. The violent nature of the game, predating the use of helmets and padding, is made quite explicit in this illustration.

in 1903. That decade also saw Ty Cobb thrilling crowds with his hitting and base-stealing feats.

While organized baseball achieved recognition as a sport played between city or town teams, football soared to prominence as a collegiate sport. Football had begun at a few colleges in the East as a simple, informal diversion for young "gentlemen." However, during the last three decades of the 19th century, American football evolved into a formalized sport distinct from its English antecedents, soccer and rugby. College football games, organized and controlled by the players, attracted thousands of enthusiastic spectators.

After some public criticism of the violent nature of the game, football regained widespread popularity during the first decades of the 20th century, with the greater acceptance of contact sports, more newspaper coverage, and the fame of player Knute Rockne.

The Rose Bowl in Pasadena, California, first played in 1902 to promote interconference competition, aroused great public interest. New stadiums were built, gate receipts increased, and alumni loyalty became an integral part of the game. Rules were continually revised in an effort to make the game less violent and more exciting to watch. It was at this time that the forward pass was introduced. Reflecting public enthusiasm, high schools and YMCAs began to offer the sport as a regular part of their physical education programs.

Two team sports, basketball and volleyball, were invented during the 1890s. James A. Naismith, a YMCA trainee who had been instructed to devise an attractive team game to be played in an indoor gym, came up with the game of basketball in Springfield, Massachusetts, in 1891. Naismith's game was especially appealing to athletes involved in outdoor team

Basketball became highly popular soon after its invention, suggesting a general preference for organized sport over gymnastic or calisthenic exercises during the winter months. This YWCA poster from around 1918 reflects the popularity of this team sport among young women at this time.

The game of curling, in which teams of players slid slightly flattened round granite stones to designated spots on the ice, was taken up by many clubs after the Civil War. This engraving from Harper's Weekly, February 9, 1884, *depicts a match between Scottish and American curlers at Cortlandt Lake, Westchester County, New York. A considerable number of "admirers of the game" as well as "local seekers after entertainment" were on hand to view the "novel scene."*

sports who were unhappy about relying on calisthenics and gymnastics for exercise during the winter. The standard, bottomless goal baskets made of cord net were introduced in 1893, replacing the peach baskets Naismith had originally used for this purpose. Within 10 years, basketball had won many adherents among YMCAs, high schools, colleges, and athletic clubs. It became the first truly active team sport for women, especially at colleges, although physical educators almost from the beginning tried to modify the rules so that the game would be less strenuous for them.

Another YMCA faculty member, William G. Morgan, developed volleyball in Holyoke, Massachusetts, in 1895. He devised this game, at first termed "minionette," for middle-aged and older men who found basketball too strenuous. Volleyball rapidly spread to grammar schools and during World War I was a favorite sport for soldiers.

Cricket continued to be played, often within the sphere of private clubs. Philadelphia became especially well known for its cricket clubs. James Muirhead alluded to its elite status, which was due in part to the extended amount of playing time needed, in *The Land of Contrasts* (1898): "A first-class match takes three days to play, and even a match between two teams of small boys requires a long half-holiday." Polo, another team sport associated with elite clubs, was introduced from England around 1875. Several matches took place in New York City soon after, and the sport spread to several other clubs and resort areas in the 1880s.

Various Indian tribes introduced lacrosse to early settlers, but it did not become popular in America until the late 19th century, after it had become an organized sport in Canada. Curling clubs proliferated by the 1870s. Ice hockey, a winter version of English field hockey, was brought to the United States from Canada in the 1890s. It caught on among amateur clubs and colleges and the first professional hockey team was formed in 1903. However, for many decades the sport continued to be most popular among youngsters.

Other nonteam spectator sports continued to attract large crowds. Horse racing remained a sport both for the wealthy and for the gambling sporting fraternity. The number of metropolitan courses increased and races were highly organized. Thoroughbred racing attained national prestige with the first Kentucky Derby, held in 1875.

Trotting continued to fascinate a wide general public. Commercialized trotting races were thoroughly entrenched features of county and state fairs. A National Trotting Association, formed in the 1870s, brought uniform rules, national contests, and the publication of statistics and records.

After the Civil War, yachting enjoyed a strong comeback. Yacht clubs organized numerous regattas, attended by masses of spectators. Ice yachting, a winter adaptation of this sport, was particularly

By the 1870s trotting had become a highly organized spectator sport, with uniform rules, scheduled contests, and hundreds of racetracks across the country. The Great Trot at East Saginaw, Michigan, of July 16, 1874, *depicted in this lithograph, set a record for trotting time.*

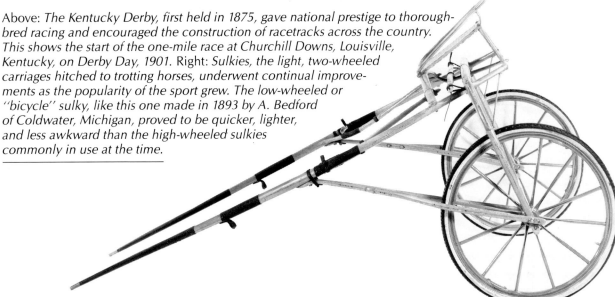

Above: *The Kentucky Derby, first held in 1875, gave national prestige to thorough-bred racing and encouraged the construction of racetracks across the country. This shows the start of the one-mile race at Churchill Downs, Louisville, Kentucky, on Derby Day, 1901.* Right: *Sulkies, the light, two-wheeled carriages hitched to trotting horses, underwent continual improvements as the popularity of the sport grew. The low-wheeled or "bicycle" sulky, like this one made in 1893 by A. Bedford of Coldwater, Michigan, proved to be quicker, lighter, and less awkward than the high-wheeled sulkies commonly in use at the time.*

popular between the 1860s and the 1880s.

Prize fighting gained nationwide recognition in the postwar years as well. Although still opposed by most religious denominations and by most respectable citizens, it was slowly gaining acceptance. The introduction of the first standardized rules in 1867 led to cleaner fights and opened the door to legal approval of boxing. Most organized fights moved to indoor arenas, where spectators paid admission and purses were awarded to the winners.

Probably the most famous boxing match of this period was the 1892 confrontation between long-standing champion John L. Sullivan and newcomer Jim Corbett. Sullivan, the favorite, was a follower of the old school of boxers with a preference for bare knuckles. The quieter Corbett shocked the country by defeating Sullivan with a new, scientific approach to boxing. The intensity of national attention focused on this match was truly momentous. The fervor even spread to respectable citizens, including the clergyman father of William Lyon Phelps, an influential literature professor at Yale University. In his *Autobiography With Letters,* published in 1939, Phelps recalled:

In 1892 I was reading aloud the news to my father. My father was a good man and is now with God. I had never heard him mention a prize fight and did not suppose he knew anything on that subject, or cared anything about it. So when I came to the headline Corbett Defeats Sullivan *I read that aloud and turned over the page. My father leaned forward and said earnestly, "Read it by [the] rounds!"*

Sullivan was considered by many to be the first great American sports hero. Colorful and outspoken, he typified the practical man of action who had raised himself up from modest origins and was revered by the American public for this achievement.

In the early 20th century, boxing gained even more respectability. Encouraged by athletic clubs, YMCAs, and colleges, it also became part of military training during World War I. Professional promotion, local boxing clubs in cities (and later in small towns), and new heroes lessened its reputation for seediness. Nevertheless, the boxing picture was clouded by racial tensions. These were exacerbated by the success of black boxer Jack Johnson, who in 1908 became the world heavyweight champion, keeping the title with victories over a series of white chal-

The 1892 match for the heavyweight championship between John L. Sullivan and "Gentleman Jim" Corbett announced in this engraving was the most famous boxing meet of its time. The resulting publicity raised the status of boxing considerably in the public eye.

Published by Arthur T. Lumley, New York Illustrated News.

FOR THE HEAVY-WEIGHT CHAMPIONSHIP OF THE WORLD.

John Lawrence Sullivan, the Champion, and James J. Corbett, the Adonis of the Fistic Arena, Who Are to Battle September 7th Next For a Purse and Stakes of $25,000 and the Big Fellow's Title.

From Photographs Taken Expressly For the Illustrated News.

lengers until defeated by the "Great White Hope," Jess Willard, in 1915.

Wrestling and weight lifting increasingly became public spectacles. They were as much a part of the entertainment world as they were displays of athletic prowess. Although YMCA classes offered training in wrestling and weight lifting, these did not become popular scholastic sports for many years.

When automobile racing began in the 1890s, it was taken up by the same well-to-do crowd that had been involved in sport carriage driving and horse racing. Races were usually organized to stimulate interest in the new American automobile industry. Cars raced short distances to set speed records, and participated in long-distance road rallies and hill climbs to display their endurance and reliability. The international long-distance road races for the Vanderbilt Cup, first held on Long Island, attracted huge crowds, especially after an American victory in 1908. Automobile races also proved to be popular features at fairs, replacing many of the earlier horse races.

Although road racing, increasingly conducted along designated circuits, remained popular, closed-course races eventually attracted even more fans. The American love of watching races on enclosed tracks provided the impetus for the construction in Indianapolis of the first permanent speedway. By the time of the first Indianapolis "500" race in 1911, automobile racing had reached truly national proportions. As automobiles became more numerous and participation in automobile races more widespread, both racing cars and races became more specialized.

Motorcycle racing began at about the same time. Although most of the early races and racing courses were in Europe, American motorcyclists won some significant early awards.

Just as automobile racing began to replace horse racing at fairs and other public gatherings, air races came along to pose a strong challenge. As soon as airplanes had developed to the point where sustained flight for a considerable distance was possible, exhibition fliers began to thrill crowds with performances at air meets; with endurance flights; with races against automobiles; and with cross-country contests. In 1910, as many as 75,000 spectators attended an aviation meet in Boston. The following year,

This 1893 park drag, made by C. P. Kimball & Company of Chicago, Illinois, was the type of carriage driven for sport by well-to-do gentlemen. They often were seen at horse races, where their passengers enjoyed an excellent view from seats on the top of the vehicle. The inside seats frequently were occupied by servants, who served the passengers food and drinks.

Right: *Automobile companies produced some of the earliest racing cars in America to stimulate interest in their models among the general public. This 1910 Ford Model T Racer was used in several hill-climbing contests. In 1911 it achieved a new speed record by completing a mile in 34 seconds. Below: American enthusiasm for automobile racing spurred the trend toward closed-track racing. The Indianapolis Speedway, the first permanent enclosed track of its kind, opened in 1909. The first 500-mile race, shown here, attracted some 80,000 spectators.*

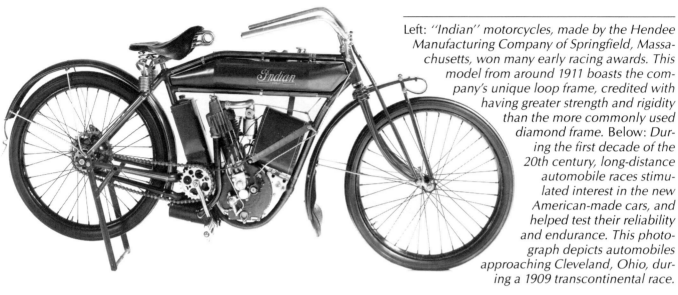

Left: *"Indian" motorcycles, made by the Hendee Manufacturing Company of Springfield, Massachusetts, won many early racing awards. This model from around 1911 boasts the company's unique loop frame, credited with having greater strength and rigidity than the more commonly used diamond frame. Below: During the first decade of the 20th century, long-distance automobile races stimulated interest in the new American-made cars, and helped test their reliability and endurance. This photograph depicts automobiles approaching Cleveland, Ohio, during a 1909 transcontinental race.*

Before air travel had become commercially viable, pilots thrilled crowds at fairs and meets with their daring feats and races. These 1922 snapshots depict some of the stunts undertaken by female pilot Lillian Boyer.

daring pilots won a reported million dollars in prizes by risking their lives in races and stunt flying. Around this time, a number of flying schools were established and aeronautical clubs organized, leading the way to a more general participation in sport aviation.

Amateurism in individual and team sports achieved its greatest success and widest exposure through the international Olympic Games. Originating in Ancient Greece but revived for modern participants in 1896 by Frenchman Baron Pierre de Coubertin, this program of games and sports was meant to bring together the most talented youth from around the world to compete on the athletic field, rather than on the battlefield. The track-and-field events were reminiscent of, although stylistically different from, those of the ancient games held at Olympia in Greece. The modern events included fencing, weight lifting, gymnastics, swimming, tennis, and bicycle racing.

This international competition, held every four years, heightened the general interest in sports and deepened the association between sports and nationalism. Although Americans participated in the first Olympics, and in fact won several medals, it was not until the second decade of the 20th century that amateur athletic associations in the United States began seriously to select, train, and subsidize athletes for these competitions. From the beginning, various ethnic groups made strong showings; American Indian Jim Thorpe achieved particular fame in the 1912 Olympics. In their scope, national exposure, ability to create heroes, and eventual commercialization, the Olympic Games truly foreshadowed trends in 20th-century sports.

Croquet and archery were genteel sporting pursuits of the 1860s and 1870s. This illustration from the 1867 book Popular Pastimes for Field and Fireside *indicates the appeal of these games for both men and women.*

Sporting Pastimes

During the post-Civil War years, American socialites took up a variety of sporting pastimes—including croquet and lawn tennis—that had become fashionable among their European counterparts. Generally they engaged in these games at exclusive clubs and resorts, treating them as social rather than competitive pursuits. When members of the middle class followed suit, the character of these pastimes changed. National groups were organized to standardize rules and set schedules for local and national meets. As these pastimes became accessible to a broader spectrum of participants, they tended to change into competitive sports.

Croquet, a modern version of an old French game, was brought to America by way of England around the time of the Civil War. An article in the *Nation,* August 1866, declared: "Of all the epidemics that have swept over our land, the swiftest and most infectious is croquet." The vogue for croquet became so great in the 1870s that manufacturers produced sets with candle-sockets attached to the wickets to facilitate night games. Women as well as men participated in this game, for it was more of a social amusement than a test of skill, and it did not require great exertion. When a National Croquet Association was formed in 1882 to revise and standardize the rules of the game, the national enthusiasm had already passed its peak. By the end of the century, a revised game called roque turned what had been a "courting game" into a contest of skill and strategy.

The ancient sport of archery had been revived in the early 19th century as a means of healthful recreation for gentlemen. However, it became enormously popular for both men and women in the 1870s and 1880s, especially at summer resorts.

Target shooting became even more popular for gentlemen than it had been in earlier decades. The growing interest in trapshooting (now more often at "clay pigeons" that imitated birds in flight) led to the establishment of standardized trap fields, the first national tournament in 1885, and the formation of

The Standard Clay·Percussion Target Ball.

PATENTED MARCH 16, 1880.

Above: *A variety of rifles were used for target shooting during the late 19th century. Among them was this pocket or bicycle rifle, patented in 1864. Compact and portable, it could be broken apart and put in a case or strapped to one's back.* Right: *During the late 19th century, trapshooting found enthusiastic adherents among gentlemen sportsmen wishing to hone their shooting skills. This advertisement from the 1880s promoted the superiority of a particular target, which, it claimed, would "save trouble, save disputing, save ammunition, save the gun and save the shooter."*

1888

Horace Partridge & Co.

BOSTON

Illustrated Catalogue of

General and Sporting Athletic Goods

T. WALTERS, 175 Main Street,
Agent for Worcester.

Facing page: *Lawn tennis first caught on at fashionable cricket clubs and summer resorts. Its relatively slow action and the custom of not keeping score made it an appealing game to women as well as men, as the cover of this 1888 trade catalog suggests.* Left: *The popularity of tennis led to the production of more standard equipment, such as this "Blue Ribbon" tennis racket, made by Harry C. Lee & Company of New York around 1908. It is set in a brace to keep it from warping.*

a national organization in 1890. By the early 20th century, the new sport of shooting skeet on a circular (later semicircular) course began to vie with trap-shooting for attention.

The social elite brought lawn tennis to America in the 1870s. An outdoor adaptation of the ancient game of court tennis, lawn tennis made its first appearance at cricket clubs and summer resorts. Its relatively slow pace and the custom of not keeping score encouraged women to take part. *Outing* magazine declared this "the one athletic game which women may enjoy without being subjected to sundry insinuations of rompishness."

In 1881, a national tennis association was formed. During the 1880s and 1890s, a growing emphasis on competition, and greater interest in exercise, led to the development of a more active form of the game. This encouraged more men to take it up as a pastime. The establishment of the International Davis Cup matches in 1900 clearly marked the transformation of tennis from a pastime to a sport. On the whole, tennis remained an upper-class diversion into the 20th century, as the well-to-do continued to play on their own courts and at private clubs.

Variations of lawn tennis, including racquets, squash-racquets, and table tennis also became popular during this time. Badminton, a cross between lawn tennis and the earlier game of battledore and shuttlecock, gained widespread attention as well.

Bowling became more respectable and by the 1890s had become tremendously popular. The national American Bowling Congress, formed in 1895, standardized rules and equipment and organized competitive matches. The game was played at exclusive clubs, at numerous fashionable alleys con-structed at the time for use by both men and women, and at more modest establishments open to the public at large. James Muirhead was struck by the popularity of the game in 1898, noting in *The Land of Contrasts:*

Bowling or ten-pins is a favourite winter amusement of both sexes, and occupies a far more exalted position than the English skittles . . . . [E]ven the fashionable belle does not disdain her "bowling-club" evening, where she meets a dozen or two of the young men and maidens of her acquaintance.

Ice skating continued to engage a large, enthusiastic public. Neighborhood skating clubs offered year-round skating at indoor rinks lit by gas and later by electricity. The 1868-69 handbook of rules and regulations for the Brooklyn Skating Rink Association emphasized the prevailing democratic attitude toward this sport:

Skating, in a moral and social point, is particularly suited to our republican ideas as a people. The millionaire and mechanic, the lady of fashion and those of humbler rank, all meet together to enjoy this fascinating and beautiful exercise. All can skate alone or associate with those most agreeable to themselves, and none are held responsible for the action or standing of others.

Figure-skating and speed-skating competitions became more popular after the organization of a national ice-skating association in 1886.

Roller skating came into vogue for adults at

TEN PIN BALLS AND PINS.

Bowling gained respectability in the course of the 19th century. By the late 1880s,
when Horace Partridge & Company put out this catalog of sporting and athletic
goods, bowling had become an accepted, even stylish, pastime for the entire family.

about the same time, becoming a craze in the mid-1880s. Almost every city and town had its rink. At the most fashionable ones patrons could rent skates and glide to the music of a live band. James Plimpton, who had invented the first "guidable parlor skates" in 1863, was instrumental in creating a proper moral environment at roller rinks. After his patent expired in 1880 and cheaper skates were produced for a wider public, rinks became more commercialized, competing with each other by means of various gimmicks and contests. Professional roller skaters also entered the field, engaging in figure skating, skating races, acrobatic stunts, and a competitive game called roller polo. When improved skates were developed after the turn of the century, roller skating was revived as a fashionable sport.

Rowing, sailing, canoeing, and walking were other noncompetitive sporting pastimes open to women as well as men. They provided exercise as well as relaxation and sociability. Yachting had helped to popularize small-boat racing and cruising, while technological improvements made a range of small boats more affordable to the general public.

But of all these pastimes, it was enthusiasm for bicycling that reached the most staggering proportions. Bicycles had first gained wide exposure in America with a display of English models at the 1876 Centennial Exhibition in Philadelphia. The high-wheeled bicycles of the 1870s and 1880s, called "ordinaries," were greeted with somewhat limited enthusiasm. They were hard to master and dangerous to ride, but they were a vast improvement over the "bone-shakers" of the 1860s.

A growing interest in bicycling in the 1880s,

Below: *The continuing appeal of ice skating during the 19th century led to the construction of an increasing number of indoor rinks so that skaters could enjoy the sport year-round. Skating rinks like the one depicted on this sheet music from 1868, were especially attractive to city dwellers, who flocked to them for exercise and sociability on evenings and weekends.* Right: *Roller skates tended to be slow and awkward prior to the 1880s, when several models allowing greater flexibility of movement were patented. These wooden skates with leather bindings probably date from between 1850 and 1880.* Below right: *During the 1870s and 1880s, roller skating became so popular that roller rinks were constructed in almost every city and town. This trade card from 1881 advertises the rink in Northampton, Massachusetts.*

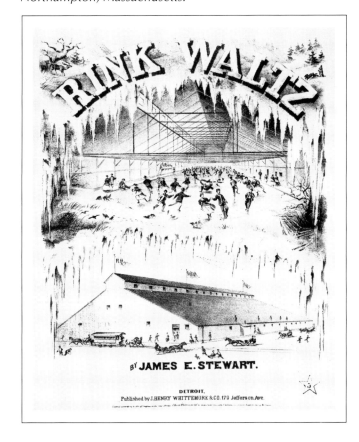

Above: *By the end of the 19th century a range of small boats was available at prices affordable by middle-class families. Rowing became a popular pastime for people of all ages, as suggested by this turn-of-the-century photograph taken at Erie Basin on Long Island, New York.* Below: *Canoeing was a non-competitive pastime accessible to women for exercise and relaxation. This photograph was taken at Belle Isle Park near Detroit, Michigan, around 1900.*

Since bicycling on high-wheeled "ordinaries" was difficult to master, its greatest appeal was to athletically inclined men. This cabinet card from the mid-1880s is of C. H. Wilkins, captain of the Manchester Bicycle Club of New Hampshire.

especially by athletically inclined men, led to the organization of clubs and cycling associations. These groups sponsored races, meets, and two- and three-day tours. The League of American Wheelmen (formed in 1880) was especially influential in promoting clothing reform, better roads, and outdoor exercise.

It was the introduction of the safety bicycle, with equal-sized wheels, a chain-gear drive, and a diamond-shaped frame, that turned bicycling into a national obsession in the 1890s. Pneumatic tires, added in 1889, and improvements in brakes and frames in the early 1890s, resulted in the production of several light, comfortable, and durable models. An extensive advertising campaign, reduced costs due to assembly-line production, and installment payment plans made bicycles even more appealing. The number of cyclists rose from approximately 150,000 in 1890 to close to a million in 1893, and to a peak of 4 million in 1896. In an issue dated July 2, 1896,

the *American Wheelman* claimed that "no one article of use, pleasure, or sport" had ever before retained "such a hold on popular appeal, popular taste, or popular fancy as the bicycle."

The sport of bicycle racing also gained enthusiasts in the 1880s and 1890s. At first the races were held along stretches of open road, but increasingly they were run on enclosed tracks. By the 1890s, trained professional racers were riding specially designed racing bicycles.

The most avid bicycle riders were from the urban and suburban areas of the Northeast and the Midwest. Bicycling received strong endorsement from the medical profession as conducive to good health. According to an article in the January 1895 issue of *Scientific American,* bicycling offset the effects of a sedentary lifestyle by providing exercise and engendering a "feeling of brain rest and mental refreshment." Despite some criticism, women took

to bicycling eagerly; it was fun, easy to learn, did not tax their strength too seriously, and did not breach contemporary standards of decorum.

Much has been written about the reasons underlying the American cycling craze of the 1890s. Of great importance was the fact that it allowed freedom from the restraints previously imposed by other methods of transportation and other forms of social activity. In an article entitled "The Great Bicycle Craze" (*American Heritage*, December 1956), Fred C. Kelly recalled his youthful cycling adventures:

Left: *The late 19th-century enthusiasm for bicycle racing spurred the invention of devices like this "Buffalo Home Trainer," produced around 1886. It would have been sold to men who wanted to train for a specific race as well as to those wishing to maintain a general exercise program during the winter months.* Below: *Bicycle road races became a summer craze during the 1880s and 1890s. As in the case of automobile races some years later, logistical problems encouraged a trend toward enclosed tracks.*

Bicycle races were a staple feature of agricultural fairs and community celebrations until superseded by automobile races and air shows. This mid-1890s poster announces a cycle race to be held as part of a Decoration Day celebration.

Above: *The Punnett Companion Bicycle, made in Rochester, New York, around 1895, was designed so that couples could ride together. The seats were movable, so that one of them could be placed on the center socket for the solitary rider, who could use either set of handlebars and the inside pedals. However, these bicycles were hard to pedal because of the wind resistance offered by two riders and because the combination of the riders' weights frequently caused tire blowouts.* Right: *The bicycling mania was instrumental in bringing about the design and acceptance of more comfortable clothing for women. By 1895 divided skirts and "bloomers"—loose-legged trousers gathered above the ankles—were admissible as cycling apparel. The wool gabardine bicycling suit and accompanying accoutrements shown here are from around 1900.* Below: *This photograph dates from the mid-1890s, when bicycling reached the peak of its popularity. Both men and women took to it avidly, since the "safety" bicycle was easy to master and cycling provided exercise, sociability, and a degree of independence and flexibility in travel that previously had been unknown.*

Golf was especially popular at hotels and resorts in natural settings. This early 1900s photograph of the Stevens House Golf Links in Lake Placid, New York, conveys the appeal of such surroundings and indicates that women shared the growing enthusiasm for this pastime.

On the bicycle you could go where you pleased, fixing your own schedule. It took you to "the city" to attend a theater matinee and be back home in time for the evening meal. Soon after I owned a bicycle I rode with two other boys the sixteen miles from our Ohio town to Dayton and, at a cost of fifty cents for a seat in the peanut gallery, saw Joseph Jefferson in Rip Van Winkle, *the first good actor any of us had ever seen. That was living.*

On a deeper level, its invention glorified America's technological progress, while providing a means of escape from the consequences of that progress—the city, congestion, and dirt—to open spaces and fresh air. That interest in bicycling declined when the automobile was introduced is not surprising, considering that the automobile supplied many of the same needs, but more quickly and comfortably. The introduction of mass-transit systems had an effect as well. From the late 1890s until several decades later, the status of bicycles declined to not much more than that of children's toys. Only professional cycle racing continued as an adult sport.

Another reason why the enthusiasm for bicycling declined, at least for many members of the upper class, was the new interest in golf. Various forms of this game had originated centuries earlier in Scotland and Holland, but golf was revolutionized in the 19th century by the introduction of the iron-headed club and the gutta-percha ball

St. Andrews Club, established in 1888 by a group of Scotsmen in Yonkers, New York, was the first permanent club for golfers. Soon after its organization the game became popular at summer resorts and was influential in the spread of country clubs. Golf was considered healthful, but not over-taxing for women.

Although golf originally was seen as a somewhat quaint and foreign game, a new hard-driving style and a livelier rubber-centered ball (introduced in 1899) helped Americans to improve their games. By 1913 America had won its first international golf championship, and before long Americans began to dominate the golfing world.

By the second decade of the 20th century, the aristocratic aura associated with golf also diminished, as business and professional men saw golf games as

The increasing availability of public golf courses, like the one at Forest Park, New York, pictured in this photograph from the early 1900s, helped change golf from a game played only by the rich to one accessible to a broader public.

potential extensions of their business activities. *Demorest's Family Magazine*, November 1895, noted the burgeoning interest in this sport:

> *[G]olf is already so popular in this country as to have nearly one hundred and fifty clubs of votaries; and it is because every day of the golfing season sees innumerable recruits drawn from the fringe of onlookers into the fascinating vortex of the game, that golf promises to soon lose its exclusiveness and take its place beside baseball and tennis as an outdoor sport in the United States.*

The construction of 472 public golf courses by 1917 suggests that democratization of the game had begun.

From the 1870s to World War I, thousands of affluent gentlemen from cities in the East took to outdoor field sports with a passion. In doing so they combined the love of sport—derived from their British counterparts who had been pursuing these activities for over a century—with an ever-increasing fascination with the American wilderness.

The Adirondacks became the most popular destination for gentlemen sportsmen at this time, probably due to the ease with which small boats could be navigated across the vast network of interconnecting lakes and streams. Moreover, logging operations and forest fires had led to a huge increase in the number of white-tailed deer in the area; these rapidly became the most popular target for hunters.

The American field sportsmen adopted the British code of sporting conduct. An issue of the *American Sportsman* from the early 1870s noted that their emphasis was not on the killing of their prey but on the demonstration of "the vigor, science, and manhood" necessary to overcome difficulties, and on the display of "the true spirit, the style, the dash, and the unalterable love of fair play" necessary to a proper gentleman. For the most part, these men did not enjoy "tramping" or "roughing it"; they brought with them as many of the comforts of home as they could, thus turning relatively primitive summer hostels into elaborate private camps and clubs.

Other wilderness areas "civilized" by gentlemen sportsmen at this time were mostly in the East and, to a lesser extent, in the Midwest. Despite the glowing reports of daring outdoorsmen like Theodore Roosevelt, only the most adventurous risked the hazards of the Far West.

Fishing was also popular in the Adirondacks, where trout abounded. As the means of transportation improved, the vogue for fishing extended to numerous other areas. Anglers' clubs proliferated, and enthusiasts organized many tournaments. Mean-

Above: *A vociferous advocate of wildlife conservation and the ideal of the hunter-naturalist, Theodore Roosevelt raised these issues in the national forum when he became president. This mechanical bank, patented in 1907, refers to the tale that Roosevelt refused to shoot a bear cub that crossed his line of fire during a hunting trip in Mississippi. This supposed event, much acclaimed by the American public, inspired the creation of the "teddy" bear. Right: Men who hunted for sport were proud to show off their prey. In this tintype Fred and Edward Bryant (Henry Ford's brothers-in-law), a friend, and their dog pose with their prize after a hunting trip in 1885. Below: During the latter decades of the 19th century, the Adirondack Mountains in upstate New York became the most popular destination for gentlemen sportsmen eager to pursue their favorite field sports while "roughing it" at primitive or elaborate camps. One of the area's chief attractions was the abundance of white-tailed deer, as can be seen in this photograph from around 1900.*

Above: *Fishing appealed not just to wealthy sportsmen, but became a pastime for Americans of all ages and from every walk of life, as this 1896 photograph suggests.* Below: *During the late 19th century the Adirondacks area became as popular for fishing as for hunting because of the abundance of trout in its lakes and streams. This photograph of fly-fishing in that region was taken around 1905.* Facing page: *The universal appeal of fishing led to its commercialization in the form of various children's games and toys, including the 1890s Fish Pond game.*

while, in rural areas and small towns average people continued hunting and fishing as leisure pastimes, using relatively unsophisticated techniques and equipment.

Throughout most of this period the belief persisted that the supply of fish and game was inexhaustible. In fact, the pursuit of fish and game for sport was so excessive that some species—including the trout in the Catskills—were pushed to the brink of extinction. Sea fishing became fashionable only after the depletion of game fish in some of the more popular rivers and lakes.

As early as the 1870s, sportsmen's clubs, state groups, and national associations were formed to propagate and protect wildlife. An International Association for the Protection of Game was organized in 1874, and the first uniform game laws were passed in 1875. Twelve years later, Theodore Roosevelt helped found the Boone and Crockett Club, an early clearinghouse for conservation ideas. However, many of these early organizations faced hostility and criticism from the general populace, which tended to feel that the privileged and wealthy were controlling the game for their own enjoyment.

Only when wholesale slaughter threatened the complete extinction of certain species of wild animals and fish were conservation measures seriously considered. Theodore Roosevelt helped bring the issue of wildlife conservation to the forefront by giving it national exposure in the first decade of the 20th century. Statements like the following, made by Roosevelt in *Outdoor Pastimes of an American Hunter* (1904), were typical of the new sentiment:

> *All hunters should be nature-lovers. It is to be hoped that the days of mere wasteful, boastful slaughter are past and that from now on the hunter will stand foremost in working for the preservation and perpetuation of wild life, whether big or little.*

Numerous game preserves were added to the three already existing in 1900, and national and state governments assumed control over the preservation of game. State game commissions supervised game wardens and established licensing systems for hunters and anglers. Anglers' clubs also promoted stricter conservation measures. The pursuit of field sports would continue into the 20th century. While gaining more adherents, these sports would increasingly provoke opposition from groups wanting to protect wildlife and the environment.

In Colonial times, sports played a minor role in the lives of Americans. This changed during the late 19th and early 20th centuries, as spectator and participatory sports were organized on a national level. After World War I, both would become commercialized, and the genteel sporting pastimes of the 19th century would evolve into a wide range of popular sports, many of which were highly competitive.

Life

PRICE 10 CENTS
Vol. 66, No. 1710.   August 5, 1915
Copyright 1915 Life Publishing Company

RARE FORM

Taking Part:
The Shaping of
Modern Sports

*S*ince World War I, sports have developed characteristics that continue to
the present day. Spectator sports have been greatly commercialized, while
participatory sports have become a significant part of many people's lives.
Over the decades, class and gender distinctions, especially in the playing of
participatory sports, have decreased.

    Sports were encouraged during World War I, both as part of military
training and as a way to pass time constructively. Ultimately this set the stage
for the tremendous surge in sporting activities that followed. After the war,
veteran soldiers joined the rest of the nation in "plunging into sport" to express their "release from years of gloom and suppression," according to an
article in the New York Times of June 1919. In the 1920s, the enthusiasm for
sports swept over the nation, engrossing the public and placing numerous
athletes in the limelight. Thereafter, sports became one of America's foremost
social institutions. As new social attitudes stressed the necessity for recreation in people's lives, the pursuit of sports came to be seen as every person's
right and both spectator and participatory sports reached unprecedented
levels of popularity.

Facing page: *Although this illustration from the cover of* Life, *August 5, 1915,
suggests that women had become quite active in competitive sports by this time,
their attempts to do so would in fact continue to encounter considerable
opposition for the next several decades.*

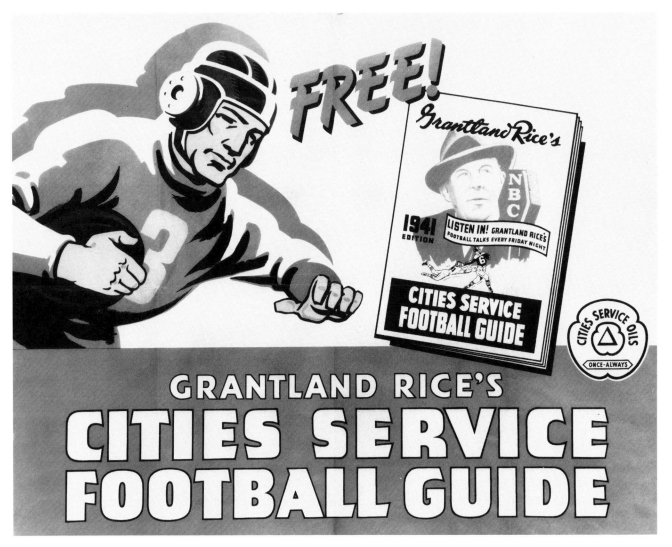

After World War I a new generation of writers and announcers helped transform sports from "hard" news to a source of entertainment. This early 1940s poster advertises a football guide and radio talk show, both featuring one of America's greatest sportswriters, Grantland Rice.

New Influences

Several major social and technological changes spurred the fascination with sports. First, sports came to be integrally associated with the emerging emphasis on youth culture. Beginning in the 1920s, participation in sports activities became a way for people of all ages to feel young.

Traditional religious prejudices toward sports all but disappeared during this period, as they came to be considered wholesome and constructive aspects of daily life. Churches wholeheartedly supported sports programs, and ordinances and laws prohibiting Sunday sports were eased or expunged from the books in communities across the country. Sports also became closely connected with industry, as companies established recreation programs and sponsored teams to promote fitness and a "team spirit"

among workers (thus strengthening their loyalty to their employers).

Racial and gender discrimination in sports declined, especially after World War II. After decades of exclusion that forced them to play in their own leagues, black athletes began to be admitted to baseball, football, and basketball teams, and to become eligible for participation in other sports. Women's sports, especially tennis, golf, swimming, intercollegiate sports, and Olympic sports, had soared in popularity after World War I. But it took Title IX of the 1972 Education Amendment Act, which forbade the exclusion of, or discrimination against, anyone wishing to participate in school sports programs, to revolutionize female scholastic sports. Sports opportunities for the handicapped also improved during the 1970s and 1980s.

Technological breakthroughs and a new emphasis on consumerism played a significant role in fanning the public enthusiasm for sports in the post-World War I era. Magazines and newspapers helped publicize sports on a national level. Sports reporting became a full-fledged profession. As sports moved from being "hard" news to being a source of entertainment, entire sections in the print media were devoted to their coverage. Sports critic John Tunis remarked upon this in an article entitled "The Business of American Sports," published in *America as Americans See It* (1932):

> *The average American newspaper devotes from one-eighth to one-quarter of its entire space to the complex business of athletes in the United States, both amateur and professional. Foreigners visiting this country casually would be pardoned for imagining that the average American citizen spends from a quarter to an eighth of his life watching or playing games.*

Advances in photography contributed to and enhanced sports publicity. While photographs illustrated many pages of publications, the development of motion picture cameras made possible the production of newsreels, shorts, and feature films on sports. These were viewed by the general public in movie theaters across the country.

Radio and, later, television greatly encouraged national enthusiasm for sports. Sports reporting became so popular on the radio that by 1930 it ranked next to popular music in the amount of air time allotted to it. But television undoubtedly played the most important role in publicizing and popularizing sports. Television introduced many sports to a

---

Television made it possible for millions of Americans to watch organized sports events in the comfort of their own homes. Programs like the baseball games promoted in this beer advertisement swelled the size of television audiences during otherwise slow viewing times like Saturday and Sunday afternoons.

1956 - MAY POSTER

During the 1920s stadiums across the country were improved and expanded to handle the ever-increasing number of sports fans. This included Detroit's Navin Field (now Tiger Stadium), whose seating capacity increased from 11,000 to 40,000 with the addition of an upper deck in 1924. This photograph dates from 1934, a year of resurging interest in Detroit baseball after several off-seasons.

larger and broader audience than had been possible in the past. Before long, spectator sports were being marketed as entertainment spectacles for home viewers. Weekend afternoon sports shows like "The Wide World of Sports" (begun in 1961), had particular impact, both by covering the major spectator sports and by introducing lesser-known ones, like winter sports, to the general public.

Some games were altered to fit television requirements: football games were revised to fit a two-and-a-half hour format, with commercial breaks scheduled to correspond to time outs. Eventually, even the Olympic Games were repackaged as extravaganzas to be offered as entertainment for home viewers. Sports shows became so popular that in 1979 a new station, the Entertainment Sports Programming Network (ESPN), began offering 24-hour sports telecasts. In the words of ESPN founder Wayne Rasmussen, the station was formed in the belief that "the appetite for sports in this country is insatiable."

College basketball, professional baseball, and boxing were frequently televised, but the game of football, with its isolated action on a specific part of the field, was especially suited to the new medium. Entertaining announcers, unusual camera angles, and instant replays all became part of the ritual of presenting the game via television. Football became such a popular television sport that a weekly Monday night game was added in 1970 to supplement the traditional Sunday afternoon games. To maintain live attendance, communities "blacked out" televised local games unless the games were sold out.

Although television has been criticized for discouraging live attendance at games, it also can be argued that the medium has helped to popularize them. Live attendance at football and baseball games has actually increased, and the professional leagues have expanded because of greater television exposure. Television also has helped the novice fan to understand and appreciate the intricacies of the various sports. As one football fan, quoted in Benjamin Rader's book *American Sports: From the Age of Folk Games to the Age of Spectators* (1983), put it:

You watched a game on television and, suddenly, the wool was stripped from your eyes. What had appeared to be an incomprehensible tangle of milling bodies from the grandstand, made sense. [Television] created a nation of instant experts in no time.

Modern forms of transportation also helped to popularize sports. Advanced railroad networks facilitated travel for teams, while public, interurban transportation increased attendance at urban sporting events. But the automobile and airplane had the greatest impact on all kinds of sports: stadiums, parks, and golf courses, as well as faraway fishing, hunting, boating, and skiing spots, all became easily accessible to a large public. Air travel made it possible for teams to compete in far-flung cross-country and international locations, and therefore also contributed to the expansion of the professional leagues.

The number of sports structures increased dramatically at this time. Electric lights facilitated the scheduling of many more indoor and evening sporting events; large clocks and public address systems became commonplace in stadiums and arenas. In the 1960s and 1970s, domed stadiums and synthetic turf began to have a major impact on baseball and football games.

The effect of the commercialization of amateur and professional sports was evident not only in the mass media but in other areas as well. "Big-time" spectator sports came to be designed for the mass audience, their character often dictated by the fans. Athletes "worked" at their sports, often for the fans, managers, and owners, rather than just for them-

College-level physical education programs offered rigorous training regimens, sometimes preparing students for careers in professional sports. This athlete is lifting weights under the close supervision of a coach at Columbia University.

Left: *The athletic feats of Harold "Red" Grange endeared him to Americans across the country. In common with other celebrities Grange endorsed a number of products, including the malted milk advertised on this soda-fountain menu from the mid-1920s. Above: By the 1950s, when this cereal bowl was produced, athletes shared the celebrity status of movie and television stars. The association of sports figures with such items was meant to increase both the exposure of the athletes and the marketability of the products. Facing page: Although every field of competition had its national heroes during the 1920s, Babe Ruth stood high among the preeminent sports stars of the time. As suggested in this sheet music cover of 1928, Ruth was a master of the offensive style of baseball that focused on hitting home runs.*

selves. Although some criticism was directed at professional athletes who pursued fame and fortune above all else, careers in sports became increasingly acceptable. The commercial success of sports brought the potential of huge profits to owners and promoters, and of large salaries to players. As a result, the tense management-labor relations often found in the business world have been mirrored in the confrontation between players and owners.

In the latter part of the 20th century, all realms of sport—from professional team sports to collegiate sports, to playground and secondary school athletic programs—have become highly organized and structured. Full-time administrators, expert coaches, special trainers, and the use of scientific methods to improve performance have all become part of the sports business.

Inevitably, sports have influenced the construction, clothing, and other industries, including the multimillion-dollar "sporting goods" industry. Sports have increased local revenues, especially during such nationally advertised spectacles as the Kentucky Derby, the Indianapolis Speedway races, and the various football bowl games. As an advertising vehicle, sports have helped to sell soft drinks, beer, and numerous other products, as well as vacation spots and housing developments. In the 1920s, the Miami Chamber of Commerce attempted to lure visitors to its city by including the following enticements in its promotional brochure:

The Climate Supreme, The Tourist's Delight, The Motorist's Mecca, The Fisherman's Paradise, The Golfer's Wonderland, The Polo Player's Pride, the Surf Bather's Joy, The Aviator's Dreamland, The Yachtsman's Rendezvous, The Tennis Player's Happiness, The Horse Racing Utopia, The Hi-Li Player's Haven . . . Truly the Outdoor City.

As players were marketed by promoters and the mass media, they were raised to larger-than-life stature. Sports heroes competed with movie, radio, and television stars for public adulation. Worship of sports heroes added excitement to people's daily

Chew
MAIL POUCH
TOBACCO

IT'S THAT WAY IN THE U.S.A.
A good workman is a good sportsman. We Americans know how to work and how to play, and we're going to keep a proper balance.
CHEWING SERVES TO STEADY NERVES

Numerous companies have promoted competitive sports as a social and physical outlet for their employees, as reflected in this late 1940s poster for Mail Pouch Tobacco. Industrial teams have been seen as strengthening company loyalty, building civic pride, and encouraging participants to maintain an interest in professional sports.

lives and offered fans a sense of collective identity.

American sports heroes since World War I are too numerous to mention, and only a few will be discussed in the context of their sports. However, of all the preeminent athletic heroes of this period, one name seems to stand out above the others: that of George Herman "Babe" Ruth. A flamboyant character and a masterful baseball player, Ruth represented the attributes of brute power, natural ability, lack of inhibitions, and disregard for authority that appealed to the American public in the 1920s. As sportswriter Paul Gallico expressed it in his book *The Golden People* (1965):

In times past, we had been interested in and excited by prize fighters and baseball players, but we had never been so individually involved or joined in such a mass outpouring of affection as we did for Ruth.

Public shrines commemorating almost every sport and its stars were constructed across the country, reflecting both the prevailing hero cult and the close association between sports and nationalism. Beginning with the National Baseball Museum and Hall of Fame, built in Cooperstown, New York, in 1939, these shrines have served to glorify sports and to reinforce the perceived positive values that most Americans have come to associate with them.

Spectator Sports

Spectator sports expanded and prospered during the post-World War I period. After an unfortunate scandal in which a number of players intentionally fixed the 1919 World Series, baseball managed to improve its image with the appointment by the team owners of a national commissioner to oversee it. When more offensive action was added to the game in the 1920s, especially a new emphasis on the home run, baseball achieved a higher level of popularity. Colorful stars, managers, reporters, and radio announcers helped to intensify enthusiasm for the game. Player drafts and minor-league farm systems also were established at this time. This raised the standard of playing and helped equalize the growing competition on the baseball diamond.

A drop in ballpark attendance occurred during the depression of the 1930s and World War II. However, popular interest in the game was maintained by the introduction of an annual All-Star Game in 1933, an abundance of spectacular players to idolize, the regular scheduling of games on Sundays and at night, radio broadcasts, and a variety of promotional gimmicks. Company and local youth teams also helped keep baseball in the forefront. Since World War II, baseball has kept the loyalty of fans by continually emphasizing offensive play and by making a strong appeal to civic pride.

College football reached a new level of popularity in the 1920s, when huge concrete stadiums were constructed and a large cast of cheerleaders,

Above: *The pitching feats of Leroy "Satchel" Paige packed ballparks throughout the country while he played both on Negro- and major-league baseball teams. Although Paige began his career in 1926, he was not able to break into the majors until 1948, a time when other black players also began to be admitted. When he signed with the Cleveland Indians at the age of 42, Paige became the oldest rookie in the majors and the first black pitcher in the American League.* Above right: *Professional baseball has made continuous efforts to keep its fans interested. The 1953 baseball schedule sponsored by Eveready Flashlight Batteries included team schedules for the upcoming year, as well as predictions, statistics, and quizzes.*

marching bands, majorettes, and fervent alumni supporters became regular features of the games. Paid trainers, coaches, and assistants became the rule, and football scholarships were instituted to recruit talented players.

As in baseball, college football rules were constantly revised to make the game more appealing to spectators. The focus on teams shifted from the East to the Midwest and the West, while annual bowl games reinforced regional rivalries. Enthusiasm for the game filtered down to younger players, and high school and sandlot games abounded.

Professional football, a minor aspect of the game for a number of decades, also became prominent during this period. The first professional foot-

ball organization, the National Football League, was founded in 1922 to improve the profitability of team ownership and enhance the public image of the game. Professional teams often recruited college football stars, including Harold "Red" Grange, whose fame helped make professional football acceptable to a national public. The 1930s saw the institution of a player draft. In spite of these developments, professional football was not much of a box-office success during the 1920s and 1930s. In contrast to college football, it remained inferior in quality and was held in low esteem by the public.

During the late 1940s and 1950s, professional football experienced a major resurgence in popularity. Returning soldiers who had played football as

Facing page: *Football became firmly entrenched on college campuses during the early decades of the 20th century, as the earlier violence abated and the use of the forward pass became more customary. This program was produced for a game between the University of Michigan and Cornell University.* Above: *School and sandlot football games, like this one played in Dearborn, Michigan, in 1934, encouraged enthusiasm for the sport.* Right: *The Super Bowl, started in 1967, pitted the best professional team from each conference against the other after a series of playoff games. This pennant and buttons are from the 1982 game between the San Francisco 49ers and the Cincinnati Bengals, held at the Pontiac Silverdome, Michigan.*

part of their military training brought home a taste for it. At the same time, exposure to the game through television stimulated spectator interest in the sport. Like other spectator sports, professional football came to be geared toward the fans' interest. The Super Bowl, a championship game between leagues, was introduced in 1967, and included an increasing number of teams in its playoffs. The appeal of football in the 20th century has undergone as much interpretation as has the American interest in baseball during the 19th century. Whereas baseball was integrally related to America's emerging industrial society in the 19th century, football has been perceived as echoing the modern corporate business world and the experiences of white-collar and professional workers, especially in the use of teamwork, in the time-bound restrictions of the game, and in the need for careful planning and coordination in order to achieve success.

During this period, basketball moved to a faster style of play, resulting in more running action than earlier. As the game shifted from being primarily recreational to being more competitive, it developed into a distinctive spectator sport. For sports enthusiasts, basketball bridged the gap between the football and baseball seasons. It was especially popular

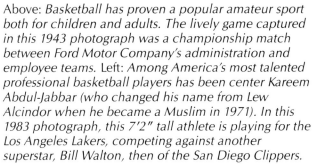

Above: *Basketball has proven a popular amateur sport both for children and adults. The lively game captured in this 1943 photograph was a championship match between Ford Motor Company's administration and employee teams.* Left: *Among America's most talented professional basketball players has been center Kareem Abdul-Jabbar (who changed his name from Lew Alcindor when he became a Muslim in 1971). In this 1983 photograph, this 7'2" tall athlete is playing for the Los Angeles Lakers, competing against another superstar, Bill Walton, then of the San Diego Clippers.*

as an inter-high school and intercollegiate sport, fostering fierce rivalries between home towns and enthusiastic support from alumni. Sociologists Robert S. and Helen M. Lynd described the fanaticism for high school basketball in Muncie, Indiana, in their book *Middletown: A Study in American Culture* (1929):

> *Hundreds of people unable to secure tickets stand in the street cheering a score board, classes are virtually suspended in the high school, and the children who are unable to go to the state capital to see the game meet in a chapel service of cheers and songs and sometimes prayers for victory.*

Like football, professional basketball gained widespread interest after World War II. The National Basketball Association, formed in 1946, experienced phenomenal growth in the 1950s. As in the other major spectator sports, a draft system was established, top players were recruited, rules were revised for the fans and for television coverage, and the quality of play was generally improved. Black players, who initially had been excluded from major national teams in most sports, came to dominate the game after 1950, making up as much as 75 percent of the team rosters by 1980.

Having served as an integral and useful aspect of World War I military training, boxing achieved a degree of public acceptance during its so-called "golden age" in the 1920s. Powerful mauler Jack Dempsey, fight promoter Tex Rickard, and the publicity generated by Madison Square Garden were instrumental in both the popularization and commercialization of boxing. Although new stars like Joe Louis and, later, television coverage, attempted to revive the sport, it rarely reached the level of popularity it had enjoyed in the 1920s. Wrestling survived mainly as an entertainment spectacle rather than a serious sport. However, both boxing and wrestling remained part of the Olympic Games and became popular sports in schools.

Other spectator sports enjoyed their greatest

Superb boxing skills and powerful knockout punches made Joe Louis a national hero. The "Brown Bomber" retained the heavyweight crown for a record 12 years, between 1937 and 1949. This included his years of service in the army during World War II when he toured overseas. This photograph is of his wartime bout in North Africa with Morton Fry, Jr., of Parkersburg, West Virginia.

Professional ice hockey teams in America attracted a growing following during the post-World War II years. This 1950 photograph shows a playoff game betwen the Detroit Red Wings and the New York Rangers for the coveted Stanley Cup.

popularity at this time as scholastic sports. These included track and field, rowing, and women's volleyball, basketball, and field hockey.

Tennis "went public" in this period, moving from the private courts of country clubs and exclusive summer resorts to stadiums and public courts. Matches were widely publicized, and the quality of play improved greatly. Again, spectators and television exposure played an influential part in determining the character of the sport. Both amateur and professional players engaged in tournaments, and women as well as men became famous for their skill at the game. Beginning with Bill Tilden in the 1920s, an array of exciting players have continued to attract spectators to the game.

In the 1920s, golf became a spectator sport for the first time in its history. Players like Walter Hagen

made the profession of golfing socially acceptable, while amateur players like Bobby Jones drew acclaim by winning tournaments. As with tennis, women were influential in popularizing this sport. The presence of celebrities and television coverage of tournaments helped establish and maintain interest in golf as a spectator sport.

Professional ice hockey first amassed a following in large metropolitan areas in the 1920s, and continued to grow in popularity and expand its territory in succeeding decades. Although many players on the professional ice hockey teams have been Canadian, the sport has drawn increasing support from American sports fans.

Responding to the American love of watching races and sporting competitions, all manner of other competitive events also have become popular spec-

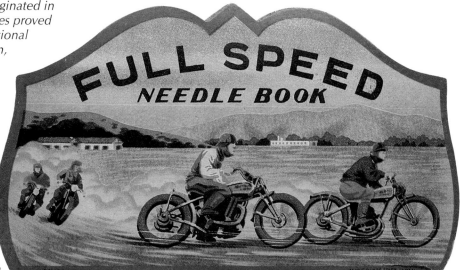

Above: *The soapbox derby, a coasting race for homemade, engineless vehicles, originated in Dayton, Ohio, in 1933. The first races proved so popular that two years later a national competition was organized in Akron, with heavy sponsorship from local tire manufacturers. This Derby Downs racetrack, a three-lane, cement-paved raceway, was constructed in that city in 1936 by the Works Progress Administration (WPA) organized by the government to combat unemployment.* Right: *Motorcycle races continued to attract large audiences in the post-World War II years. This depiction of a race appeared on the cover of a needle packet produced for the American market in occupied Japan.*

tator sports. Among these are competitive skating, sled racing, ski racing and jumping, competitive aquatics, bicycle racing, and such spectacles as roller derbies (which evolved in the 1930s from dance marathons). Races and competitions involving animals also have proven extremely popular, including horse racing, rodeos, greyhound racing (especially in Florida), and dogsled racing (especially in the Northern states).

Races involving motorized vehicles have attracted thousands of spectators. Huge throngs have attended motorcycle, speedboat, and air races. However, automobile races have drawn the largest following. Technological developments in high-speed automobile engines after World War II resulted

in the production of highly diversified and specialized racing cars suitable for drag, track, and road races. Dozens of new tracks were constructed as sites for weekly, monthly, and annual events, which were highly commercialized.

The international Olympic Games have continued to serve as a prime vehicle for popularizing certain spectator sports and raising the most talented athletes to celebrity status. Although they have remained one of the last bastions of amateur sport, an increasing degree of importance has been placed on winning and breaking records. In recent years, following the example set by the United States, the Olympic Games have become as much entertainment extravaganzas as they are sports competitions.

Top: *Harness racing remained a popular spectator sport at county fairgrounds and at specially lighted race tracks that made night racing possible. This photograph by Marion Post Wolcott shows a harness race at the 1940 county horse show and fair in Shelbyville, Kentucky.* Above: *From the time the Piper Aircraft Corporation began to manufacture small planes in 1937, its name became synonymous with low-priced, light airplanes. This Piper J-3 Cub airplane was produced in 1946, during the postwar enthusiasm for flying.* Right: *The efforts of early aviators helped make airplane flying a viable sport as well as a form of transportation. This trophy, produced in 1926 and sponsored by Edsel Ford, was awarded to the winning aircraft of the National Air Commercial Reliability Tour, an annual event held during the 1920s and 1930s to promote the commercial aircraft industry.*

Right: *Automobile "hot rodding" became a highly diversified and commercialized hobby after World War II. Scores of periodicals, such as this December 1961 issue of* Rod & Custom, *kept devotees up to date on the latest trends and styles and suggested ways to improve the performance and appearance of their own vehicles.* Below: *Automobile companies were heavily involved in racing during the 1960s, producing immensely powerful and showy machines. This Ford Mark IV racer, sporting an all-aluminum body held together with an epoxy resin, set new lap and overall speed records at the LeMans race held in 1967.*

JULY 10, 1924

PRICE 15 CENTS

OLYMPIC NUMBER

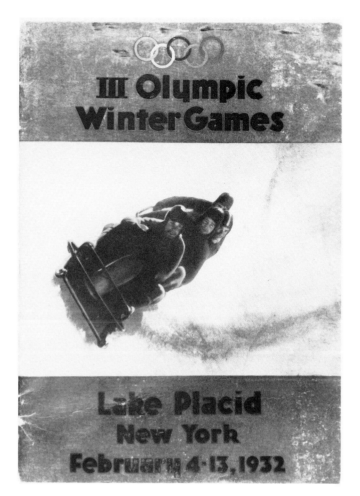

III Olympic
Winter Games

Lake Placid
New York
February 4-13, 1932

Facing page: *The tremendous interest in sports during the 1920s extended to the international Olympic games. This* Life *magazine cover from July 16, 1924, depicts some of the diverse contests that took place at the Olympics held that summer in Paris, France. Above: The Winter Olympics, first organized in 1924, were held in America at Lake Placid, New York, eight years later. The rich variety of events encouraged an enthusiasm for winter sports that has continued ever since. The cover of this 1932 program depicts a bobsled competition.*

Sports for Everyone

According to Dulles, in *America Learns to Play*, 20th-century critics have denounced America as "a nation of onlookers," its people inflicted with "spectatoritis." But in fact, at the same time that spectator sports have become so popular, more people than ever have been actively engaging in sports themselves. Especially since the late 1930s, a far greater number of people have participated in athletic activities than have watched others play.

Extensive sports facilities were added to parks and schools in the 1920s. However, it was during the 1930s that several new developments greatly expanded the scope of public recreation. A new recreation movement, evolving out of the earlier children's play movement, came to the forefront during the Great Depression. Leaders of this movement believed that organized play for people of all ages, not just children, would help solve many of society's problems. They thought that organized recreation would not only help people to relax and recover from work, but would also help the unemployed to organize their free time more productively. It was at this time that sports came to be regarded as hobbies that could provide a way for people to find more meaning and personal fulfillment in their lives.

The Works Progress Administration (WPA), born out of the Great Depression, stimulated this recreation movement by assigning substantial amounts of time and money to expand parks and recreational facilities, including thousands of public tennis courts, baseball diamonds, athletic fields, outdoor basketball courts, and swimming pools. Between 1935 and the beginning of World War II, the WPA spent more than a billion dollars on some 40,000 new sports and recreation facilities.

At the same time, the newly formed Civilian Conservation Corps (CCC) constructed new golf courses, ice-skating rinks, gymnasiums, and ski runs and trails. The National Recreation Association (as the original Playground Association of America was renamed in 1930) helped to furnish equipment and train recreation specialists. All of these organizations ultimately provided the impetus for other city, town, and federal agencies to promote the healthful aspects of adult sports and to devote time and money to organized recreation programs and facilities. By 1953, as many as 2,000 cities were expending over $100 million annually on public recreation.

The enthusiasm for spectator sports, combined with this new interest in adult recreation and the construction of numerous new facilities, encouraged a tremendous number of Americans to engage in sports. Thousands of new public tennis courts made tennis accessible to a wide public. *Hobbies for Everybody*, published in 1934, noted this trend:

Public parks and playgrounds, particularly in the large cities, now abound with tennis courts that may be used for a small fee and rackets and balls can be purchased at prices within the reach of all. An enormous amount of the most healthful

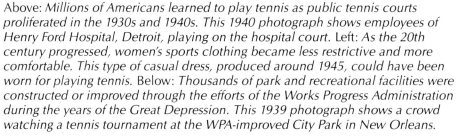

Above: *Millions of Americans learned to play tennis as public tennis courts proliferated in the 1930s and 1940s. This 1940 photograph shows employees of Henry Ford Hospital, Detroit, playing on the hospital court.* Left: *As the 20th century progressed, women's sports clothing became less restrictive and more comfortable. This type of casual dress, produced around 1945, could have been worn for playing tennis.* Below: *Thousands of park and recreational facilities were constructed or improved through the efforts of the Works Progress Administration during the years of the Great Depression. This 1939 photograph shows a crowd watching a tennis tournament at the WPA-improved City Park in New Orleans.*

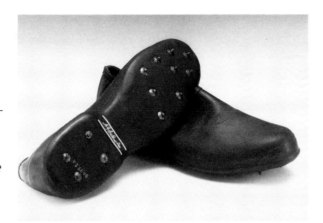

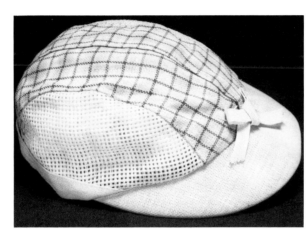

Popular interest in golf led to the development of an array of clothing accessories and specialized equipment. By the mid-20th century this included items like the golf shoes above right, made to offer extra traction and durability; the woman's hat below right, designed to screen out the blazing sun; and packaged golf balls in a range of quality and prices, far right.

and invigorating exercise can be obtained in a short period of time. With daylight saving effective the ordinary business man or woman is able to play three sets of tennis before dinner on any week-day, provided the court is reasonably accessible and hardly a section of the land is without its reasonably accessible court.

In 1939, the *Recreation Yearbook* estimated that 11 million people played tennis.

Similarly, golf became more popular, especially in suburban areas with space for new municipal and private courses. In 1939, an estimated 8 million people played golf, even though course fees, equipment, and the exclusivity of country clubs continued to separate the wealthy and upwardly mobile golfers from the rest of the public. Recommended for older people because it is less strenuous than other sports, golf became a major off-season draw for resorts.

Softball, which developed from indoor and children's games that used a soft or "mush" ball, witnessed a spectacular rise in popularity at this time. Adults were encouraged to play this game in the late 1920s and 1930s in an effort to revive a declining interest in baseball. The National Recreation Association sponsored tournaments and an Amateur Softball Association of America was formed in 1933. Within five years, about 8,000 softball diamonds, many fitted with electric lights for night games, were in use across the country. In 1940, some 300,000 organized softball clubs boasted more than 3 million players. Workplace teams were particularly popular, but many church, school, and college teams also were formed.

Bowling is another sport that gained thousands of new adherents at this time. Inexpensive and casual, bowling became extremely popular with church groups, employee teams, and community leagues. Although often still associated with drinking and gambling, bowling became more respectable as more women took up the game. As the *New York Times Magazine,* April 3, 1949, put it, "Mom took it out from behind the pool room and put it in the church basement." Most of the new alleys constructed at this time were luxuriously outfitted, well lighted, and neatly kept, to increase their appeal to women. By the 1950s, automatic pin setters made the game more enjoyable. In the early 1960s, an estimated 30 million people bowled—more than participated in any other organized sport at that time.

Above: *Baseball games played between teams in formalized leagues or between informal teams chosen at the time of the game, continued to be popular at community events through the 20th century. In this 1940 photograph, residents of Inkster, Michigan, play baseball as part of their town's Independence Day celebration.* Left: *Softball appealed to Americans in search of exercise and relaxation. Playing softball was recommended in this Beautyrest Mattress advertisement from the* Ladies' Home Journal, *April 1943, as a way to "take the tightness out of little-used muscles" and to keep from worrying about "priorities and taxes" during wartime.*

The first skiing club had been formed in 1883 by a group of Norwegians in Red Wing, Minnesota, and skiing had become popular among trendsetters in the 1920s. But participation in winter sports, including skiing, skating, sledding, and ice hockey, reached much higher levels after the first Winter Olympic Games of 1924, and especially so after the 1932 Winter Olympics were held in the United States. New ski slopes and trails were constructed in the 1930s, and vast transportation networks, above all special ski trains, were developed to reach them. Railroad companies, resort owners, and manufacturers of sporting goods and sports clothing con-

tributed to the commercialization of the sport. In 1938, Americans spent some $9 million on skiing, with $6 million alone devoted to the purchase of ski clothing! By 1940, there were some 2 million skiers in the United States, and many communities were holding ski meets.

Technological advances improved and expanded winter sports after World War II. Indoor ice rinks became more numerous, and larger ski slopes with more complex lifts were developed. Ski lodges and resorts expanded to include swimming pools, ice-skating rinks, and nightly entertainment, and ski attire began to influence general trends in fashion.

When natural snow was insufficient, ways were found to create artificial snow, and manmade hills and runs for sledding and tobogganing were constructed by winter resort owners.

The varieties of winter sports also expanded. Motorized snowmobiles were developed, and challenging trails were laid out for them. Cross-country skiing, chiefly pursued by hardy outdoors enthusiasts decades earlier, became a full-blown sport for seekers of a strenuous yet solitary winter sport. Both of these sports became especially popular in the 1970s and 1980s, and were greatly commercialized by resort owners, land developers, and manufacturers of sporting goods and clothing.

In the 1920s, affordable automobiles and mass-produced rifles and shotguns put sport hunting within the means of almost everyone. The number of licensed hunters doubled during that decade. It became necessary to institute conservation controls and elaborate wildlife management programs to help maintain adequate levels of fish and wildlife for sportsmen, and licensing restrictions were enforced more widely. Despite opposition, sportsmen have continually adopted modern technological advances

Above: *By the mid-20th century women's enthusiasm for bowling lent the game a respectability it had never known before. This page from* McCall's *magazine, January 1941, displays the latest fashion in bowling outfits for mothers and daughters.* Below: *Downhill skiing experienced a tremendous boom following the 1932 Winter Olympics. Railroads transported thousands of skiers to New England slopes, and automobiles provided even greater mobility. By 1940, when this photograph of the Cranmore Mountain ski slope in North Conway, New Hampshire, was taken, some 2 million Americans had become devoted skiers.*

to aid them in their hunting activities, including overland vehicles, long-range rifles, and small airplanes and helicopters. There has obviously been less criticism of their resort to newly developed outdoor clothing, artificial heating devices, trail foods, and a tremendous range of other specialized equipment. In 1970 there were over 14 million sport hunters in America, a sign of continued enthusiasm for the sport.

Fishing, too, has become even more widespread as a result of improvements in spinning reels, fishing rods and tackle, and specialized fishing boats. Since the 1950s, artificially created bodies of water have become increasingly popular places to fish, while fly-fishing experienced a revival in the 1970s. The study of fish ecology has given fishing advocates a growing knowledge and understanding of the habits of the gamefish they pursue.

Since the 1930s, trap and skeet shooting have become major participatory sports, providing some

Above: *In the late 1960s and 1970s, snowmobiles were second in popularity only to minibikes as all-terrain sporting vehicles. This trade catalog cover advertises two models of Bolens snowmobiles available in 1967.* Left: *In contrast to downhill skiing, which appealed to those avid for speed and competition, cross-country skiing combined strenuous exercise with solitude. The couple on this cover of a 1953 travel brochure are exploring the backcountry of upstate New York on cross-country skis.*

of the satisfactions of the hunt close to home. These sports have become particularly popular in suburban communities and country clubs; they allow hunters to test their skill during the off-season and also make it possible for nonhunters to compete with them. Participants in both sports can vie for national championships, and both trap and skeet shooting have become part of the Olympic Games.

Swimming has become one of the most popular outdoor participatory sports in America. The quest for a suntan, symbolizing the "healthy glow of youth" in the youth-oriented culture of the 1920s, helped significantly in stimulating interest in swimming. Greater freedom in dress, fewer moral restrictions, and increased construction of swimming pools all contributed to the growing popularity of the sport. In 1939, the *Recreation Yearbook* revealed that 200 million people engaged in swimming at public bathing beaches and in pools. At first pools were constructed in parks and summer resorts, but they spread to motels and suburban back yards after World War II. Diving became a specialized sport of its own.

Above: *Automobiles and less expensive equipment brought hunting within the reach of large numbers of Americans. This 1943 photograph of a triumphant hunter was taken in front of the Ford Motor Company's Rouge plant in Detroit, Michigan.* Below: *With increased interest in target shooting, especially after World War II, rifle clubs proliferated. This club was located in New York City.*

Above: *Attracting all members of the family, swimming became a highly popular sport during the 1920s, as suggested by this photograph, which was taken at Belle Isle Park, Michigan.* Left: *A large assortment of men's and women's bathing suits came on the market as swimming caught the public fancy and as attitudes about modesty became more relaxed. This woolen women's swimsuit is from the 1930s.*

The development of the outboard motor lent great impetus to speedboating. After World War II, the development of artificial lakes and reservoirs and the mass manufacture of all kinds of motorboats allowed great numbers of people to pursue this sport. Other aquatic sports also boomed with the increased number of artificial bodies of water, the manufacture of new equipment, and the interest in outdoor recreation, including water skiing, skin-diving, and scuba diving. Interest in exercise and the desire for solitude helped revive the popularity of rowing and canoeing, while the development of light, efficient craft led to a renewed interest in sailing. By the 1960s, millions of people owned and operated pleasure boats.

The sport of surfing was brought to California from Hawaii just prior to World War I, but became especially popular after World War II. New materials made surfboards lighter, smaller, and more efficient. In the mid-1960s, surfing gained national publicity through the mass media, influencing music, language, and clothing. In the 1980s, windsurfing on boards

In the post-World War II years the number of pools to be found in public parks, resorts, motels, and in suburban back yards increased enormously. As this advertisement for bathing suits from Life *magazine, June 10, 1946, indicates, pool parties became a popular diversion after the war.*

fitted with sails became a widespread sport for both inland and ocean surfing enthusiasts.

Technological developments allowed a large public to pursue various aerial sports. A growing number of people took up the sport of flying, especially after World War II, when kits enabling enthusiasts to build their own planes became available. Improvements in the design of parachutes, allowing for greater accuracy in directing the descent, made sky-diving a sport of growing popularity. The energy shortage and advances in technology during the 1970s contributed to the popularity of "ultralight" planes and hang-gliding. Ballooning also gained a following, due to the development of safer, stronger, and less expensive balloons.

In addition to snowmobiles, a number of motorized land vehicles were used for sport after World War II, including motorcycles, minibikes, jeeps, and dune buggies. Racing cars, however, retained their primacy in competitive motorized sports.

*new, quiet **Evinrudes!** smooth as sailing... horsepower with a* **hush!**

A wide variety of sports and games that were popularized in the 19th century have become even more widespread as participatory sports during the 20th century. This includes games like badminton, volleyball, pool, shuffleboard, and horseshoes, which are played in public recreation centers, resort areas, and in the back yards and basements of private homes. Roller skating, long beloved as an informal pastime for children, was revived again for adults with the construction of new roller rinks and more versatile skates.

Organized sports came to serve as one of the most pervasive forces in the lives of American children, especially boys. Sports and recreation facilities for children continued to expand, while some of the highly organized and bureaucratized adult sports filtered down to the youth level. Nationally organized leagues in some sports were first formed in the 1930s, including Pop Warner football (1930) and Little League baseball (1939). Similar youth programs were formed for basketball and hockey in the early 1950s.

These sports became "big business," as financial sponsors for them came to include business firms, professional sports organizations, Olympic committees, and colleges.

Capitalizing on the youth market, certain pastimes were aimed directly at children and adolescents. Some of them became so popular that they evolved into organized sports, with standardized rules, play variants, and special competitions. These included hoola hoops (especially popular among the young in the late 1950s), skateboards (introduced in California in the early 1960s as "sidewalk surfboards"), and Frisbees (particularly popular in colleges; reportedly introduced after World War II, but standardized by the Wham-O Manufacturing Company in the late 1950s).

Some sports drew a large following as a result of the stress on physical fitness. This campaign began at the urging of President Eisenhower in the 1950s, and gained momentum with the youth fitness programs sponsored by President Kennedy in the early

Facing page: *More economical production methods and greater prosperity brought motorboats within the reach of a larger public in the post-World War II era. This advertisement in* Collier's *magazine, October 15, 1954, assured potential buyers that riding in this motorboat was "blissfully quiet" and "smooth as the glide of a sailboat in a kindly breeze."* Left: *Like many other sports activities, motorcycling as a sport became accessible to the general public after World War II. Although this advertisement in* Collier's *magazine, June 10, 1950, promoted motorcycling as a healthful outdoor activity, its prime appeal was to men who loved the sensation of speed and the thrills that this sport afforded.* Below: *Beach movies geared to the youth market and featuring surfing proved great money-makers in the mid-1960s. The trendsetting movie* Beach Party *(1963), starring teen idols Frankie Avalon and Annette Funicello, set box-office records nationwide soon after its release and undoubtedly spurred the interest in surfing.*

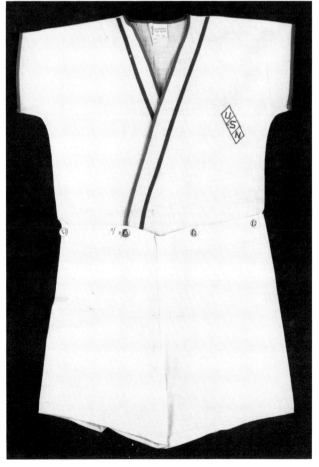

Above: *Carl Statz of Williamsport, Pennsylvania, founded Little League baseball in 1939 as a way of directing the physical energy of youth into constructive channels. At the time it was just one of several highly organized, adult-sponsored programs for the young. This photograph depicts a group of Little Leaguers in Manchester, New Hampshire, in 1954.* Left: *The pervasive influence of sports on children's lives extended to their daily clothing. This muslin play suit, evocative of a baseball uniform, is from around 1930.*

1960s. But it received major impetus in the 1970s as part of a new emphasis on the "inner joys" of maintaining good health and a trim physique.

In a reaction to automobile congestion and air pollution during the late 1960s and the energy shortage of the early 1970s, a vast number of Americans rediscovered the sport of bicycling. Avid cyclists, especially college students and adults living in suburban communities, became a vocal force in the development of bicycle paths and trails. The ready availability of multispeed bicycles, especially in the 1970s and 1980s, made bicycling an even more popular sport throughout the country.

Sports like squash, racquetball, handball, and tennis reached new heights of popularity, both at outdoor and indoor courts. Mountain climbing, backpacking, martial arts, and weight lifting joined

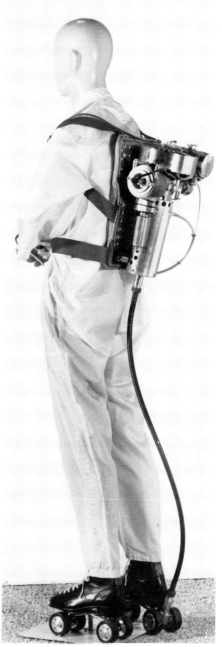

the list of sports recommended for their contribution to fitness. Aerobic and other exercise routines, including those using special machines, were much encouraged, whether performed at health clubs, in classes, or in the privacy of one's home.

But the largest group of fitness advocates were joggers and runners. According to the *New York Times,* December 30, 1979, this group numbered upwards of 20 million during the decade of the 1970s. In 1980, a staggering 14,000 people participated in the annual New York Marathon, while 20,000 more were turned away—a dramatic contrast to the 126 runners who had turned out for the 1970 race. Although the popularity of specific sports has changed, the pursuit of sports for the healthful benefits they provide shows no sign of diminishing.

Above left: *Although an earlier version of shuffleboard had been popular in England for centuries, it assumed its current form in Florida in the years just before and after World War I. Appealing to men and women of all ages, the game continues to be played at hospitals, recreation centers, parks, and at vacation lodgings like the Sarasota Terrace Hotel, depicted in this postcard from around 1960.* Above right: *These motorized roller skates were invented by Antonio Pirello of Detroit around 1956. A pull cord started the engine which, strapped to the rider's back, transmitted power to a differential in the rear axle of the right skate causing it to move at speeds of up to 17 miles per hour. The inventor suggested that these skates be used in races, roller derbies, and roller-skate hockey games, and that they be rented out at rinks on an hourly basis. The skates received worldwide publicity, but were not a commercial success.*

Left: *Improvements in the mechanisms of bicycles during the late 1960s and 1970s allowed them to go farther and faster, while innovations in the materials used for their construction made them more affordable for the general user. This 10-speed Schwinn bicycle, produced in 1970, faced fierce competition from bicycles made by foreign manufacturers. Below left: The ''Tour of the Scioto River Valley'' (TOSRV) symbolized the ''Great American Bicycle Boom'' more than any other event, claimed a 1975 brochure. Originating in 1962, this annual bicycle tour between Columbus and Portsmouth, Ohio, grew to involve thousands of riders from across the country and abroad. This snapshot from the early 1970s shows cyclist Calvin Law and other riders preparing for the two-day, 210-mile tour. Below: Protective helmets became an important safety measure for serious bicycle riders. This helmet from around 1970 was manufactured by Erb Plastic, Inc., of Woodstock, Georgia.*

Increasingly, it is unusual to find a person of any age who is not involved with or interested in a sport. Two hundred years ago, sports in America were engaged in by few, disapproved of by many, and, for the most part, took up an extremely limited portion of people's lives. During the 19th and early 20th centuries, both spectator and participatory sports were organized and expanded so that they became national in scope.

Since the 1930s, sports have become an important part of the daily lives of men and women of all ages. Indeed, all Americans are *expected* to devote a certain amount of their leisure time to sports. Children grow up with a knowledge of and interest in a variety of sports, carrying their enthusiasm into adulthood. John Tunis's remarks in "The Business of American Sports," remain true today:

To this religion of sports then, the American turns naturally. For sports come to him instinctively, he is taught to hit, kick, and throw balls of all kinds, baseballs, footballs, golf balls, tennis balls, basketballs, and so forth, from his earliest youth. His boyhood heroes are never soldiers, sailors or explorers as in other lands; they are athletes, airmen, champion football or golf players. The young American cannot go through a school or a college without being obliged to fall into the habit of playing games; in some places this is compulsory. He cannot as a rule graduate from a university without knowing how to swim, without taking part in games as a regular part of the curriculum. No wonder, therefore, that the American nation, trained to think, play, and compete in athletics, is sport mad.

The enthusiasm for physical fitness in the 1970s and 1980s has led to a great specialization in foot apparel. This early 1980s poster for Kinney shoes points out the many sports for which these shoes were designed.

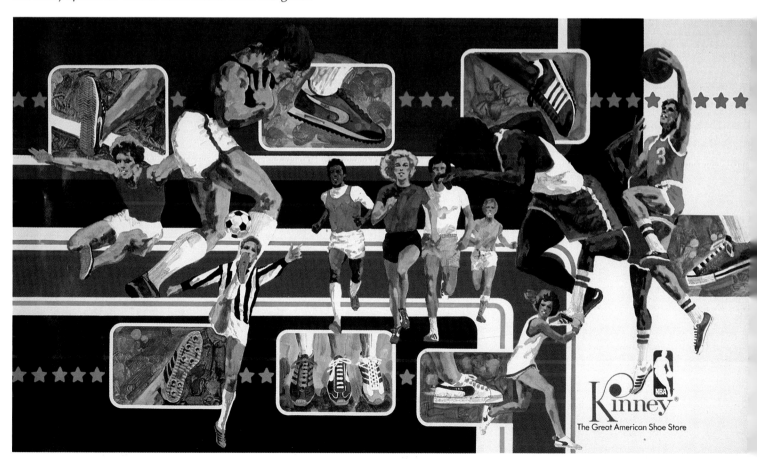

GETTING AWAY:
Travel and Tourism

*A*mericans have always been known as a restless, wandering people. But their appetite for travel has not been motivated solely by the search for new opportunities; early on they began to display a predilection for travel as an end in itself. Since the 18th century, traveling for pleasure has progressively become less exclusive and, as it became a feasible diversion for larger numbers of people, it also became more commercialized.

The nature of pleasure travel largely has been shaped by two considerations: the traveler's desire to go to a particular place, and the means available to get there. Among the motivations for pleasure trips have been the search for better health, relaxation, knowledge, and adventure. These inducements have grown with the increasing availability of discretionary time and money, and with the urge to escape from the country's spreading urban-industrial environment.

At the same time, the rise of rapid and efficient modes of transportation has allowed vast numbers of Americans to go increasingly farther more cheaply and more comfortably. Nevertheless, despite these innovations, large numbers of the population have been unable to afford more than day-long outings or visits to relatives.

Before World War I, in what can best be described as a ''ripple effect,'' loners led the way to scenic areas in search of solitude. They were followed by members of the upper class, with the middle class in hot pursuit. As resort areas and other travel destinations became crowded, the loners and wealthiest travelers struck out in new directions in search of more isolated areas. New forms of transportation in the 20th century, especially automobiles and airplanes, democratized travel and made the experiences of travelers more homogeneous.

Other important factors in the development of pleasure travel included the availability of more free time with increasingly shortened work weeks and, eventually, with the institution of paid vacations. Also significant was the relaxation of religious restrictions on Sundays in many parts of the country.

Facing page: *World's fairs and expositions served as popular vacation destinations for tourists during the late 19th and 20th centuries. Coming at the end of a decade of worldwide economic depression, the 1939–40 New York World's Fair advertised in this poster placed a distinct emphasis on consumerism as the means to prosperity and social unity.*

These developments coincided with changes in attitude, leading to the commonly held view that "getting away" was as much a necessity for one's physical and mental health as it was a pastime.

During the 19th century, tourism evolved into a specialized and complex industry. The word "tourist," denoting a person who travels for pleasure, appeared in print as early as 1800. Many studies in recent years have attempted to reexamine the phenomenon of tourism. In one of these works, The Image, or What Happened to the American Dream *(1962), historian Daniel Boorstin pointed out that the word "travel" is related to the word "travail," meaning work. Originally the term signified a laborious or troublesome journey. "Travelers" engage in active, strenuous work; "tourists" are more likely to be passive pleasure-seekers who expect interesting things to happen to them. The extreme example of the tourist experience is the package tour, in which attractions are pleasantly and conveniently "sold in packages."*

Boorstin maintained that because tourists seek to confirm the expectations they have conceived prior to reaching their destinations, attractions like resort areas, world's fairs, national parks, and historical sites have been purposely structured and promoted to attract and satisfy them. Even in the 19th century, obvious or "contrived" attractions like historic markers and scenic lookouts offered the "experience" of these spots in a form that required a minimum of thought and effort. These deliberately contrived attractions, which Boorstin described as "pseudo-events," have become major aspects of pleasure travel and have proven highly profitable for the tourist industry.

A spate of roadbuilding during the early decades of the 19th century, and the availability of passenger stagecoaches like this one from the 1830s, increased the numbers of people who ventured away from home. At the same time poor road maintenance and unregulated coach service, combined with unpredictable weather, made many trips less than pleasurable.

Canal travel was slow, but much smoother than overland journeys. Following the completion of the Erie Canal to Niagara Falls in 1826, a canal tour across New York State became fashionable for the well-to-do. This 1830s engraving depicts an excursion boat approaching the complex canal-lock system at Lockport, 30 miles east of Buffalo, New York.

AMERICANS BECOME TRAVEL CONSCIOUS: TO THE CIVIL WAR

Travel before the 19th century was an arduous, grueling experience for Americans. Heavy expenditures of time and money, poor roads, and inadequate modes of transportation tended to limit trips primarily to ones that were absolutely necessary. Adventurous youths and members of the upper class were most likely to take trips for the sole purpose of pursuing pleasure.

As modes of transportation and roads improved in the early 19th century, pleasure travel became more viable. Passenger stagecoaches traversed new and improved roads, usually dropping travelers off at inns, taverns, or private homes for overnight stops. Roads, weather, and lodging were quite unpredictable, however, and stagecoach travelers often found that unwittingly they had embarked on an adventure.

Improvements in water travel transformed inland journeys into pleasure trips rather than ordeals. Developed in the 1820s, travel via canals was admittedly slow (about four miles per hour), but smoother and far more comfortable than overland travel. When conveniences like sleeping and dining facilities were added to canal boats, this means of travel became fashionable for a time. After the initial novelty wore off, however, complaints about slowness, tedious meals, mosquitoes, and low bridges increased, and soon canals were being used primarily for commercial transportation.

By the 1840s, elegant steamboats carried passengers across major lakes and rivers. Steamboats were faster and more luxurious than canal boats, and cheaper and more comfortable than stagecoaches. But it was the development of the railroads from the 1830s on that added a new dimension to travel in America. The 3,000 miles of railroad track in place by 1840 had tripled by 1850, traversing almost every state east of the Mississippi River. Until the Civil War, however, railroad travel remained far from comfortable. Accidents were frequent, and travelers spent a great deal of time and money changing trains because of the lack of a unified gauge system among

From the 1830s on railroads added a new dimension and flavor to American travel. Although still dangerous and unpredictable, trains were the fastest means of transportation available for long-distance travel. This engraving depicts an American railway car "of the best sort" from around 1850.

the railroad networks in various parts of the country. Nevertheless, trains were the fastest vehicles yet, traveling at speeds of up to 15 and 20 miles per hour, and reaching areas that had been inaccessible to most people a generation earlier.

Despite the rigors of travel, increasing numbers of Americans embarked on pleasure trips. Among them were explorers, adventurers, government surveyors, and merchants. The latter often engaged in pleasure trips while pursuing their business interests. Others were writers, poets, and painters seeking solace among the beauties of nature. As accounts and pictures of newly discovered scenic areas were published, an increasing number of travelers set out to experience their splendor at first hand. The wealthy, able to afford the time and expense of the trips, were among the first of the avid travelers. As early as 1826, Timothy Flint wrote in *Recollections of the Last Ten Years* that the better classes were carrying the desire

for travel "to a passion and a fever." In time, less well-to-do people also undertook pleasure trips, as new transportation methods enabled them to travel great distances at less expense. As the desire to escape the constraints of crowded urban life became stronger, and as epidemic diseases like cholera ravaged the cities, travel gained even more appeal.

Foreign visitor Francis J. Grund, author of *The Americans,* published in 1837, marveled that:

> *There is scarcely an individual in so reduced circumstances as to be unable to afford his "dollar or so," to travel a couple of hundred miles from home, in order to see the country and the improvements which are going on.*

By the mid-19th century, the tradition of leaving home for a day-long excursion or a seasonal vacation was well under way.

Destinations

People who could afford only short excursions away from home took advantage of an increasing number of scenic picnic groves and rural retreats located on the outskirts of towns and cities. These included some rural cemeteries, like Mt. Auburn Cemetery outside Boston, and Greenwood Cemetery on Long Island, both specifically landscaped to provide reposeful surroundings. At first many of these places were intended exclusively for the upper class, but before long they were being frequented by all classes of people seeking a respite from city crowds and daily routines.

Resorts became the favorite destinations of long-distance travelers. Usually they offered magnificent scenery and pleasant climates. The oldest and most fashionable resorts centered around springs that were reputedly laden with health-giving minerals. Rationalizing that their visits were in the interest of good health, the wealthy transformed these watering-places from invalid retreats into bustling social centers. Relaxation and "taking the waters" were soon superseded by sporting pastimes, public entertainment, dancing, and railroad or stagecoach excursions to nearby attractions.

The increasing scope of railroad and canal travel led to the discovery of mineral springs farther inland. Saratoga, New York, was the most popular and fashionable of these inland spas, sporting a hotel as early as 1803. Before long, however, Saratoga became known for its drinking, dancing, and "looseness" rather than its health-giving qualities. To escape the heat and epidemics associated with the summer months, Southern planters and their families fled to Saratoga by the thousands until sectional political tensions forced them to stay at home. As the Civil War became imminent, they turned instead to Southern resorts like White Sulphur Springs in what is now West Virginia.

Resorts also grew up around various natural wonders that had been visited by sightseers since the late 18th century. The most popular of these curiosities was Niagara Falls, in New York State. Thronged with visitors after the Erie Canal reached it in 1826, Niagara Falls quickly became commercialized. As early as the 1830s visitors complained about "the abominable fungus" of souvenir vendors polluting its environs.

When sea bathing caught on as a healthful and invigorating pastime, dozens of beaches along the

By the mid-19th century improved means of travel via railroad and steamboat encouraged women to attempt the kinds of long-distance trips they had previously avoided. The heightened interest in travel led to the design of more efficient luggage, including the all-purpose traveling case humorously pictured in this engraving from Harper's Weekly, *August 22, 1857.*

NEW PATENT TRAVELING-CASE.

Facing page top: *During the 1850s the most favored destinations for urban dwellers were outlying parks and picnic groves that could be visited on a day trip. On a Sunday afternoon, for example, New Yorkers of all classes could enjoy beer and other refreshments, and the live musical and theatrical performances, mechanical pleasure rides, and games and sports depicted in this engraving of Jones's Woods, which appeared in* Harper's Weekly, November 5, 1859. Facing page bottom: *During the early 19th century, Nahant, Massachusetts, became a popular coastal resort for upper-class Bostonians. This engraving portrays some of the amusements available to visitors to that spot around 1830. Above: During the 1850s Newport, Rhode Island, became the most fashionable resort on the East Coast. Sea bathing had become the rage in Newport's fairly sheltered waters and would soon become popular at other beach resorts as well.* The Bathe at Newport *appeared in* Harper's Weekly, *September 4, 1858.*

East Coast—especially those close to cities—attracted bathers. Some beaches became so popular that special boardinghouses were built to accommodate the crowds that flocked to them. In several areas, lavish hotels and resorts eventually replaced these boardinghouses. As new beach resorts became crowded, members of the upper class moved to less accessible spots. Newport, Rhode Island, soon emerged as the most fashionable resort for the wealthy. However, even Newport was soon besieged by tourists, and the old elite cordoned itself off from the ordinary folk by erecting luxurious and secluded private "cottages."

In contrast to the elegance and exclusiveness of Newport, the beach resorts of Atlantic City, New Jersey, and Coney Island, New York, became popular in the late 1850s as summer havens for the middle class. There, everyone could take advantage of the mixed bathing made popular at Newport by the rich.

As these East Coast resorts became crowded, areas farther north and inland were developed. After a few appreciative artists directed attention to Mount Desert Island, on the coast of Maine, it was invaded by "armies of summer pilgrims." Others sought a respite from city life and summer crowds at more tranquil and less accessible resorts on inland lakes like Lake George, New York, and Lake Winnepesaukee, New Hampshire. By 1860, the English novelist Anthony Trollope noted in *North America,* that "It is the habit of Americans to go to some watering-

The breathtaking views to be seen from the summit of Mt. Washington, New Hampshire, made this mountain a popular destination for sightseers. By 1849 some 5,000 travelers had climbed the steep path to the top, and luxurious hotels had been constructed at its summit to accommodate those who wished to stay overnight.

place every summer, that is, to some place either of sea water or of inland waters."

Mountains held a particular appeal for summer travelers because of their healthful air and scenic views. First made known by artists and writers, many mountain retreats became popular stops on sightseeing routes as well as seasonal destinations for those escaping the cities for the summer. Mt. Washington in New Hampshire and the Catskills in New York were early tourist destinations, with the initially primitive shelters there giving way to luxurious resorts by the 1840s and 1850s. As new, more secluded resort areas were sought, the Adirondacks area in upper New York State attracted attention as a place where people could relax and regain their health.

Before long, critics attacked the resorts for encouraging false responses to nature in the frenzied search for continual amusement. The revelry and gay life of the resorts were severely condemned by ministers and other like-minded people. Such critics found more appropriate opportunities for relaxation at a number of Methodist camp meetings like the ones at Ocean Grove and Round Lake, New Jersey, and at Eastham, Massachusetts. There they could count on finding healthful activities and sociability

in what they considered to be a moral atmosphere.

Both rural and urban residents visited a variety of cities in search of pleasure and novelty. Cities like New York, Boston, Philadelphia, and Baltimore offered live entertainment and exciting sporting events. By the 1850s, cities located farther inland, such as Pittsburgh, Cincinnati, and New Orleans, also had become popular travel destinations. Foreign and American tourists alike enthusiastically visited industrial, civic, and social institutions to observe the nation's rapid growth at first hand. In 1853, the first international exposition held in America, at the Crystal Palace in New York City, encouraged Americans to compare their own industrial and cultural progress with that of the rest of the world.

Beginning in the 1830s, improvements in steamships made transatlantic pleasure trips more viable for Americans. Artists, writers, students, and members of the upper class, in particular, embarked on trips to Europe. The Grand Tour, which usually included England, France, and Italy, with the addition of briefer excursions into Switzerland, Germany, and the Low Countries, was well on its way to becoming a defined itinerary for future American tourists visiting the European continent.

TOURISM GETS ORGANIZED: 1865 TO 1915

Following the Civil War, the number of pleasure travelers grew dramatically. The combination of increasing prosperity and lower travel costs swelled the ranks of those who could afford to travel. A growing number of people of all classes sought to escape the cities, while the relaxation of religious restrictions on Sundays provided yet another impetus to travel. By the end of the 19th century, getting away for "periodical rest and change" had become a "must" for those who could afford it. As the June 1909 edition of *Cook's Excursionist* warned:

> *The "dull boy" who takes all work and no play, is outclassed by his bright and energetic competitor who has learned the value of occasional recreation and change.*

The desire to travel was stimulated by a spate of books, guides, and accounts that were widely read at this time. A number of new magazines, including *Outing* (1881), *Outdoor Life* (1898), and *Travel* (1901), specialized in travel subjects. Some transportation companies even published their own travel periodi-

Right: *Organized to encourage technological innovation and to bolster international trade, world's fairs served as great attractions both for local residents and for visitors to cities. New York's 1853 World's Fair of the Works of Industry of All Nations (also known as the New York Crystal Palace Exposition), pictured on this soda-water bottle, was America's first international fair.* Below: *By the mid-19th century, the promise of a pleasant transatlantic steamship voyage encouraged an increasing number of Americans to visit their "Old World" homelands. But the going was not totally free of vexation, as this engraving from Harper's Weekly, July 25, 1857, suggests. The illustration, depicting the departure of a Mr. Roe and family, was accompanied by the remark, "We gather that the embarkation of the Roe family on board the steamer last year was a severe and trying operation."*

Improved modes of transportation in the post-Civil War years increased the possibilities of "getting away" for vacations. This engraving from Harper's Weekly, *August 1, 1868, shows throngs of New Yorkers at the railroad station, heading for the country during a particularly "torrid term" that summer.*

cals. Among these was the Southern Pacific Railroad, whose *Sunset* magazine marketed the pleasures of tourism to a large public.

Newspapers also abounded with travel suggestions, advertisements, and travel accounts. Starting in 1867, the *New York Tribune* was the first to include a column of travel tips and information. In 1906 both the *New York Times* and the *Tribune* began to include Sunday travel sections. Americans also were spurred to travel by paintings, prints, stereoscopic views, illustrated promotional literature, and a growing number of picture postcards and snapshots depicting scenic spots.

Especially significant to the expansion of pleasure travel at this time was the development of a standardized travel network on a growing number of passenger railroad and steamship lines. These forms of travel offered regular schedules and predictable routes. Both trains and steamships became increasingly more comfortable and luxurious in their

appointments, giving travelers a feeling of elegance and sophistication.

The proliferation and increased reliability of the railroads checked the zeal for road improvement, and gradually lessened the use of inland waterways. Railroad mileage quintupled between 1865 and 1885 as the railroad networks spanned the United States. Fierce competition led to the development of faster and larger trains and improved service. Between 1885 and 1900, railroad passenger traffic increased almost 70 percent. Improvements in the design and manufacture of passenger cars reduced the cost of railroad travel as well as ensuring greater comfort and safety. Pullman's comfortable, indeed elegant, railroad cars—beginning with the sleeping cars of the early post-Civil War years—set a high standard for the railroad industry as a whole. By the 1890s, railroads offered special excursion rates that substantially increased the number of those who could afford long-distance trips.

During the first two decades of the 20th century, railroads continued to dominate long-distance public transportation. In 1915, almost a billion train tickets were sold, about triple the figure for 1885. Because it remained the chief mode of transportation for the multitude not yet able to buy cars, the railroad acquired the nickname of the "poor man's automobile."

During the 1890s and into the early years of the 20th century, urban mass transportation also improved dramatically. More efficient, electrically powered trolley cars replaced many horse-drawn omnibuses and cable cars, while larger cities built underground or elevated rapid transit systems. These advances in urban mass transportation allowed the general populace to undertake day excursions and outings.

Above right: *Portable cameras developed by the end of the 19th century allowed amateur photographers to capture their vacations on film. This Pony Premo No. 5 camera was manufactured in 1891 by the Rochester Optical Company of Rochester, New York. Right: Snapshots helped travelers relive their journeys, as well as encouraging their friends and families to undertake similar trips. As this 1901 snapshot makes clear, the placement of the people being photographed was often carefully planned.*

Facing page: *Railroad travel during the 19th century not only tied travelers to rigorous schedules, but also imposed on them codes of behavior and dress considered appropriate to public places. These women's traveling costumes were depicted in* Demorest's Family Magazine, *June 1876.* Right: *This 1890s domed trunk for railroad travel was modeled after earlier stagecoach trunks designed to withstand the stress of baggage handling. Its interior features a removable bonnet box for the convenience of female travelers. In the early 20th century such cumbersome trunks were replaced by lighter, hand-grip luggage.* Below: *Between the Civil War and World War I railroads became the dominant form of long-distance travel, offering a structured travel experience to a specific destination. As reflected in this postcard from around 1910, railroad stations were centers of lively activity.*

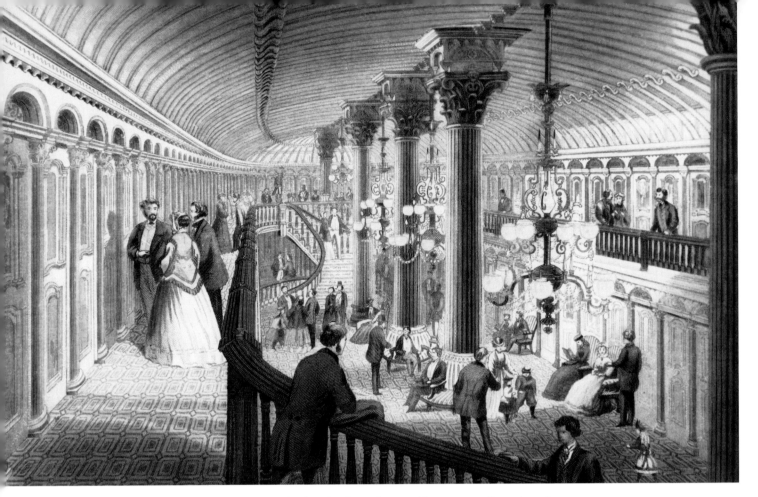

Above: *In the post-Civil War years the levels of comfort and luxury on all modes of transportation increased markedly. Formal dress and high standards of decorum were the rule on trips on this elaborately outfitted Hudson River steamer of the early 1880s.* Facing page: *By 1900 American tourists were dominating the passenger lists of transatlantic steamers. The increasing comfort of steamship travel is reflected in this advertisement for Ivory soap, which appeared in the* Ladies' Home Journal, *July 1903.*

The tremendous popularity of the safety bicycle in the 1890s began to refocus attention on the road for the first time in several decades. Heeding the promotion of manufacturers and the encouragement of printed travel accounts, millions of bicyclists fled from "the psychic and moral void of the city" to the promised peace and serenity of the countryside. For those who could afford it (the cost of a bicycle still averaged a rather expensive $100 in 1895), the bicycle's convenience and flexibility helped to offset the growing dissatisfaction with public transportation. In "Twenty Years of Cycling" (*Fortnightly Review*, August 1897), J. and E. R. Pennell commented on the superiority of cycling over public modes of travel as follows:

[A]s [the cyclist] rides on, there is absolutely nothing to shut out the prospect; no fellow passengers to dispute it with him, no carriage top to obscure it, no silly driver to intrude inane remarks.

The popularity of bicycle touring not only led to a renewed interest in road improvement, but also revived almost obsolete travel services along the roadside. Wherever the bicyclist went, proprietors of inns and hotels geared up for business. An article in the *New York Times*, July 28, 1895, entitled "On the Old Merrick Turnpike," noted:

The truck farmers, whose produce-laden wagons could formerly be seen at any time in great numbers stopping at the various road houses, now hurry over this portion of their cityward journey, or take other routes to avoid "them dern bicycle fellers." . . . *Bicycle riders, the road house keepers have found, are a better class to cater to . . . . Not only are their numbers greater, but they spend money more freely . . . . Hence they have altered the character of their hotels entirely. The names once so common of "Farmer's Home," "Marketman's Hotel," etc., have been supplanted by "Bicyclers' Retreat," "Wheelman's Rest," and*

ONE of the greatest conveniences travelers can take with them
for their own exclusive use is a supply of Ivory Soap. It
will save them much annoyance and discomfort. To have a pure
soap always at hand is a great source of satisfaction. Ivory Soap
is a quick and thorough cleanser, and speedily removes the dirt
and stain of travel.　　　IT FLOATS.

Above: *As bicycling became popular local clubs organized and sponsored long-distance tours. Extended trips like this 1885 tour to Niagara Falls not only helped revive the use of roads for pleasure travel, but also encouraged a general interest in cycling. Facing page: Periodicals and newspapers abounded in bicycle touring suggestions and activities. This 1895 advertising poster marked out a pleasant route for cyclists north of New York City.*

similar names. Every hotel keeper has supplied himself with a foot pump and repair kit for the use of the wheelmen.

Ironically, while trying to escape from the city, bicyclists ended up by bringing urban amenities with them to the roadside.

What the bicycle tourist began, the automobile tourist perfected. Not only did roads and roadside services improve tremendously, but the automobile itself represented the greatest comfort, flexibility, convenience, and independence of any vehicle thus far used for pleasure travel.

Before around 1905, the high cost of purchasing, maintaining, and operating an automobile kept it primarily as a "plaything" for members of the upper class, who looked on motoring as a fast, exciting replacement for sport carriage driving. As early as the 1890s, members of this "motor fraternity" enthusiastically participated in races, meets, and group tours.

Travel guides for motorists advanced beyond anything imagined by bicyclists. They were prepared and published by such organizations as the American Automobile Association, founded in 1902, as well as by dozens of smaller highway associations and local touring clubs.

Like the bicycle, the automobile freed travelers from the "bondage of the timetable." Its slow speed (in contrast to the railroad) and the freedom and intimacy it allowed, were nostalgically compared to earlier travel by stagecoach and carriage. Others equated the automobile with a return to an active, "strenuous" life, an individual and spiritual test against hardship in contrast to relatively smooth and passive transportation on a train or ship.

During World War I, frustration with public transportation increased, while the comfort and safety of the automobile improved. Better highways and cheaper, more dependable automobiles portended the transformation of motoring into a major means of pleasure travel for the public at large. In the years after World War I, the growing comfort and speed of the newer models belied the earlier likening of automobiles with both the hardships and the leisurely pace of stagecoach travel.

Between the Civil War and World War I, pleasure travel was organized and promoted on a national scale. The desire of many more people to travel and the improvements in transportation led to the development of a full-fledged travel industry. The tremendous expansion of promotional literature, the growth of travel agencies offering standardized package tours, and the introduction of conveniences like travelers' checks in the 1890s, further facilitated pleasure travel and the growth of tourism.

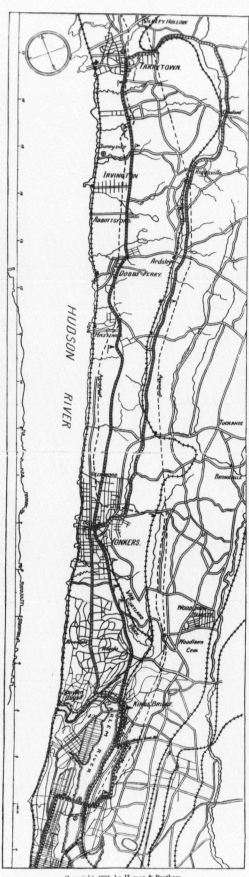

BICYCLE ROAD MAPS

IN

HARPER'S ROUND TABLE

PRICE FIVE CENTS
ON ALL NEWS STANDS

Left: *The cost, upkeep, and operation of automobiles limited them to "playthings" for the wealthy until around 1905. This 1904 Packard Touring car, which sold for a then-phenomenal $3,000, was designed to compete with the power, luxury, and quality of similar European models. Below: The wealthy and adventurous were the first to attempt long-distance trips by automobile. Although faced with many obstacles, including resentment from horse owners, unpredictable weather, bad roads, and frequent mechanical problems with their cars, groups like this one forged on to their destinations inspired by a sense of freedom and independence lacking in railroad travel.*

By the end of the 19th century excursion steamers offered day trips for sightseers. Excursions on the Hudson River's Dayline steamer were particularly popular for New Yorkers wishing to escape the city. This photograph was taken around 1905.

Heading Farther Afield

Short day excursions were the easiest, least expensive, and thus the most possible pleasure trips for the average person at this time. By the 1890s, railroads offered trips by day coach or weekend "sleeper" to neighboring towns, especially for planned community celebrations and sporting events. Steamboats also ran excursion trips along rivers, around bays, and to popular bathing beaches.

At the same time, to encourage weekend business, trolley companies developed their own recreation grounds on the outskirts of cities and towns. Trolleys also allowed people to explore their hometowns. They appealed especially to the working classes, who had little other means of escape from their often cramped quarters.

For those who chose to undertake more extended vacations, resorts continued as the favorite destination. Large resort hotels, often associated with railroad or steamship lines, were geared increasingly to a middle-class clientele as the wealthy moved to more exclusive summer homes. Resorts promised healthful pursuits, relaxation, and a change of scenery and climate, as well as pleasures and luxuries not available at home. The veranda, where guests relaxed and engaged in idle conversation, became the symbol of the leisurely atmosphere of resort hotels. Women and children predominated at these hotels, their vacations paid for by the heads of the household, whose economic viability and social status were secured by obsessive attention to their business careers.

As more Americans found their way to resort areas, tourist services and contrived attractions inevitably followed. Day excursions from the resort hotels by horseback, horse-drawn vehicle, railroad, or boat became extremely popular. Souvenir shops, photographers, ice-cream parlors, and other refreshment stands abounded near many resort hotels. Live entertainment and other amusements directed at tourists proliferated. Important among these were amusement parks, the first of which were built at the seaside resort of Coney Island, New York, in 1895. (*See "Going Out."*)

Continuing the pre-Civil War trend, the major resort areas generally centered around mineral

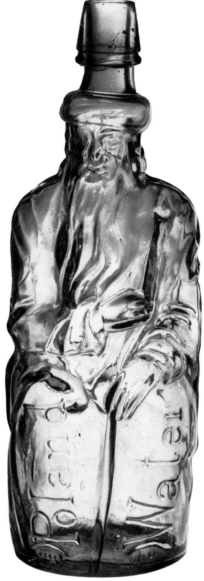

Above: *The spread of railroads after the Civil War made the once-exclusive spa of Saratoga Springs accessible to a broader clientele. A horse-racing track, added in the mid-1860s, inspired even more people to attempt the journey. Guidebooks like this one from 1882 described the town's hostelries, mineral springs, and sporting events for the first-time visitor. Above right: As early as the 1820s, the bottling and sale of spring waters had become a thriving business. Once the medicinal value of the water at Poland Springs, Maine, was established in the 1850s, it was bottled and sold throughout the country, even in the renowned mineral-spring town of Saratoga! This bottle was produced between 1870 and 1890 for Hiram Ricker and Sons, who owned the property on which the Poland Springs were located.*

springs, magnificent scenery, or a comfortable climate. Fashionable spas like Saratoga Springs and White Sulphur Springs continued to draw the well-to-do. Springs even farther inland, like French Lick, Indiana, and Hot Springs, Arkansas, also became popular. By the 1870s, greater accessibility to these springs attracted what an article in the *Independent*, June 1, 1911, recalled as a more "dense, democratic, and vulgar" clientele. In seeking privacy from the increasing hordes of vacationers, members of the upper class began to frequent mineral springs in Colorado's Rocky Mountains. Colorado Springs became a particularly fashionable spot for East Coast socialites to visit during the 1870s, although many criticized it for being overcrowded while lacking the amenities offered by resorts in the East.

Seaside resorts continued to be as crowded as ever. Newport remained the most exclusive, while a succession of lesser communities, such as Long Branch, New Jersey, and various beaches along the Long Island coast rose and fell in favor. By the 1890s, however, even Newport was being invaded by "mammoth loads of excursionists," people of modest means who crowded the beaches and tried to catch a glimpse of the palatial summer homes with their beautifully landscaped grounds.

As in the case of the mineral spring resorts, the wealthy responded by seeking ever more distant watering places like Bar Harbor, Maine, and the Thousand Islands area of the St. Lawrence River. The beaches of Florida also became fashionable winter

destinations, and luxurious resorts and private estates multiplied there. Palm Beach, accessible by private yacht or railroad car, was particularly favored. By the 1880s, seacoast destinations in California, such as San Francisco, San Diego, and Monterey, were accessible by rail to those with plenty of time and money.

For the less well-to-do, smaller hotels, cottages, and boardinghouses provided accommodations at seaside and lakeside resort areas. Denominationally sponsored summer resorts and campgrounds, often located on the sites of earlier camp-meeting grounds, provided recreation and relaxation in a morally inspiring atmosphere. The New Jersey shore sported

Immense hotels were constructed to accommodate the great influx of people of "modest means" who were patronizing resort areas by the 1870s. The passion for sea bathing was in full swing by the time this sheet music honoring the Long Island, New York, resort of Brighton Beach was published in 1883.

At the elite Florida resort of Palm Beach vacationers could frequently be spotted relaxing in hand-pushed rolling chairs, as in this turn-of-the-century photograph showing the avenue in front of the Royal Poinciana Hotel. Rolling chairs were introduced to Atlantic City in an effort to convey the sense of luxury and refinement associated with the more fashionable resort areas like Palm Beach.

a number of these, including ones at Ocean Grove and Asbury Park. Several towns modeled after the original Chautauqua site in upstate New York also served as summer resorts, providing instruction and entertainment within an uplifting environment.

Coney Island and Atlantic City became more crowded than ever. Both had begun as relatively quiet resort areas, until commercialized attractions superseded the lure of their beaches and scenery. A boardwalk erected in 1870 in Atlantic City soon became a crowded promenade lined with concessions, a place to "see and be seen." This resort came to be known as a "Mecca of Millions," where the middle and working classes could imitate the ways of the rich. The size and variety of its amusement areas made Coney Island particularly famous during the first decade of the 20th century. Heavy visitation encouraged further expansion, and by 1900 both Coney Island and Atlantic City sported numerous concessions, contrived attractions, live entertainments, and mechanical rides.

Mountain resorts continued to cater to upper-class vacationers until, like other types of resorts, they experienced an influx of a more mixed clientele, and old hotels were replaced by new, larger ones.

Resorts in New York's Catskills and in New Hampshire's White Mountains remained popular, but people with more time, money, and the desire for exclusivity sought relaxation in the less accessible Adirondacks area of upper New York State and in the Rockies in the West. As modest hotels sprouted in the Adirondacks, the wealthy moved to private camps and estates in more secluded areas.

By the 1890s, the large resort hotel was beginning to lose some of its popularity. Vacationers increasingly expressed concern about the heavy food, outmoded sanitary facilities, and overheated, badly ventilated rooms of these large establishments. Many wanted some relief from the imposed idleness of traditional resort life and looked to hiking, horseback riding, bicycling, tennis, and golf to provide some vigorous activity. Growing numbers of middle-class families began to rent rooms in farmhouses and smaller hotels, as well as summer cottages so as to be in closer contact with nature and "old-fashioned rural values." Entire middle-class families—now including the tired, overworked men of the household—began to vacation together. Some pundits advocated vacationing in farmhouses or cottages as a way of cementing family unity.

Right: *This 1880s omnibus saw daily service at the Hotel del Monte in Monterey County, California, a grand hotel for fashionable tourists located at the end of the Western travel circuit. Reportedly the largest hotel omnibus of its time, this vehicle transported guests across the hotel's "twenty-six acres of paradise," which included a golf course, polo field, racetrack, tennis courts, and glass-enclosed bathing pavilion. The vehicle, with its characteristic rear door and longitudinal facing seats, remained in operation until 1928. Right below: Although San Francisco had been accessible to well-to-do tourists by the 1870s, Southern California did not become a viable destination for the more general public until railroad travel became less expensive at the end of the century. This railroad advertisement from the Saturday Evening Post, February 21, 1903, emphasizes the state's year-round mild climate.*

Go Where Comfort Is

You can't be comfortable at home and it is useless to try.
To be comfortable you must go where comfort is — California.
In California — even in midwinter — wraps and overcoats are unnecessary. The sun shines bright and clear, and there is just enough "snap" in the air to make it invigorating; just enough warmth to tempt you to spend all day and every day out-of-doors.
In California — even in midwinter — you can hunt, bathe and play golf. You can catch the biggest fish ever snared by hook and line. You can pick flowers, climb mountains, go a-picnicking. or stroll through the prettiest valleys in America; palms and orange groves all about you and the bluest of blue skies above you.
The way to go to California is via the

Golden State Limited

Newest, handsomest and most luxuriously equipped of trans-continental trains.

Leaves Chicago daily at 7.45 P. M ; Kansas City at 10.40 A. M. Less than three days to Los Angeles. Through cars to Pasadena, Los Angeles, Santa Barbara and San Francisco. Lowest altitudes and most southerly course of any line across the continent. Compartment and standard sleeping cars; dining, buffet-library and observation cars. Electric lights; electric fans; bath; barber. Route: Rock Island and El Paso-Northeastern Systems, Chicago to El Paso; Southern Pacific Company, El Paso to Los Angeles and San Francisco.

Tickets and full information at all railroad ticket offices in the United States and Canada. Beautifully illustrated literature descriptive of California sent on receipt of six cents in stamps.

Rock Island System

JOHN SEBASTIAN,
Passenger Traffic Manager, Rock Island System,
Chicago, Ill.

Above: *The ultimate example of a commercialized attraction that became a regular feature of resort areas was the amusement park. From the mid-1890s to World War I, Coney Island's several amusement parks dominated all others in size, variety of entertainments offered, and renown. The wildly eclectic and exotic environment of Dreamland, shown in this photograph from the turn of the century, represented the Coney Island amusement park at its peak. Below: The atmosphere and amenities of Atlantic City, New Jersey, proved particularly enticing to middle- and working-class Americans. While sea bathing promised health-giving benefits, it was undoubtedly such features as the boardwalk, rolling chairs, and various amusements, including mechanical rides, that made Atlantic City a "Mecca for Millions." This view is from the early 1900s.*

Above: *From the 1870s to World War I the Adirondack Mountains area of New York State was one of the most fashionable and popular resort regions in the nation. Those who sought privacy, informality, and relief from city living built their own private "camps"—if they could afford them—or rented a cottage like the one shown here at The Antlers on Raquette Lake.* Below: *The veranda came to symbolize the pleasures of idleness at the great summer resort hotels. As reflected in this early 1900s photograph of Manhanset House on Shelter Island, New York, hotel verandas usually were dominated by women or couples relaxing and engaging in leisurely conversation.*

Left: *Among the manmade attractions of many resort areas were inclined or "switchback" railways, which became popular in the decades following the Civil War. This depiction appeared on the cover of a Lehigh Valley Railroad brochure.* Below: *When travelers began to visit the natural attractions near popular resort areas, observation decks and towers were constructed both to focus the visitors' attention and to prevent them from intruding on the natural features of the landscape. The observatory in this turn-of-the-century photograph was built for sightseers at Steamboat Rock and Balanced Rock, in Colorado's Garden of the Gods.* Facing page top: *Boating satisfied the hankering for more strenuous activity at resort hotels, as can be seen in this late 1890s photograph taken at Sylvan Lake in the Black Hills of South Dakota.* Facing page bottom: *By the end of the 19th century, a host of services had evolved at resort areas to cater to the needs and whims of tourists. This photograph of "The Midway" in Petoskey, Michigan, from the early 1900s, depicts some of the souvenirs and attractions available to tourists.*

Top: *By the end of the century, some of the country's larger cities offered guided sightseeing tours on motorized vehicles to orient out-of-town visitors to important attractions and landmarks. The passengers on this sightseeing bus, photographed around 1910, are passing Grant's Tomb on Riverside Drive in New York City.* Above: *This Liberty Bell plate was part of a set of glass dinnerware made in quantity for the 1876 Centennial Exposition in Philadelphia by the local firm of Gillinder and Sons. It is an early example of the myriad items for domestic use that would be produced for sale at various world's fairs.*

More and more tourists chose to spend vacation time in a major urban center. Cities not only delighted tourists with artistic and scientific curiosities and live entertainment, but in general offered variety, adventure, and freedom from the routines of daily life. Exhibitions and world's fairs held in the major American cities confirmed perceptions of the nation's industrial and cultural progress, and evoked admiration for the accomplishments of the cities in which they were held. The popularity of cities as tourist destinations spurred the growth of commercial sightseeing tours, and such auxiliary services as restaurants, hotels, and guidebooks.

As railroad networks extended across the country, the West gained new distinction as a travel destination. In the 1870s and 1880s, a vacation trip westward was expensive, available only to the rich. Although travel literature identified the West with Old World beauty and a certain amount of "roughing it," vacationers nevertheless expected to find a considerable number of amenities to make the experience as "civilized" and familiar as possible.

Except for those who vacationed in resort areas like Colorado Springs or San Diego, California, most tourists followed a standard sightseeing circuit, traveling by railroad and spending only a few days in any given area. During the 1870s, a typical route might start at the Chicago stockyards, continue through the Colorado Rockies to Salt Lake City, Utah, then go on through the California Sierras to Yosemite Valley and San Francisco, ending up at the luxurious Hotel del Monte in Monterey. By the 1880s, Yellowstone National Park in Wyoming and scenic areas of Alaska, Canada, and Mexico had been added to the railroad package tours offered by various travel agencies. Side trips off the main circuit were more difficult and expensive. However, by the 1890s many railroad excursion cars and stagecoaches could provide sufficient convenience and comfort to make day-long sightseeing trips appealing.

By the end of the 19th century, the West had come to be closely associated with the vanishing wilderness and an idyllic past. In an era of growing nationalism and nostalgia, the West became a mecca

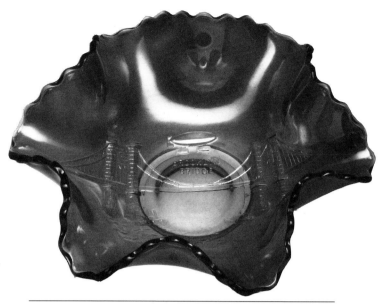

Above: *Buying souvenirs, like taking snapshots, has always added to the pleasure of vacation trips. This bowl, made by the Dugan Glass Company of Indiana, Pennsylvania, around 1910, offers a view of the Brooklyn Bridge.* Below: *Produced by the Rapid Motor Vehicle Company of Pontiac, Michigan, in 1906, this vehicle was particularly suited to provide jitney service between railroad stations and hotels as well as longer distance transportation for sightseeing excursions. Its open design and forward-facing seats allowed passengers to enter from either side.*

Left: *Amusements and concessions had become integral features of world's fairs by the time of the Louisiana Purchase Exposition, held in St. Louis in 1904. This embroidered handkerchief was one example of the types of souvenirs that could be purchased there.* Below: *The World's Columbian Exposition, held in Chicago in 1893, was the first American fair to offer a distinctive amusement area in addition to formal exhibits. The fair's Midway Plaisance, shown in this illustration from the Portfolio of Photographs of the World's Fair, included an international village of restaurants and entertainment, and a variety of concessions, side shows, and mechanical rides. Dominating the Midway was the spectacular giant revolving wheel designed by George W. G. Ferris.*

By the end of the 19th century, the popular perception of the West included a romanticized image of the American Indian. Tourists were most likely to encounter Indians selling souvenirs at railroad stations, as in this turn-of-the-century postcard from Albuquerque, New Mexico.

for tourists wishing to gain a sense of their country's frontier heritage. Rodeos, fairs, and festivals, and a few early dude ranches all added to the West's distinctive character and appeal.

As the dangers and uncertainties of cross-country travel faded, and as Americans sought more active pursuits, a substantial "back-to-nature" movement developed to spur pleasure travel to backwoods areas. Although it was English in origin, Americans associated this movement with their own frontier and pioneer past.

Members of the urban middle class were particularly vocal advocates of this return to nature. These people considered resorts, the outlying areas of cities, and country roads to be natural buffers against unhealthy and crowded urban conditions; a home in the suburbs or the country provided yet another form of escape from urban ills. Larger, more unspoiled natural areas were looked on as particularly revitalizing to the spirit, and thousands of people joined conservation crusades to help preserve federal and state lands from economic exploita-

tion. In *Our National Parks*, published in 1901, naturalist John Muir enthusiastically reported:

> *The tendency nowadays to wander in wildernesses is delightful to see. Thousands of tired, nerve-shaken, over-civilized people are beginning to find out that going to the mountains is going home; that wildness is a necessity; and that mountain parks and reservations are useful not only as fountains of timber and irrigating rivers, but as fountains of life.*

An interest in camping also arose out of this new appreciation of natural scenery. As early as August 1874, *Scribner's Monthly* reported that "camping out" was "rapidly growing in favor," providing city dwellers with temporary relief from artificiality and confinement.

The back-to-nature movement was organized and institutionalized through the formation of various clubs, including the Appalachian Club (1876), the American Scenic and Historical Preservation Society

While hunters and woodsmen had "roughed it" for generations, camping out became a popular form of vacationing for city dwellers during the late 19th century. According to the rhetoric of the period, the couple camping in this secluded spot at Glen Eyrie, Lake George, New York, would find relief from the artificiality and confinement of the city and attain a more wholesome life by communing with nature.

(1895), and the Sierra Club (1892). Local garden clubs, women's clubs, and horticultural societies augmented the movement, and an increased interest in bird-watching led to the formation of several local Audubon societies and Junior Audubon clubs during the first two decades of the 20th century.

Nowhere was the ideal of living a more strenuous life in the out-of-doors more successfully embodied than in the Boy Scout movement. Organized in 1908 by a British general, Sir Robert Baden-Powell, the movement took root in the United States in 1910. It was thought that, as members of the Boy Scouts, American boys could develop the sort of frontier skills and values that would lead the nation to emphasize once more the rugged outdoor life that their ancestors had experienced. The Boy Scouts rapidly

became the largest youth organization in the country. Soon other "Backwoods Brotherhoods" were organized, along with similar girls' organizations, including the Girl Scouts and Campfire Girls.

The importance accorded to children's appreciation and understanding of nature contributed to the proliferation of summer camps for them. These camps evolved from day-long excursions to natural areas into semipermanent resorts where city children could enjoy communion with nature while engaging in a variety of organized activities. Almost unknown in 1900, summer camps had become "the customary thing" for affluent children by 1915.

The popular interest in nature led to increased governmental regulation of parks and forests. Even before the back-to-nature movement gained hold, the government had moved to preserve certain "freaks and phenomena of Nature" for public enjoyment. In 1864, for example, it set aside Yosemite Valley in California expressly for "public use, resort, and recreation." And in 1872, the government created Yellowstone National Park in Wyoming as a "public park or pleasuring-ground for the benefit and enjoyment of the people." In the 1880s, the growing belief that exposure to nature could serve as an antidote to urban problems contributed to the designation of Niagara Falls as a public park and the establishment of the Adirondack Forest Preserve. The view that the Adirondacks were "a place where rest, recuperation and vigor may be gained by our highly nervous and overworked people" became a major rationale in changing its status to a state park in 1892.

Theodore Roosevelt was a keen advocate of wilderness conservation, and many more natural areas were given governmental support during his term of office. During the first decade of the 20th century, the government designated several more landmarks as national parks and the national forest system was greatly expanded. The passage of the Antiquities Act in 1906 allowed Roosevelt and succeeding presidents to designate "objects of historic or cultural interest" as "national monuments."

In 1908, some 69,000 people visited national parks, and that number multiplied astronomically as parks began to admit automobiles. Railroads provided access to the parks via elegant railroad cars that made the trips fairly comfortable. An increasing number of hostelries, roads, trails, and other tourist amenities "softened" the rawness of the parks. But the major development of tourism in the national parks did not take place until after World War I.

Improvements in the speed, comfort, and cost of transatlantic voyages by steamer led many more Americans than before to travel abroad for pleasure, while new tourist services in Europe made the sightseeing trips there more inviting. Although such trips were still too expensive for the average American, a growing number of upper-middle-class families

Below: *Nature lovers in the Western region of the country founded the Sierra Club in 1892. Under the leadership of naturalist John Muir, the club was instrumental in the growth of a national preservation movement. This 1908 photograph shows Muir, left front, with Sierra Club members on one of many expeditions through the Sierra Nevada mountain range of California.* Right: *A new interest in birdwatching led to the organization of the Audubon Society in 1886. Reorganized in 1896, the Society established local chapters in 37 states during the next two decades. This membership button is from the early 20th century.*

Top: *During the late 19th century nature study was emphasized at city schools and summer camps because it was believed that keeping children in touch with nature was beneficial for society as a whole. This turn-of-the-century photograph shows a nature study group in Bedford Park, New York.* Above: *The Boy Scouts organization, founded in 1910, was dedicated to the "revival of Woodcraft as a school for Manhood," and its handbook emphasized woodlore, campcraft, and other frontier skills. Specialized equipment like this firemaking kit was developed to help teach Boy Scouts how to survive the hardships of outdoor living.*

began to vacation abroad. Many took advantage of travel agents and standardized package tours to lessen the risks and uncertainties of travel in foreign countries. The tremendous popular success of Mark Twain's travel satire, *Innocents Abroad,* published in 1869, further enhanced the appeal of foreign travel.

Between the 1860s and the 1880s, the number of Americans traveling abroad had doubled, and by the turn of the century Americans were "looking outward" as never before. Foreign destinations closer to home became accessible to American vacationers as resorts were developed in the Caribbean countries, Canada, and Mexico. American travel to the "exotic lands" of the Middle East, India, South America, and the Orient also increased at this time.

Large numbers of Americans were traveling in Europe at the outbreak of World War I. One *New York Times* writer hailed the cessation of European travel with relief, noting, "At last we are delivered from the tyranny of the Chateaux of the Loire, the canals of Venice, and the glaciers of Switzerland." According to the 1914 summer issue of *Travel,* the wartime suspension of travel to Europe lent "an immense filip" to a new "See America First" campaign. The Pan-Pacific International Exposition held in San Francisco in 1915 served as a potent inspiration to national travel, attracting some 13 million visitors.

When Congress gave Yosemite Valley to the State of California in 1864, it set a precedent for future national park sites by specifically reserving the area for "public use, resort and recreation." By 1906 the valley and its surrounding environs had been merged into a larger national park.
Right: *This photograph from around 1910, showing the "Half Dome" in Yosemite from the New Glacier Point Hotel, reflects the growing emphasis on tourist services near major points of interest in these parks.* Below: *Among the tourist services at Yosemite were the recreational facilities at Camp Army, evident in this photograph from around 1913.*

Above: *Established as America's first national park in 1872, Yellowstone soon became a popular stop on the Western tourist circuit because of its geysers and other natural wonders. In the following decades hotels were constructed at Yellowstone to provide a break for tired travelers and to help soften the bleakness of the landscape. The Old Faithful Inn (1903), whose rustic interior is shown here, was situated as close to Old Faithful (the park's most famous geyser) as regulations would allow.* Below: *Popular interest in the Grand Canyon was first aroused in the late 1860s by the publication of a hair-raising account of a journey through its interior. The area was designated a national monument in 1908 as part of the Antiquities Act, and declared a national park in 1919. As was typical of other tourist spots, the rim of the canyon was embellished by a lookout tower complete with telescope. This postcard is from around 1915.*

American interest in foreign travel was augmented by improved, more comfortable steamships, the introduction of package tours, and the publication of Mark Twain's Innocents Abroad *(1869), a humorous account of his travels overseas. Above left: This engraving from* Harper's Weekly, *March 1, 1890, points to the "awe...akin to reverence" shown by American tourists toward famous European works of art. Above right: A number of board games capitalized on the growing interest in foreign travel, including this game produced by the Milton Bradley Company around 1900.*

THE ERA OF MASS PLEASURE TRAVEL: SINCE WORLD WAR I

Increased discretionary time, rising income levels, and technological advances in transportation led to a further democratization of pleasure travel after World War I. Shorter work weeks (especially after New Deal labor legislation in the 1930s) and the introduction of paid vacations (customary for both white-collar and production workers after World War II) provided new incentives for people to travel. Automobiles and, eventually, jet planes also helped transform travel from a diversion of the privileged to a major leisure activity for the general public.

After World War I, the automobile emerged as the principal mode of pleasure travel. In the first two decades of the 20th century, the number of private automobiles increased a thousandfold to 8 million in 1920, and nearly tripled again by 1930. From the

1930s on, about 80 to 85 percent of all vacation trips were taken by automobile. Motorists continued to emphasize the freedom, speed, and comfort offered by automobile travel as opposed to other forms of transportation. No longer were the upper and middle classes bound by the dictates of railroad and steamship lines, nor were the working classes trapped within their home cities or towns. Moreover, in many places blacks for the first time were able to avoid segregated travel on public means of transportation.

Increased automobile ownership after World War I intensified the demand for improved roads. The highway organizations of the teens (the most famous being the Lincoln Highway Association, founded in 1913) expanded in the early 1920s into more than 100 groups that sponsored at least 250 marked trails and installed every shape and size of road sign. The inauguration of a federal road system in 1925 for the first time standardized numbered

routes and road signs across the country. Affixed to posts at every turn or crossroads "too plainly for even the worst blunderer to miss," these signs became a "blessing to wanderers," according to Frederic F. Van de Water in *The Family Flivvers to Frisco* (1927). Many roads were graded, straightened, widened, and improved with asphalt. During the 1930s, lesser roads were brought into the federal highway system, the number of landscaped "parkways" increased, and Portland cement was introduced as a smooth, quiet, and inexpensive road-paving material.

As automobiles became faster and more comfortable to ride in, travelers tended to become less interested in the passing scene. Motoring became a means to an end rather than an enjoyable experience in itself. The obsession with speed in automobile travel was reflected in Dallas Sharp's *The Better Country,* published in 1928:

> *To push on from dawn to dark, and after dark, seeing nothing, resting nowhere, hailing no traveler nor station, is quite truly American.*

Many maps, guidebooks, and itineraries transformed automobile touring into a more goal-oriented activity, while the installation of heaters, air-conditioners, and radios in cars increased the traveler's reluctance to stop. Ironically, rapid driving from destination to destination came to resemble closely the railroad-to-resort mode of travel that motorists had so fervently sought to avoid.

By 1956, a system of divided, limited-access interstate freeways had been adopted to cope with the overwhelming number of vehicles on the roads. These freeways and the system of toll highways increased travel speeds and eliminated congestion, but they also contributed to the increased monotony and homogeneity of automobile travel. Reflecting on

In 1925 the United States government adopted a national numbered road system to help standardize and simplify travel directions. Even after roads were numbered, however, highway directional signs like this one photographed in Rutland, Vermont, in 1939, were still often cluttered with town names, mileage figures, and an array of arrows.

this, John Steinbeck gloomily predicted in *Travels with Charley in Search of America* (1962):

> *When we get thruways across the whole country, as we will and must, it will be possible to drive from New York to California without seeing a single thing.*

A host of services to facilitate the motorist's passage, including gas stations, repair shops, eating places, and lodgings evolved along the growing network of paved roads. At first eating and lodging places were fairly primitive, and were located at unpredictable distances from one another, so that many motorists found it cheaper and more convenient to camp and cook their own meals along the side of the road. Large groups of these so-called "tin can tourists" traversed the countryside just after World War I, and specialized automobiles and equipment were designed for this purpose. During the heyday of autocamping, the campers were likened to wandering gypsies and vagabonds or to America's self-reliant pioneers.

By the early 1920s, the nomadic, independent nature of autocamping was curtailed, as campers began to use centralized, municipal campgrounds. These free campgrounds, which offered security and such amenities as sanitation and cooking and laundry facilities, helped obviate complaints that autocampers were defiling private property and littering the roadside. Most autocampers welcomed these campground conveniences as a relief from their earlier self-sufficiency.

The free municipal autocamp was short-lived. By the middle of the 1920s, camps began to charge entrance fees and institute registration requirements,

---

Local highway organizations and touring associations were instrumental in marking important roads, publishing guidebooks, and serving as clearinghouses for travel information. This 1925 travel brochure described four distinct "trails" in New York State for the motorist, each with its "own individual charm and providing the most interesting scenery, the finest macadam and concrete roads, historical landmarks, and the most convenient and comfortable hotels and inns."

The game of "Touring," introduced in 1925 by Parker Brothers, Inc., reflected the current American preoccupation with automobile travel. Updated versions of this popular game appeared on the market for the next several decades.

occupancy limits, and police supervision, claiming that this separated the "better class" of tourists from the "undesirables" (migrant workers, transients, and the unemployed). In truth, it was not so much the "undesirables" that caused problems, but general crowding, rowdiness, and sanitation problems. As the wealthy left the autocamps to tour Europe or spend their time at private summer estates, and the municipalities' enthusiasm for establishing camps waned, there was a major shift from public to private camps. From the late 1920s on, private operators controlled most of these facilities.

In an attempt to attract more tourists to their autocamps, private owners began to add permanent tents, and eventually, small cabins to their sites. Motorists found they could enjoy the same flexibility in travel as before, but with added privacy and convenience. Soon the word "cottage" crept into the names of these lodging sites, implying more permanent, winterized facilities with private bathrooms

The wealthy were among the first to combine motoring with camping out. These early enthusiasts included, left to right, inventor Thomas A. Edison, industrialist Harvey Firestone, naturalist John Burroughs, and industrialist Henry Ford, seen here at Camp Wolf Creek, West Virginia, in 1918. Likening themselves to gypsies or vagabonds roaming the countryside at will and learning "God's truths in nature" through hardship and self-reliance, they managed to temper their privations with the help of "six big cars," two "flivvers," two trucks, a service crew of seven men, and a "luxurious outfit" of camping equipment.

Above: *Rather than face the relatively primitive conditions of autocamping, many motorists continued to frequent hotels like this one, which Henry Ford and his traveling companions visited in 1924. Outdated facilities and dress codes, and poor service at such hotels eventually encouraged travelers to seek alternative lodgings, first at autocamps and, later, at motels.* Right: *The collapsible "Gold Medal" Folding Camp Chair made around 1920 was said to "adjust itself perfectly to the body," and to "support the weight of the heaviest man or woman." These particular examples were used by Henry Ford during his 1921 camping trip.* Below: *As more Americans took to the open road some automobiles were designed specifically for camping. This 1924 photograph shows one such vehicle equipped with a foldout tent and, undoubtedly, several other cleverly devised comforts as well.*

and running water. As individual units became integrated under a single roof, "cottage courts" evolved into "tourist courts." During the Great Depression, these types of lodgings dotted the roadside, offering affordable yet private accommodations.

At the same time that roadside lodgings became more sophisticated, restaurant meals began to supplant picnic lunches and campfire meals for hungry travelers on the road. During the 1920s, downtown cafes evolved into tearooms and roadside stands, and in the 1930s into all manner of "drive-in" restaurants, diners, and roadhouses.

After World War II, larger and more luxurious "motels" were built. The number of motels doubled in the decade from 1939 to 1948, and by 1960 there were twice as many again. Air-conditioning, television, and swimming pools became standard motel amenities. Aging hotels were forced to modify their rates, spruce up their interiors, and provide new enticements. Most of the motels were small-scale and individually owned, and fierce competition caused many to close.

The trend toward massive highway development in the 1950s led to the construction of more elaborate, often multistoried, motor hotels and motor inns. These integrated the formality of a hotel with the recreational facilities and convenience of motels. Chain systems of motor inns featured recognizable architecture and familiar signs all across the country, easing travelers' anxieties with the assurance that, as the promotional materials of the Holiday Inn chain put it, "the best surprise is no surprise."

Left: An outing or long-distance automobile trip usually necessitated the preparation and eating of portable meals. These collapsible cups, produced in 1933, were convenient for picnics or camp dinners on the road. Below: Preparing food and eating out-of-doors were considered a pleasurable part of the autocamping experience, as suggested in this illustration from the 1926 Motor Camping Manual.

II—*Cooking and Eating Outdoors*

Atten-*shun*' Knives and forks ready! Eat!! With Dad at the coffee-pot and frying pan and Mother in the rear to keep reinforcements coming up, the family won't go hungry. And, oh, how good food tastes out of doors!

As the design and function of highways and lodgings became more standardized, roadside restaurants followed suit. Diners, cafes, and drive-ins serving simple, predictable food were largely superseded by fast-food and chain restaurants offering identical menus across the country.

Innovations in the design of motorized recreational vehicles corresponded with advances in automobiles. Before World War I, wealthy Americans had toured the countryside in luxurious, custom-built "house cars," just as they might have traveled in a

Above: *In contrast to autocamp facilities, tourist cabins and cottages were permanent winterized structures with private bathroom facilities and indoor plumbing. With their promise of comfort, convenience, and informality, lodgings like this Arkansas tourist camp from the 1930s proved attractive both to autocampers and to travelers who had previously stayed at hotels.* Right: *Until relatively recently black families, especially when traveling through the South, would have to plan their routes carefully to avoid racial discrimination. Publication of this "Green Book," which began in 1936, was intended to "give the Negro traveler information that will keep him from running into difficulties, embarrassments, and to make his trips more enjoyable." This 80-page edition from 1949 listed hotels, boardinghouses, restaurants, beauty shops, barber shops, and various other services "which cater to the Negro trade."*

Above: *The 1949 Kaiser Traveler, made by the Kaiser Frazer Corporation of Willow Run, Michigan, was one attempt to meet the pent-up demand for cars after World War II. Its appearance was thoroughly modern and its innovative hatch-back design, with fold-down rear seat, anticipated other hatchbacks by 20 years. The car's roominess made it popular for family vacations. Left: The station wagon, as represented by this mechanical toy, became the favored family vacation vehicle of the 1950s.*

yacht or a private railroad car. Members of the middle class followed their lead, fashioning their own house cars or trailers. In the 1920s several small companies produced specialized truck and car bodies for autocamping, but the popularity of these vehicles was shortlived. By the early 1930s, however, portable trailers had evolved into fully furnished house trailers, which far surpassed the earlier house cars in affordability and convenience.

After World War II, and especially from the 1950s on, the production of recreational vehicles developed into a major industry. Large numbers of luxurious, comfortable vacation vehicles were produced, including trailers, pickup campers, vans, and

motor homes. In 1973, Americans spent almost $2.5 billion on recreational vehicles.

Passenger railroads reached the peak of their popularity around 1920, and declined thereafter. From that time on, the attention of the various railroad lines tended to focus on improving passenger comfort. Railroad companies made a valiant effort to revive their business in the late 1930s and 1940s by improving their operating efficiency through the use of new power sources and by adopting new, streamlined designs for their trains. The railroads continued to modernize and upgrade passenger service after World War II, but most of these improvements merely slowed the decline of the railroad as a major means of pleasure travel.

Railroad passenger travel shrank for a number of reasons, including the popularity of private automobiles, but also because of the appearance of motorized buses. Increasingly comfortable buses were built in large numbers during the 1920s by several small companies. In 1929, many of these merged into the Greyhound bus system. Along with its major competitor, Continental Trailways, the

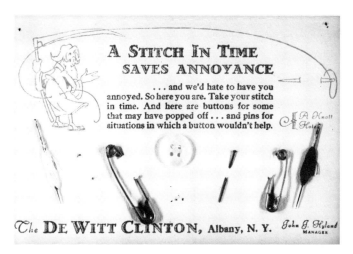

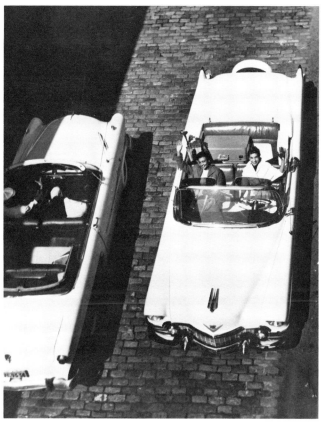

Above: *In an effort to compete with motels, hotels offered an increasing variety of free services to their guests. One example was this sewing kit, made for the DeWitt Clinton Hotel in Albany, New York.* Right: *In 1950 the* Saturday Evening Post *reported that 80 percent of the long-distance pleasure trips undertaken by Americans were by automobile. In this 1950s photograph, a Mrs. Olivia Clarke and friend are setting out on a vacation in their automobile, complete with golf clubs.* Below right: *The motor inns of the 1960s were larger and more luxurious than the motels of previous years. Typically they offered such amenities as air-conditioning, television, and enticing swimming pools like the one shown in this 1965 brochure. Often these lodgings were located at the exits of major interstate highways, such as route 75, which ran from Michigan to Florida.* Below: *The Holiday Inn Corporation offered standardized signage and packaging to promote its facilities and to reassure travelers that they would always get what they expected at one of its motels. Examples included towels, soap, and matches, as shown here.*

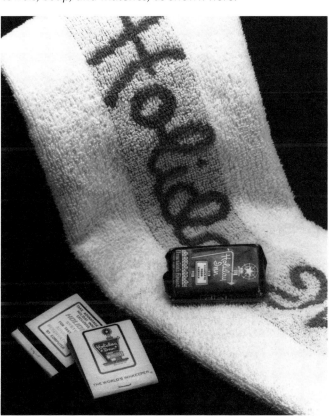

Greyhound system became a significant factor in vacation travel. Bus service has expanded tremendously since the 1930s, providing an inexpensive alternative to other forms of travel. Buses also have become a major mode of transportation for group travel on package tours and chartered trips.

Passenger airlines were first developed in the 1910s and 1920s, but it was not until considerable technological advances were made in aircraft design during the 1930s that they began to be considered a means of pleasure travel. After World War II, the airplane became a quick and dependable means for long-distance travel. By the mid-1950s, travel by air had become so efficient and affordable that millions of passengers chose this form of transportation, compared to only thousands before World War II.

From their inception in 1958, jet-powered passenger airplanes revolutionized American travel habits and patterns. Long-distance pleasure travel became affordable for people of all classes; those with the money and inclination to travel farther and see more of the world than the rest of the crowd became known as the "jet set." The speed of jets put an end to special sleeping accommodations on airplanes, and made once-remote countries easily accessible to pleasure travelers.

Stuckey's

**Now, coast to coast!
The place for travelers to relax, refresh, refuel**

You can find a lot of happiness beside the highways now. Make every trip easier, more fun by stopping at Stuckey's all along your way. Stuckey stores are located at convenient intervals on main highways throughout the nation. Welcome stops to break fatigue of driving; to refresh in whistle-clean facilities. Enjoy tempting pecan candies; free samples, too. Tasty snacks, beverages. Discover exciting food packs, uncommon gifts. Only at Stuckey's, with one stop, can you relax, refresh, refuel in such happy holiday fashion.

Every trip's a pleasure trip when you stop at Stuckey's

PET INCORPORATED STUCKEY STORES DIVISION

Left: *As uninterrupted travel became possible along the new limited-access freeways, tourist services and souvenir shops were confined to freeway exit ramps. Stuckey's shops, shown in this advertisement from* Better Homes & Gardens, *August 1967, capitalized on the use of freeway billboards to entice travelers to "relax, refresh, refuel" at their establishments.* Facing page: *The recognizable colors and signage of Howard Johnson's promised the traveler a consistent eating experience. By December 24, 1956, when this* Life *magazine advertisement appeared, Howard Johnson's "coffee shop" had become something of a roadside landmark.*

Landmark for Hungry Americans

From happy experience millions of Americans know they will find a wide range of prices and courteous, friendly service under the familiar orange roofs. Howard Johnson's restaurants — featuring full-course meals, salads, sandwiches and tempting desserts — can be found on important highways. Today there are over 500 and we're still growing.

HOWARD JOHNSON'S

Restaurants · Motor Lodges · Ice Cream · Candies

Juicy charcoal-broiled steaks

Grilled-in-butter frankforts

Tendersweet fried clams

28 flavors of pure, rich ice cream

LOCATIONS FOR HOWARD JOHNSON'S restaurants and motor lodges are desired on main highways and in shopping centers. Write Howard D. Johnson Co., 89 Beale St., Wollaston, Mass.

Left: *The "Nomad" motor coach was advertised as "A Highway Home Uniting Comfort with Economy." This 1923 coach gained additional power when remounted from its original Model T chassis onto a Graham Bros. chassis in 1928. Its first owners, John Stanton Chapman and Mary Isley Chapman, wrote some 42 novels between them while traveling in this vehicle. Below: Fully furnished house trailers appeared on the market in the early 1930s. Their use for everyday and vacation housing created a major manufacturing industry. By 1939, when this photograph was taken, some 300,000 trailers had been sold in the United States.*

Right: *Motorcycles presented an alternative mode of travel for day outings and longer vacations. This top-of-the-line Harley-Davidson motorcycle, produced in 1941, featured a matching sidecar, a small luggage compartment, and long, semi-elliptical springs for a ''floating ride.''* Below: *By the mid-1960s trailers were competing with all manner of recreational campers and motor homes that simulated the comforts of home. This photograph of two of the most up-to-date Chrysler Newport automobiles hauling a trailer and a boat was taken in 1966.*

The Milwaukee Road's
SUPER DOME CARS
Delightfully new for a wonderful view
ON THE OLYMPIAN HIAWATHA
AND ON THE TWIN CITIES HIAWATHAS

Above: *After World War II passenger railroads modernized their trains in an attempt to revive business. Among the innovations were the addition of air-conditioning, dining and lounge cars, and, as shown here, specially designed sightseeing cars. This travel brochure from the early 1950s claimed that 68 passengers could ''relax in perfect comfort'' in the new ''Super-Dome cars'' while their eyes ''sweep the wide horizons, look down into canyons and deep valleys, look up at cliffs and mountain peaks.''* Below: *Buses proved an especially useful mode of transportation for sightseeing excursions and package tours. This 1937 photograph shows chartered buses touring Alaska.*

Right: *Although flying remained a minor form of passenger transport until the post-World War II era, some airlines began to offer passenger flights during the 1920s and 1930s. As evident from the stress on luxury in this 1928 Ford Tri-Motor advertisement, only the most affluent tourists and businessmen could afford these flights. Below: When airplanes became fast and dependable means of long-distance travel during World War II, the future mass production of light aircraft for private flying seemed imminent. Although this early 1950s photograph of an outing via one of these airplanes appears inviting, the contemporary prediction of an "airplane in every garage" has as yet remained unfulfilled.*

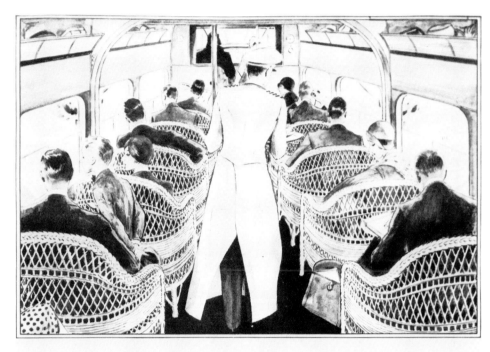

FIRST TIME UP!

 ‑‑"Fun is never out of season

once you learn about year-'round Flagship travel!"

"We don't let the weather slow us down. In every season, we keep on doing the things we enjoy ...visiting people and places we want to see —by AMERICAN AIRLINES Flagship."

Yes, your favorite form of fun is *all yours all year* when you travel American, riding high above the wintry weather that hampers surface transportation. A sunny weekend in the Southwest... a gay visit to the big city ... swimming or skiing, sightseeing or just lazin' around: they're yours for the flying, right now, with *economical* Flagship travel.

All year 'round, travel is better by air...

best by **AMERICAN AIRLINES**

AMERICAN AIRLINES, INC. • AMERICAN OVERSEAS AIRLINES, INC.

After World War II passenger airlines usurped the role of railroads as the means for moving masses of people. The promise of quick, easy, year-round travel is the crux of the message in this American Airlines advertisement from Life magazine, February 28, 1949.

Time to Travel !

Travel Tip: carry...

AMERICAN EXPRESS TRAVELERS CHEQUES
Convenient as Cash—100% Safe!

*Most Widely Accepted Cheques
in the World!*

Wherever you travel, however you go, never carry, in cash, more than you can afford to lose! Instead, carry *American Express* Travelers Cheques—the safe and sensible way to protect your travel and pocket cash. If they're lost or stolen, you get a prompt refund. And *these* are the travelers cheques you can spend *anywhere*—for they're the most widely accepted in all the world! The only identification you need is your signature . . . Only 75¢ per $100.

Ask for AMERICAN EXPRESS TRAVELERS CHEQUES at Railway Express and Western Union offices

From their inception in 1891 travelers' checks did much to ease fears of losing or running out of money on long-distance trips. This advertisement from Life *magazine, April 11, 1949, reminded vacationers that the ones issued by American Express were the most widely accepted in the world.*

Above: *The promotion of travel was greatly refined in the course of the 20th century, especially through the use of the media, through centralized tourist bureaus, and through the accelerated production of printed literature. This mid-1940s brochure is typical of state travel promotion in combining the appeal of scenic beauty with the promises of sports opportunities, pleasant climate, and historic attractions. Above right: Polaroid Land cameras, introduced in 1948, appealed to amateur photographers because they combined all the processes of developing and printing pictures within a filmpack inside the camera. This early 1970s Polaroid "Swinger" was a compact, fully automatic, inexpensive box camera whose name attracted aspiring photographers of all ages.*

Since World War I, the tourist business has become a more lucrative economic enterprise than ever. As author Norman Miller put it in *The Leisure Age* (1956):

> *Literally thousands of business enterprises in scores of states flourish and grow as a direct result of the tourist industry. Hundreds of thousands of jobs are made possible by it. A large portion of money which is spent goes for meals, lodgings, and refreshments. Millions are spent on gasoline and oil, rail, plane, bus, and steamship fares. The golf courses, theaters, gift shops, and stores benefit as do the dealers who outfit the tourist before he even starts on a vacation.*

By the late 1970s, about 8,000 travel agencies planned and arranged trips for domestic and foreign travelers. While travelers' checks and gasoline company credit cards had been in use earlier, multipurpose credit cards (introduced in the late 1950s) have come to offer increased convenience to the pleasure traveler. Travel promotion through the media of film, radio, and television has become extremely sophisticated, while travel-related pamphlets, guidebooks, and newspaper and magazine articles abound.

Right: *The insulated "Ther-Mo-Pack," produced in the late 1930s by Lockport Products of Chicago, incorporated a quart-size fruit jar to "keep food or drinks, hot or cold, for hours." The convenient carrier, or "Outing Grip," could be used to take the Ther-Mo-Pack on any kind of outing. Below: Day outings became much more frequent as a result of widespread automobile ownership. Such expeditions might include a specific destination like the picnic grounds depicted in this 1953 Plymouth owner's manual, or a casual ramble through the countryside.*

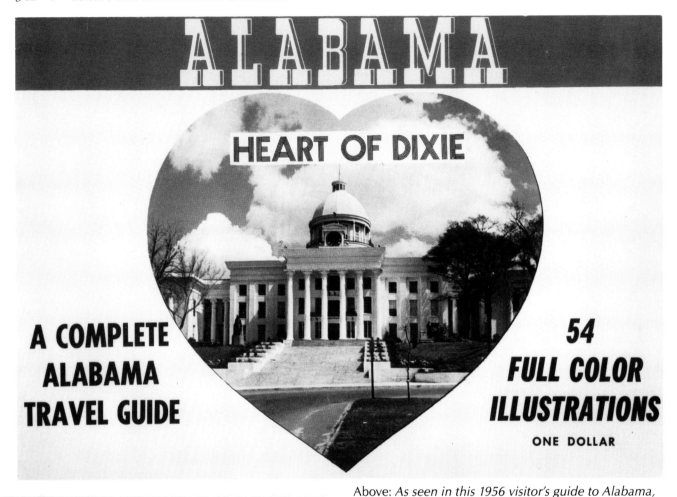

Above: *As seen in this 1956 visitor's guide to Alabama, the promotional travel literature of Southern states often emphasized the grandeur and leisurely lifestyle of the pre-Civil War era. This guidebook boasted that "historic spots, beautiful gardens, rugged mountains, beaches, hunting, fishing, golf, resort fanfare, and quiet retreat" all beckoned visitors to this "Heart of Dixie." Left: New England, with its blend of history, distinctive natural scenery, and lovingly preserved Yankee culture, has often been considered a separate region. That sense of regional character is reinforced in this advertisement for the Greyhound Lines from* Life *magazine, May 20, 1946. Facing page: Of all Southern states, Florida experienced the greatest influx of tourists. The attraction of Florida—especially of the Miami beaches—for sunbathers is expressed in this image from a piece of 1933 sheet music.*

Expanding Horizons

New and improved modes of transportation, especially the expanded use of the automobile, increased the number of short outings and excursions undertaken by families and groups of friends. The amusements of nearby towns and cities, the scenery of the countryside, and the attractions of outlying recreational facilities and bathing beaches were finally brought within the practical reach of millions of people.

The independence and flexibility of pleasure travel after World War I led to the tendency to view the country in terms of geographical regions rather than in terms of resort areas or towns. As the accelerating speed of the automobile and other modes of transportation blurred the landscape, the region became an organizing concept for the tourist—a means to impose order on the diversity of sights encountered in the course of travel. At the same time, with increasing cultural homogeneity nationwide, genuine regional diversity has become more muted, and is often overlooked in favor of stereotyped generalizations. These regional stereotypes have included the perceived Yankee culture of New England, the wholesome, hometown image of the Midwest, and the slow-paced way of life in the South.

The West, considered the quintessential American region, has proven the most alluring to tourists. Its embodiment of the American frontier experience and its outstanding scenic beauty led John A. Jakle to write in *The Tourist: Travel in Twentieth-Century North America* (1985) that "one couldn't know North America without traveling west." Its vast scale and seemingly primitive character, together with romantic stereotypes of cowboys and Indians, have been publicized and popularized by moviemakers, who, according to Jakle, "elaborated on the myths of the frontier to produce a national fantasy." The epitome of the Western stereotype lives on at Disneyland's Frontierland in California.

In contrast to the civilized amenities stressed in 19th-century literature advertising the West, early 20th-century promotional literature depicted the region as wilder than it actually was. Romantic Western stereotypes were perpetuated through rodeos, festivals, recreations of Western towns, and at dude ranches. In 1933, Edward Dunn remarked on the contrived experience of the dude ranch in his *Double-Crossing America by Motor:*

> *Everyone dressed in western costumes from sombreros to high-heeled boots, and there was much talk of "wrangling," "roping," and "rounding up," despite the fact that there was not a sign of cattle within fifty miles.*

During the 1930s, the desert of the Southwest, which had been relatively untouched by tourism until then, became a fashionable destination for pleasure travel. Desert areas like Phoenix, Arizona, and Palm Springs, California, gained popularity with sun-seekers, while sites like Lake Tahoe (on the California-Nevada border) and Lake Mead (on the Arizona-Nevada border) appealed to sports enthusiasts. Las Vegas, Nevada, also achieved new popularity, particularly after several large gambling casinos were constructed there in the 1950s. As automobiles became more efficient, and especially as airlines reduced cross-country travel time and expense, California became the favored destination for huge numbers of tourists. Many of them were eager to visit Hollywood, Los Angeles, and, beginning in 1955, Disneyland. For more adventurous souls, tropical Hawaii and the "last frontier" of Alaska came to serve as popular vacation spots (especially after both obtained statehood in 1959).

The traveler in Arizona will find excellent highways to serve him on his journey through this delightful land of Sunshine and Scenic Grandeur.

The state is crossed east and west by four transcontinental highways — U. S. 60, 66, 70, and 80 — while the Canada to Mexico highway — U. S. 89 — crosses the state north and south. A network of hard surfaced highways ties all parts of the state together, and so compact and well planned is the Arizona highway system that modern highways lead to the very door of many of the state's famed Scenic Shrines, and others are of easy access.

Arizona's highways are built and maintained to render the greatest amount of service to the traveler. Adequate signing and

striping has been scientifically incorporated into the highway system to insure swift travel with the utmost of safety. The comfort and convenience of the traveler is the first consideration of the Arizona highway department. The traveler into this Empire of the West will find Arizona's highways his constant and good companions.

Left: *During the 1930s and 1940s the Southwestern desert became popular among sunseekers and those interested in exploring an area not yet "taken over" by civilization. The traveler using this "friendly guide" to Arizona, published around 1948, is assured that the state's highways will serve as "his constant and good companions" throughout this "delightful land of Sunshine and Scenic Grandeur." Below: Dude ranches in the West offered a comfortable and colorful setting where tourists could experience first hand what they considered to be the cowboy lifestyle. As such ranches became more popular they spread to the Southwest, where they attracted winter vacationers. This 1930s photograph taken in Arizona shows the combination of Western, recreational, and social elements typical of the dude ranch. Right: Watch fobs, connected to a pocket watch by a leather strap, hung outside the wearer's pocket and insured a good grip. Available in a variety of shapes and designs, they made ideal souvenirs and gifts. This watch fob from Pendleton, Oregon, depicts the "roundup saddle," an enduring symbol of the West.*

This visitor's button from the 1939 New York World's Fair depicts that fair's architectural emblem—the trylon and perisphere. A souvenir from Chicago's 1933 Century of Progress Exposition, the bracelet displays some of the futuristic, machine-inspired design motifs associated with that fair.

The attraction of cities—with their abundant nightlife and major sporting events—is an enduring one for tourists, especially if a world's fair or exposition is in progress. For general sightseeing, scores of guidebooks, pamphlets, and bus tours orient visitors to particular districts and points of interest.

History of every sort has been a major attraction to tourists since World War I. Mass automobile travel has stimulated popular interest in historical restorations and local history. Signs and markers have sprouted at numerous historic spots along the roadside; larger attractions include historic houses, museums, and town and village restorations.

While many tourist destinations offer the flavor of an area or a greater understanding of America's past, numerous other places lure travelers with nothing more than pure entertainment. A prime example is the theme park, conceived at Disneyland in 1955. Disneyland—along with the much more extensive Walt Disney World (near Orlando, Florida, 1971) and numerous other theme parks scattered across the country—features organized amusement areas centered around historical and other contrived themes. (*See "Going Out."*) Secluded resort clubs, weekend hotel "getaways," and ocean cruises also offer entertainment and relaxation.

The automobile proved an enduring feature at world's fairs, both in marketing displays and as a means to transport visitors between and through fair exhibits. At the 1964 New York World's Fair, for example, visitors to the Ford Motor Company Wonder Rotunda could travel "in the comfort of new Ford-built convertibles" to view "sights unseen for millions of years on earth." These animated scenes were created by the Walt Disney studios for the Ford Motor Company.

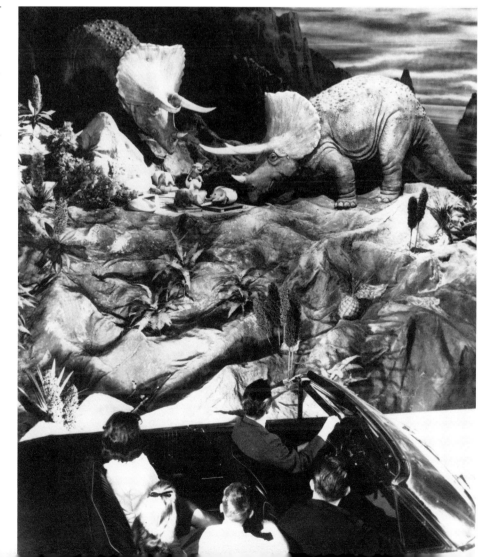

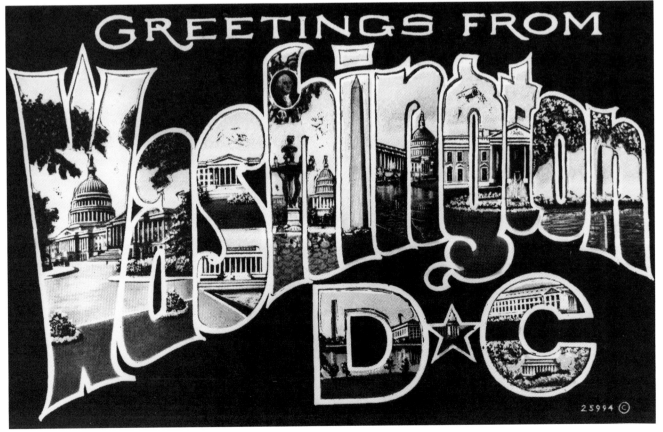

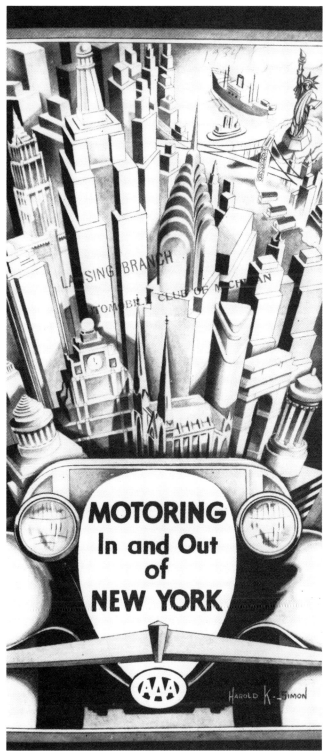

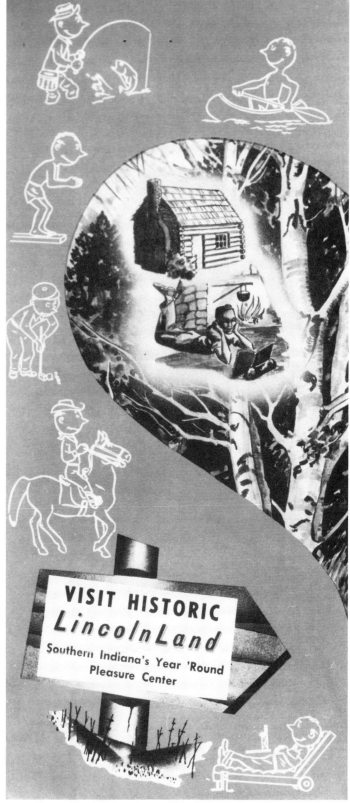

Facing page top and above: *Guidebooks, pamphlets, and other promotional literature, like these New York City and Chicago guides, were produced in increasing numbers to help orient tourists on visits to cities. Facing page bottom: Once in the city tourists could buy postcards like this one from Washington, D.C., relatively cheaply to send home to friends or to remind them of their trips. Above right: Historic points of interest have proven to be major drawing cards for travel to many regions of the country. This brochure for southern Indiana, for example, focuses on the appeal of sites connected with Abraham Lincoln, while also pointing out special nature spots and recreational activities.*

Walt Disney World®
MAGIC KINGDOM GUIDE BOOK

Compliments of Eastman Kodak Company

Kodak

Pleasure travel in the 20th century has continued to have a significant outdoor orientation; viewing nature and scenery has proven to be a major attraction in itself. Automobile travel led to the revival of many resort areas, as lodges and motels offering extensive sports facilities attracted visitors. Following World War II, private cottages and cabins began to dot the great vacation regions of the country. Increased prosperity put these within the reach of growing numbers of Americans.

Tent camping underwent phenomenal growth from the 1920s on, as millions of travelers bypassed hotels, tourist courts, and lodges to experience the more rigorous life of the outdoors. The emphasis on family togetherness helped renew the interest in camping. The majority of tent campers were city vacationers unaccustomed to outdoor life. As a result, specific areas were designated for public use, and rules and regulations were enacted to preserve the sanctity of particularly crowded spots. In the post-World War II years, camping became more convenient, and even luxurious, a trend reflected in the tremendous growth of the recreational vehicle industry and the proliferation of convenience-oriented campgrounds like the Kampgrounds of America (KOA), founded in 1962.

Children's summer camps have spread across the country since the 1920s. Since the 1950s, a new type of day camping has evolved, combining recreational activities with the flavor of camping. Summer camps have increasingly concerned themselves with helping youngsters acquire athletic, artistic, and social skills, although special wilderness and survival camps continue the rugged traditions beloved by Theodore Roosevelt.

Nowhere has the interest in the outdoors, its accessibility by automobile, and its increasing regula-

The promise of pure entertainment at theme parks stimulated tourism across the country. Walt Disney World (1971), located near Orlando, Florida, dwarfed Disneyland (built 16 years earlier) by covering an area twice the size of Manhattan. In addition to its replication of theme areas and amusement-park features popularized at Disneyland, it offered theme resorts linked with the amusement areas. Since 1982 it has had the added attraction of the Experimental Prototype Community of Tomorrow (EPCOT).

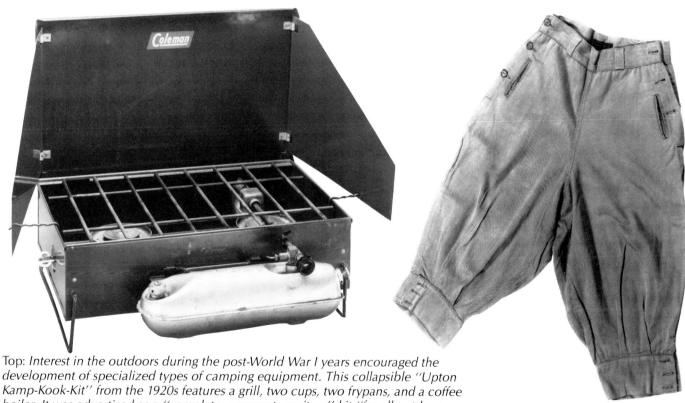

Top: *Interest in the outdoors during the post-World War I years encouraged the development of specialized types of camping equipment. This collapsible "Upton Kamp-Kook-Kit" from the 1920s features a grill, two cups, two frypans, and a coffee boiler. It was advertised as a "complete, compact, sanitary" kit "for all outdoor people."* Above: *Encouraged by the popularity of their fuel-burning lanterns and domestic stoves, the Coleman Corporation began to manufacture camp stoves in 1923 to meet the needs and pocketbooks of campers and picnickers. Touted as "The Smooth Way to Rough It," Coleman products helped convert millions to camping in the 1920s and 1930s. This Coleman stove, with characteristic wind baffle, retracting fuel tank, and folding strap legs, was purchased and used by the Ettema family of Lincoln, Nebraska, in the late 1950s.* Above right: *Specialized clothing for hikers and campers also became available. This pair of women's camping knickers was manufactured by Everywoman's Garment Company of Los Angeles, California, during the mid-1920s.*

Above: *The passion for family camping became so acute after World War II that crowded sites and lists of regulations became standard. The proximity of groups of campers to one another at this Biloxi, Mississippi, campground indicates one of the ways in which the camping experience became more restricted.* Left: *Automobile touring led to a new appreciation for America's national parks, attracting attention to features that had previously gone unnoticed and encouraging the construction of tourist hotels and other services. This postcard, sent by William F. "Buffalo Bill" Cody to Henry Ford in 1916, shows the already prominent place of automobiles as a means of transportation into and through Yellowstone Park.*

tion been as evident as at the national parks. Park Service statisticians claimed that the one in every three hundred Americans who visited a national park in 1916 had dramatically increased to one in three by 1954. And during the next two decades, visitation more than tripled.

The National Park Service, instrumental in national park development since 1916, made an early commitment to the concept of parks as public playgrounds. The Park Service not only helped make the parks more accessible to automobile travelers, but also enhanced the appeal of the various parks by increasing the number of tourist accommodations and recreational facilities, distributing millions of maps and guidebooks, instituting conducted tours and lectures by ranger-naturalists, and calling attention to special features at trailside museums. While

Hot Springs

NATIONAL PARK
ARKANSAS

Illinois Central
THE ROAD OF TRAVEL LUXURY

the Park Service has been criticized for gearing the parks to visitors' whims rather than to the complex needs of their own ecological systems, the Service has helped to ensure permanent public support by making the parks easily accessible and understandable to the general public.

In an attempt to alleviate increasing congestion in the long-established national parks, additional scenic and natural areas have been incorporated into a massive national park system, encompassing national recreation areas, seashores, parkways, lakeshores, and rivers. National and state forests, state and metro-politan parks, and federal reclamation projects multiply the opportunities for outdoor recreation.

Since World War I, renewed public concern has evolved for preserving undeveloped wilderness areas. In 1924, the Gila National Forest, New Mexico, became the first of a number of such areas to be preserved. During the 1930s, an upsurge of interest in wilderness areas led to the extension of roads and trails into such areas, and river and pack-train excursions became popular. During the 1970s, wilderness recreation experienced a boom of unprecedented proportions, leading to the fear that these areas might be "loved

Above: *During the 1970s wilderness travel experienced an unprecedented boom, and various industries evolved to cater to the needs of back-country treckers. Magazines like* Backpacker *provided helpful travel information and published advertisements from wilderness outfitters. This cover is from the first issue of the magazine, which appeared in the spring of 1973.* Above right: *The interest in back-country travel spurred the manufacture of specialized hiking equipment. This backpack was bought in 1954 from the A. I. Kelty Manufacturing Company of Glendale, California, an early producer of this type of equipment.*

to death." This has resulted in the imposition of quota restrictions on the use of back-country areas.

Travel abroad resumed after World War I. The pull of Europe remained as strong as ever, especially for the many Americans with family ties to the Old World. Foreign travel was encouraged by more efficient modes of transportation both en route to and in the European countries, and by improved tourist facilities there. Travel via ocean liner reached a peak in 1929. Even after the Great Depression curtailed such trips, the number of Americans traveling abroad remained surprisingly high.

Airplanes brought foreign travel within the reach of many more Americans in the post-World

War II period. The speed and affordability of flying, especially after the introduction of jet airplanes in the late 1950s, allowed large numbers of people to consider travel abroad even during brief vacations. By 1960, some 75 percent of American travelers in Europe had gone there by plane; within a decade only 3 percent of all travelers abroad had journeyed to their destinations by sea. Since the advent of jet planes, distant lands—including the Orient, Australia, the Middle East, and the African continent—have become popular destinations, while Canada, as well as countries in Central and South America and in the Caribbean, have continued to appeal to tourists who wish to stay closer to home.

Those who have crossed more than once invariably choose their ship with care

S.S.
RELIANCE
ALBERT BALLIN

.AND OTHER SPLENDID STEAMERS

S.S.
RESOLUTE
DEUTSCHLAND

UNITED AMERICAN LINES
(HARRIMAN LINE)
joint service with

HAMBURG AMERICAN LINE

Write for fascinating travel booklet P. Q.

39 BROADWAY, NEW YORK

171 W. RANDOLPH ST., CHICAGO   230 CALIFORNIA ST., SAN FRANCISCO

In the 1920s a larger number of Americans than ever before crossed the Atlantic to see the sights of Europe. Some four decades later grand ocean liners like the one pictured in this 1924 advertisement would succumb to the public preference for more speedy airplane travel.

Travel to foreign countries increased after World War I. Caribbean cruises originating in Florida were particularly appealing during the Prohibition years, as hinted at in this early 1930s travel brochure for Cuba.

A Bonus Pack of
HONG KONG *"Pearl of the Orient"*

DETACH THESE CARDS AND MAIL TO YOUR FRIENDS
DISTRIBUTED BY SWINDON BOOK CO., HONG KONG

Above: *As jet planes made distant spots more accessible, tourists began to travel to exotic destinations throughout the world. This packet of souvenir cards was available to travelers visiting Hong Kong.* Right: *Travel to Canada offered American tourists the feel of a foreign country while allowing them to remain close to home. This brochure for Toronto emphasized the city's role as a "centre of culture, art, and education."* Next page: *Even before the advent of jet planes, the scope and speed of world travel had become phenomenal. This Trans World Airlines advertisement from Collier's magazine, March 4, 1955, focused attention on travel destinations around the world previously accessible only in one's "fondest vacation dream."*

METROPOLITAN
TORONTO
CANADA

CANADA'S
"Queen City"
THE
METROPOLITAN TORONTO
CONVENTION AND VISITOR
ASSOCIATION

TORONTO   CANADA

THE ROYAL CANADIAN YACHT CLUB

PRINTED IN CANADA

The opportunities for Americans to travel for pleasure have changed and grown tremendously over the past 200 years. Improved modes of transportation and the growing ability and desire of Americans to "get away" for a break have worked hand in hand to expand tourism. The initial discovery of many travel destinations was made by loners attempting to avoid crowds; but they often ended up beating a path for the very people they were trying to avoid. As areas close to home became crowded, the wealthy and, increasingly, the general public, sought destinations farther away. As the numbers of tourists increased, a specialized and highly complex industry evolved to guide, serve, and occasionally exploit them.

Since World War I, tourism has become a well organized and lucrative feature of America's and the world's economy. The democratization of travel has come close to eliminating the possibility of an exclusive few claiming a specific vacation spot for themselves. The desire to get away shows no signs of abating as Americans travel toward the farthest reaches of the globe in search of relaxation, variety, adventure, and, sometimes, even their own identities.

JUST A SMALL DOWN PAYMENT AND *Off you go on o*

Paris $47.00 DOWN *

Rome $55.40 DOWN *

Los Angeles $8.60 DOWN *

*Round trip from New York via TWA Sky Tourist during Thrift Season, now to March 31. Cash fare, $461.

*Round trip from New York via TWA Sky Tourist during Thrift Season, now to March 31. Cash fare, $551.40.

*One way from Chicago via TWA Sky Tourist. Cash fare, $76.00, plus tax.

This year, with TWA's faster, finer Constellation fleet...and new "TIME PAY PLAN"...it's easier than ever to visit faraway places!

Too little time? Too little cash on hand? You'll leave both problems far behind when you plan a TWA vacation. Two weeks is all you need for a complete vacation anywhere with TWA's swift Constellations to speed you to your destination. And with TWA's "Time Pay Plan" you can go now for as little as 10% down. For example, TWA's Two-Week Bargain Tour of Europe is yours for just $49 down in Thrift Season—including round-trip TWA Sky Tourist fare, hotels, sightseeing trips and other expenses. Pay the balance in up to 20 easy monthly installments. And it's so simple to arrange. No cosigners, no collateral, no delays of any kind. Dust off your fondest vacation dream and then start planning your trip...today!

TWA's TRAVEL ADVISOR, MARY GORDON, will tell you how to plan your trip from start to finish—advise you on what to wear, how to pack; give you helpful hints on passports, currency, other details. For reservations and information, call your nearest TWA office, see your travel agent, or write TWA, 380 Madison Ave., New York 17, N.Y.

SELECTED BIBLIOGRAPHY

The following is a selective list of published works that proved useful in preparing this publication. Special attention has been given to books and articles that place leisure activities within a broad social-historical context. Many of these works contain excellent bibliographies that will direct the reader to further sources on specific subjects. This bibliography begins with a list of general works that proved helpful for the publication as a whole or in more than one section; books and articles on more specific subjects are listed under the appropriate headings. Those marked with an asterisk were particularly useful in developing the conceptual framework for this publication.

General Works

Atherton, Lewis. *Main Street on the Middle Border.* Bloomington, Indiana: Indiana University Press, 1954.*

Atkeson, Mary Meek. *The Woman on the Farm.* New York: The Century Co., 1924.

Bird, Isabella Lucy. *The Englishwoman in America.* 1856. Reprint. Madison, Wisconsin: University of Wisconsin Press, 1966.

Curtis, Henry S. *The Play Movement and Its Significance.* New York: The Macmillan Co., 1917.

Dick, Everett. *The Sod-House Frontier, 1854-1890: A Social History of the Northern Plains from the Creation of Kansas and Nebraska to the Admission of the Dakotas.* New York: Appleton-Century Co., Inc., 1937.

Dulles, Foster Rhea. *A History of Recreation: America Learns to Play.* 2nd ed. New York: Appleton-Century-Crofts, 1965.*

Duteil, H. J. *The Great American Parade.* New York: Twayne Publishers, Inc., 1953.

Fletcher, Stevenson Whitcomb. *Pennsylvania Agriculture and Country Life, 1640-1840.* Revised ed. Harrisburg, Pennsylvania: Pennsylvania Historical & Museum Commission, 1950.

Fletcher, Stevenson Whitcomb. *Pennsylvania Agriculture and Country Life, 1840-1940.* Harrisburg, Pennsylvania: Pennsylvania Historical & Museum Commission, 1955.

Garland, Hamlin. *A Son of the Middle Border.* Revised ed. New York: Grosset & Dunlap, 1927.

Green, Harvey. *The Light of the Home: An Intimate View of the Lives of Women in Victorian America.* New York: Pantheon Books, 1983.

Hine, Robert V. *The American West: An Interpretive History.* Boston, Massachusetts: Little, Brown & Co., 1973.

Hooker, Richard J. *Food and Drink in America: A History.* Indianapolis, Indiana: The Bobbs-Merrill Co., Inc., 1981.

Inge, M. Thomas. *Concise Histories of American Popular Culture.* Westport, Connecticut: Greenwood Press, 1982.

Kaplan, Max. *Leisure in America: A Social Inquiry.* New York: John Wiley & Sons, Inc., 1960.

Lape, Fred. *Farm and Village Boyhood.* Syracuse, New York: Syracuse University Press, 1980.

Larrabee, Eric, and Rolf Meyersohn, eds. *Mass Leisure.* Glencoe, Illinois: The Free Press, 1958.

Lingeman, Richard. *Small Town America: A Narrative History, 1620 to the Present.* Boston, Massachusetts: Houghton Mifflin Co., 1980.

Lundberg, George A., Mirra Komarovsky, and Mary Alice McInerny. *Leisure: A Suburban Study.* New York: Columbia University Press, 1934.

Lynd, Robert S., and Helen Merrell Lynd. *Middletown: A Study in American Culture.* New York: Harcourt, Brace & Co., 1929.

Lynd, Robert S., and Helen Merrell Lynd. *Middletown in Transition: A Study in Cultural Conflicts.* New York: Harcourt, Brace & Co., 1937.

Mergen, Bernard. *Play and Playthings: A Reference Guide.* Westport, Connecticut: Greenwood Press, 1982.

Miller, Norman P., and Duane M. Robinson. *The Leisure Age: Its Challenge to Recreation.* Belmont, California: Wadsworth Publishing Co., Inc., 1963.

Nichols, Dr. Thomas L. *Forty Years of American Life.* 2 vols. London, England: John Maxwell & Co., 1864.

Nye, Russel. *The Unembarrassed Muse: The Popular Arts in America.* New York: The Dial Press, 1970.*

Rainwater, Clarence E. *The Play Movement in the United States: A Study of Community Recreation.* Chicago, Illinois: The University of Chicago Press, 1922.

Reynolds, Lucile Winifred. *Leisure-Time Activities of a Selected Group of Farm Women.* Chicago, Illinois: The University of Chicago Libraries, 1939.

Richards, Caroline Cowles. *Village Life in America: The Diary of Caroline Cowles Richards.* Williamstown, Massachusetts: Corner House Publishers, 1972.

Rosenberg, Bernard, and David Manning White, eds. *Mass Culture: The Popular Arts in America.* Glencoe, Illinois: The Free Press, 1957.

Smith, Robert Jerome. "Social Folk Customs: Festivals and Celebrations." In *Folklore & Folklife: An Introduction,* edited by Richard M. Dorson. Chicago, Illinois: The University of Chicago Press, 1972.

Somers, Dale A. "The Leisure Revolution: Recreation in the American City, 1820-1920." *Journal of Popular Culture* 5, no. 1 (1971): 125-47.

Steiner, Jesse Frederick. *Americans at Play: Recent Trends in Recreation and Leisure-Time Activities.* New York: McGraw-Hill Book Co., Inc., 1933.

Toll, Robert C. *The Entertainment Machine: American Show Business in the 20th Century.* New York: Oxford University Press, 1982.*

Trollope, Francis. *Domestic Manners of the Americans.* 1832. Reprint. Gloucester, Massachusetts: Peter Smith, 1974.

Weaver, Robert B. *Amusements and Sports in American Life.* Chicago, Illinois: The University of Chicago Press, 1939.

Community Gatherings

Bender, Thomas. *Community and Social Change in America.* Baltimore, Maryland: The Johns Hopkins University Press, 1978.

Bryant, Carolyn. *And the Band Played On 1776-1976.* Washington, D.C.: Smithsonian Institution Press, 1975.

Calkins, Raymond. *Substitutes for the Saloon.* Boston, Massachusetts: Houghton Mifflin Co., 1919.

Fredrikson, Clark L. *The Picnic Book.* New York: A. S. Barnes & Co., 1972. Pub. for the National Recreation Association.

Galpin, Charles Josiah. *Rural Life.* New York: The Century Co., 1918.

Howells, William Dean. *Recollections of Life in Ohio, from 1813-1840.* Cincinnati, Ohio: The Robert Clarke Co., 1895.

Lutes, Della T. *The Country Kitchen.* Boston, Massachusetts: Little, Brown & Co., 1946.

Neely, Wayne Caldwell. *The Agricultural Fair.* New York: Columbia University Press, 1935.

Yoder, Paton. *Taverns and Travelers: Inns of the Early Midwest.* Bloomington, Indiana: Indiana University Press, 1969.

Home Amusements

Bogart, Leo. *The Age of Television: A Study of Viewing Habits and the Impact of Television on American Life.* New York: Frederick Ungar Publishing Co., 1956.

Calkins, Earnest Elmo. *Care and Feeding of Hobby Horses.* New York: Leisure League of America, 1934.

Daniels, Les. *Comix: A History of Comic Books in America.* New York: Outerbridge & Dienstifrey, 1971.

Earle, Edward W., ed. *Points of View: The Stereograph in America — A Cultural History.* New York: Visual Studies Workshop, 1979.

Gelatt, Roland. *The Fabulous Phonograph, 1877-1977.* Revised ed. New York: Macmillan Publishing Co., 1977.

Hart, James D. *The Popular Book: A History of America's Literary Taste.* New York: Oxford University Press, 1950.

Heininger, Mary Lynn Stevens. "Children, Childhood, and Change in America, 1820-1920." In *A Century of Childhood 1820-1920.* Rochester, New York: The Margaret Woodbury Strong Museum, 1984.

Hoover, Cynthia. *Music Machines — American Style.* Washington, D.C.: Smithsonian Institution Press, 1971.

Lichty, Lawrence W., and Malachi C. Topping. *American Broadcasting: A Source Book on the History of Radio and Television.* New York: Hastings House, Publishers, 1976.

Public Entertainment

Loesser, Arthur. *Men, Women and Pianos: A Social History.* New York: Simon & Schuster, 1954.

Lutes, Della Thompson. *The Gracious Hostess: A Book of Etiquette.* Indianapolis, Indiana: The Bobbs-Merrill Co., 1923.

Marx, Herbert L., ed. *Television and Radio in American Life.* The Reference Shelf 25, no. 2. New York: The H. W. Wilson Co., 1953.

Mergen, Bernard. "Games and Toys." In *Handbook of American Popular Culture,* edited by M. Thomas Inge. Westport, Connecticut: Greenwood Press, 1980.

Settel, Irving. *A Pictorial History of Radio.* New York: The Citadel Press, 1960.

Settel, Irving, and William Laas. *A Pictorial History of Television.* New York: Grosset & Dunlap, 1969.

Sherwood, Mary Elizabeth Wilson. *Home Amusements.* New York: D. Appleton & Co., 1881.

Smart, James R., and Jon W. Newsom. *"A Wonderful Invention." A Brief History of the Phonograph from Tinfoil to the LP.* Washington, D.C.: Library of Congress, 1977.

Stowell, Marion Barber. *Early American Almanacs: The Colonial Weekday Bible.* New York: Burt Franklin, 1977.

Tice, Patricia. *Gardening in America, 1830-1910.* Rochester, New York: The Margaret Woodbury Strong Museum, 1984.

Waugh, Coulton. *The Comics.* New York: Luna Press, 1947.

Allwood, John. *The Great Exhibitions.* London, England: Studio Vista, 1977.

"The American Lyceum." *Old South Leaflets,* vol. 6. Boston, Massachusetts: Directors of Old South Work, 1829.

Armour, David A. *Film: A Reference Guide.* Westport, Connecticut: Greenwood Press, 1980.

Bohn, Thomas W., and Richard L. Stromgren. *Light and Shadows: A History of Motion Pictures.* Port Washington, New York: Alfred Publishing Co., Inc., 1975.

Case, Victoria, and Robert Ormond Case. *We Called It Culture: The Story of Chautauqua.* Garden City, New York: Doubleday & Co., Inc., 1948.

Chase, Gilbert. *America's Music from the Pilgrims to the Present.* 2nd ed. New York: McGraw-Hill Book Co., Inc., 1966.

Erenberg, Lewis A. *Steppin' Out: New York Nightlife and the Transformation of American Culture.* Chicago, Illinois: The University of Chicago Press, 1981.

Flint, Richard W. *Step Right Up! Amusement for All: Show Business at the Turn of the Century.* Rochester, New York: The Margaret Woodbury Strong Museum, 1977.

Harris, Neil. *Humbug: The Art of P. T. Barnum.* Chicago, Illinois: The University of Chicago Press, 1973.

Hart, Philip. *Orpheus in the New World: The Symphony Orchestra as an American Cultural Institution.* New York: W. W. Norton & Co., 1973.

Hitchcock, H. Wiley. *Music in the United States: A Historical Introduction.* 2nd ed. Englewood Cliffs, New Jersey: Prentice-Hall, Inc., 1974.

Jowett, Garth. *Film: The Democratic Art.* Boston, Massachusetts: Little, Brown & Co., 1976.

Kasson, John F. *Amusing the Million: Coney Island at the Turn of the Century.* New York: Hill & Wang, 1978.

Kasson, John F. "Urban Audiences and the Organization of Entertainment in the Late 19th and Early 20th Centuries." *Henry Ford Museum & Greenfield Village Herald* 14, no. 1 (1985): 3-13.

Katz, Herbert, and Marjorie Katz. *Museums, U.S.A. A History and Guide.* Garden City, New York: Doubleday & Co., Inc., 1965.

Krivine, J. *Juke Box Saturday Night.* Secaucus, New Jersey: Chartwell Books, Inc., 1977.

McCue, George, ed. *Music in American Society, 1776-1976.* New Brunswick, New Jersey: Transaction Books, 1977.

McNamara, Brooks. "'A Congress of Wonders': The Rise and Fall of the Dime Museum." *ESQ (Emerson Society Quarterly)* 20 (3rd quarter, 1974): 216-32.

McNamara, Brooks. *Step Right Up: An Illustrated History of the American Medicine Show.* Garden City, New York: Doubleday & Co., Inc., 1976.

Mangels, William F. *The Outdoor Amusement Industry: From Earliest Times to the Present.* New York: Vantage Press, Inc., 1952.

Matlaw, Myron, ed. *American Popular Entertainment: Papers and Proceedings of the Conference on the History of American Popular Entertainment.* Contributions in Drama and Theatre Studies, no. 1. (Especially essays by Flint, Brasmer, Winsted, Bierman.) Westport, Connecticut: Greenwood Press, 1979.

May, Lary. *Screening Out the Past: The Birth of Mass Culture and the Motion Picture Industry.* Chicago, Illinois: The University of Chicago Press, 1980.

Mead, David. *Yankee Eloquence in the Middle West: The Ohio Lyceum, 1850-1870.* Reprint. Westport, Connecticut: Greenwood Press, 1977.

Nye, Russel B. "Saturday Night at the Paradise Ballroom: or, Dance Halls in the Twenties." *Journal of Popular Culture* 7, no.1 (Summer 1973): 14-22.

Rosenzweig, Roy. *Eight Hours for What We Will: Workers and Leisure in an Industrial City, 1870-1920.* Cambridge, England: Cambridge University Press, 1983.

Russell, Don. *The Wild West: A History of the Wild West Show.* Fort Worth, Texas: Amon Carter Museum of Western Art, 1970.

Sklar, Robert. *Movie-Made America: A Social History of the American Movies.* New York: Random House, Inc., 1975.

Slout, William Lawrence. *Theatre in a Tent: The Development of a Provincial Entertainment.* Bowling Green, Ohio: Bowling Green University Popular Press, 1972.

Sobel, Bernard. *A Pictorial History of Vaudeville.* New York: The Citadel Press, 1961.

Toll, Robert. *Blacking Up: The Minstrel Show in 19th-Century America.* New York: Oxford University Press, 1974.

Toll, Robert. *On With the Show: The First Century of Show Business in America.* New York: Oxford University Press, 1976.*

Wernick, Robert. "Getting a Glimpse of History from a Grandstand Seat." *Smithsonian* 16, no. 5 (Aug. 1985): 68-85.

Wilmeth, Don B. *Variety Entertainment and Outdoor Amusements: A Reference Guide.* Westport, Connecticut: Greenwood Press, 1982.*

Zellers, Parker R. "The Cradle of Variety: The Concert Saloon." *Educational Theatre Journal* 20 (Dec. 1968): 578-85.

Sports

Baker, William J. *Sports in the Western World.* Totawa, New Jersey: Rowman & Littlefield, 1982.*

Betts, John Rickards. *America's Sporting Heritage: 1850-1950.* Reading, Massachusetts: Addison-Wesley Publishing Co., 1974.*

Durant, John, and Otto Bettmann. *Pictorial History of American Sports from Colonial Times to the Present.* [New York]: A.S. Barnes & Co., Inc., 1952.

Gelber, Steven M. "Working at Playing: The Culture of the Workplace and the Rise of Baseball." *Journal of Social History* 16 (Summer 1983): 3-22.

Hardy, Stephen. *How Boston Played: Sport, Recreation, and Community, 1865-1915.* [Boston, Massachusetts]: Northeastern University Press, 1982.

Holliman, Jennie. *American Sports (1785-1835).* Perspectives in American History, no. 34. Philadelphia, Pennsylvania: Porcupine Press, 1975.

Journal of Sport History, 1974 to present.

Krout, John Allen. *Annals of American Sport.* New Haven, Connecticut: Yale University Press, 1929.

Lewis, Guy. "Sport, Youth Culture and Conventionality, 1920-1970." *Journal of Sport History* 4, no. 2 (Fall 1977): 129-50.

Lucas, John A., and Ronald A. Smith. *Saga of American Sport.* Philadelphia, Pennsylvania: Lea and Febiger, 1978.*

Mitchell, John G. "Gentlemen Afield." *American Heritage* 29, no. 6 (Oct.-Nov. 1978): 94-100.

Rader, Benjamin G. *American Sports: From the Age of Folk Games to the Age of Spectators.* Englewood Cliffs, New Jersey: Prentice-Hall, Inc., 1983.*

Reiss, Steven A., ed. *The American Sporting Experience: A Historical Anthology of Sport in America.* (Especially articles by Adelman, Harmond, Betts.) West Point, New York: Leisure Press, 1984.

Smith, Robert A. *A Social History of the Bicycle: Its Early Life and Times in America.* New York: American Heritage Press, 1972.

Terrie, Philip G. "Urban Man Confronts the Wilderness: The Nineteenth-Century Sportsman in the Adirondacks." *Journal of Sport History* 5, no. 3 (Winter 1978): 7-20.

Travel and Tourism

Belasco, Warren James. *Americans on the Road: From Autocamp to Motel, 1910-1945.* Cambridge, Massachusetts: The MIT Press, 1979.

Bilstein, Roger E. *Flight in America, 1900-1983: From the Wrights to the Astronauts.* Baltimore, Maryland: The Johns Hopkins University Press, 1984.

Boorstin, Daniel J. *The Image, or What Happened to the American Dream.* New York: Atheneum, 1962.

Borne, Lawrence. "Dude Ranches and the Development of the West." *Journal of the West* 17, no. 3 (July 1978): 83-94.

Bossemeyer, James L. "Travel: American Mobility." *Annals, American Academy of Political and Social Science* 313 (Sept. 1957): 113-16.

Buchholtz, C. W. "No Trail Too Steep: The Dream and Reality of Recreation in Our Western National Parks." *Journal of the West* 13, no. 3 (July 1978): 96-106.

De Santis, Hugh. "The Democratization of Travel: The Travel Agent in American History." *Journal of American Culture* 1 (1978): 1-17.*

Dulles, Foster Rhea. *Americans Abroad: Two Centuries of European Travel.* Ann Arbor, Michigan: University of Michigan Press, 1964.

Huth, Hans. *Nature and the American: Three Centuries of Changing Attitudes.* Berkeley, California: University of California Press, 1957.*

Jackson, Kenneth T. *The Crabgrass Frontier: The Suburbanization of the United States.* New York: Oxford University Press, 1985.

Jakle, John A. *The Tourist: Travel in 20th-Century North America.* Lincoln, Nebraska: University of Nebraska Press, 1985.*

Liebs, Chester H. *Main Street to Miracle Mile: American Roadside Architecture.* Boston, Massachusetts: Little, Brown & Co., 1985.

Lundberg, Donald E. *The Tourist Business.* New York: Van Nostrand Reinhold Co., 1985.

Mergen, Bernard. *Recreational Vehicles and Travel: A Resource Guide.* Westport, Connecticut: Greenwood Press, 1985.

Nash, Roderick. *Wilderness and the American Mind.* Revised ed. New Haven, Connecticut: Yale University Press, 1979.

Paxson, Frederic L. "The Highway Movement, 1916-1935." *American Historical Review* 51, no. 2 (Jan. 1946): 236-53.

Pomeroy, Earl. *In Search of the Golden West: The Tourist in Western America.* New York: Alfred A. Knopf, 1957.*

Rae, John B. *The Road and the Car in American Life.* Cambridge, Massachusetts: The MIT Press, 1971.

Rinhart, Floyd, and Marion Rinhart. *Summertime: Photographs of Americans at Play, 1850-1900.* New York: Clarkson N. Potter, Inc., 1978.

Rockland, Michael Aaron. *Homes on Wheels.* New Brunswick, New Jersey: Rutgers University Press, 1980.

Runte, Alfred. *National Parks: The American Experience.* Lincoln, Nebraska: University of Nebraska Press, 1979.

Schlereth, Thomas J. *U.S. 40: A Roadscape of the American Experience.* Indianapolis, Indiana: Indiana Historical Society, 1985.

Schmitt, Peter J. *Back to Nature: The Arcadian Myth in Urban America.* New York: Oxford University Press, 1969.

Sears, Stephen W. *The American Heritage History of the Automobile in America.* New York: American Heritage Publishing Co., 1977.

Spitulnik, Karen. "The Inn Crowd: The American Inn, 1730-1830." *Pennsylvania Folklife* 22, no. 2 (Winter 1972-3): 25-41.

Stover, John F. *American Railroads.* Chicago, Illinois: The University of Chicago Press, 1961.

Sutton, Horace. *Travelers: The American Tourist from Stagecoach to Space Shuttle.* New York: William Morrow & Co., Inc., 1980.

Tobin, Gary Allan. "The Bicycle Boom of the 1890's: The Development of Private Transportation and the Birth of the Modern Tourist." *Journal of Popular Culture* 7, no. 4 (Spring 1974): 838-49.

White, Roger B. "At Home on the Highway." *American Heritage* 37, no. 1 (Dec. 1985): 98-105.

PICTURE CREDITS

Unless otherwise indicated, photographs and illustrated artifacts are from the collections of Henry Ford Museum & Greenfield Village.

Page 13: John Dominis, Life Magazine ©Time Inc., New York, New York.

Page 20: Massillon Museum, Massillon, Ohio.

Pages 28, 29, 53 above, 57 left, 58 bottom, 82, 86 right, 107 above right, 170, 171 above, 180 below, 182 below, and 268 top: Farm Security Administration, Library of Congress, Washington, D.C.

Page 30: University of Oregon, Eugene, Oregon.

Pages 40 left, and 198: The New-York Historical Society, New York, New York.

Page 51 above: Kansas State Historical Society, Topeka, Kansas.

Page 59: National Archives: State Department—Werner, Washington, D.C.

Pages 105 below, 266, and 324: Library of Congress, Washington, D.C.

Page 127 right: Hoblitzelle Theatre Arts Library, The Harry Ransom Humanities Research Center, The University of Texas at Austin, Austin, Texas.

Pages 128, 129, 141 above, and 144: Harvard Theatre Collection, Cambridge, Massachusetts.

Page 145: State Historical Society of Wisconsin, Madison, Wisconsin.

Pages 153 above, and 177: Ravinia Festival, Highland Park, Illinois.

Page 156: Chicago Historical Society, Chicago, Illinois.

Page 164: Quigley Photographic Archives, Special Collections Division, Georgetown University Library, Washington, D.C.

Pages 165, 182 above, 187, and 188: Museum of Modern Art/Film Stills Archives, New York, New York.

Page 176 top: The Carnegie Library of Pittsburgh, Pittsburgh, Pennsylvania.

Pages 178 below, 179 below, 257, 261 left, 264 below, 265, and 277 below: Schomburg Center for Research in Black Culture, The New York Public Library, Astor, Lenox and Tilden Foundations, New York, New York.

Page 183: Music Division, The New York Public Library at Lincoln Center, Astor, Lenox and Tilden Foundations, New York, New York.

Page 184 above: Paul Schutzer, Life Magazine ©Time Inc., New York, New York.

Page 192: National Archives: State Department, Washington, D.C.

Page 197: Reproduced by courtesy of the Trustees, The National Gallery, London, England.

Page 272 bottom: National Archives, Washington, D.C.

Page 281 right: Stephen Rahn, photographer, Courtesy of the Oakland Museum History Department, Oakland, California.

Page 282 above: Yale Joel, Life Magazine ©Time Inc., New York, New York.

Page 319 below: Sierra Club, San Francisco, California.

Page 331 above right: Morgan and Marvin Smith, photographers, Schomburg Center for Research in Black Culture, The New York Public Library, Astor, Lenox and Tilden Foundations, New York, New York.

Page 337 below: National Archives: Aircraft Industries, Washington, D.C.

Page 344 below: National Archives: Santa Fe Railroad, Washington, D.C.

Page 350 above: National Archives: Black Star, Washington, D.C.

We thank the following for permission to use copyrighted materials in the collections of Henry Ford Museum & Greenfield Village:

Page 36: The American Tobacco Company.

Page 47: Courtesy of The Goodyear Tire & Rubber Company.

Page 67 left: Reproduced with permission of AT&T Corporate Archive.

Page 72 below left: Gorham, division of Textron, Inc.

Page 98 above: The Seven-Up Company.

Page 105 above: Hall of History, General Electric Company.

Page 106: Louis Faurer, photographer.

Page 107 below: Hiram Walker, Inc.

Page 109: The Stroh Brewery Company.

Page 123: Motorola, Inc.

Page 269 above: Petersen Publishing Company; George Barris, Barris Kustom Industries.

Page 274 below: Simmons Universal Corporation, division of Wickes Companies, Inc.

Page 275 above: Valentino Serra, photographer.

Page 280: Outboard Marine Corporation.

Page 281 left: Harley-Davidson Motor Company, Inc.

Page 332: Stuckey's Corporation.

Page 333: Franchise Associates, Inc.

Page 338: American Airlines.

Page 339: American Express Corporation.

Page 342 below: Greyhound Lines, Inc.

Page 352 left: CBS.

Page 356–57: Trans World Airlines, Inc.